Invisible Work

Invisible Work

Borges and Translation

EFRAÍN KRISTAL

VANDERBILT UNIVERSITY PRESS
Nashville

This book is printed on acid-free paper.
Manufactured in the United States of America

Library of Congress Cataloging-in-Publication Data

Kristal, Efraín, 1959-
Invisible work : Borges and translation / Efraín
Kristal.— 1st ed.
    p. cm.
Includes bibliographical references and index.
ISBN 0-8265-1407-3 (cloth : alk. paper)
ISBN 0-8265-1408-1 (pbk. : alk. paper)
    1. Borges, Jorge Luis, 1899—Criticism and
interpretation. 2. Borges, Jorge Luis, 1899—Views
on translating and interpreting. 3. Translating and
interpreting. 4. Borges, Jorge Luis, 1899—Transla-
tions—History and criticism.
I. Title.
PQ7797.B635 Z77155 2002
868'.6209—dc21
                                    2002002607

To Christopher Maurer,
one of the happy few

Contents

Acknowledgments

I first presented my ideas on Borges and translation in a conference held at the Federal University of Rio de Janeiro, organized by Guillermo Guicci in 1996. I continued discussing various aspects of my ongoing research in lectures and conferences in Peru, Australia, Germany, and the United States, as well as in graduate seminars at UCLA, Vanderbilt University, and the University of Göttingen during my tenure as Mercator Visiting Research Professor. In Göttingen I profited from conversations with Professors Manfred Engelbert and Armin Paul Frank.

For five years during my research I received annual grants from UCLA's Faculty Senate with which I enlisted the assistance of several graduate students to gather materials and to prepare aspects of the manuscript for publication: Kelly Austin, Nataly Tcherepashenets, Zaia Alexander, Philip Walsh, Kirsten Mcleary, and Susan Bausch.

I would like to express my gratitude to several individuals for their support during this project and for their valuable advice and counsel: Herbert Morris, Charles Backus, Randal Johnson, Dietrich Briesemeister, Karsten Garscha, Alexander Coleman, Roy Boland, Roberto Alifano, Dominic Thomas, Kathleen Komar, Franco Betti, Kryztof Urban, Cathy Jrade, Marcelo Abadi, Erick Felinto de Oliveira, Jorge Wanderley, Carmela Zanelli, Susanne Grosse, José Luiz Passos, Jonathan Post, H. A. Kelly, Suzanne Jill Levine, and Saúl and Gladis Yurkievich.

I also would like to offer my gratitude to the wonderful staff at Vanderbilt University Press and to Bard Young for his superb editorial work.

María Kodama, Borges's widow, graciously met with me on two occasions in Buenos Aires to discuss the translation works on which she and her late husband collaborated. She also gave me permission to look at many books that belonged to Borges and that contain his marginalia.

In order to study Borges's translation of Snorri Sturluson's *Prose Edda*, I audited Professor Jesse Byock's Old Norse language course at UCLA for a year. Subsequently, Professor Byock allowed me to quote from the manuscript of his translation of the *Edda* (forthcoming at Penguin Press) and was generous in his willingness to answer many queries.

Nicolás Helft allowed me to read unpublished letters, rare publications, and manuscripts (including the manuscript of an unpublished translation of a story by Martin Buber) at the San Telmo Foundation in Buenos Aires.

Marcelo Gilardoni of the Argentine Consulate in Los Angeles assisted me in the acquisition of microfilm copies of rare materials held at the National Library of Argentina, including the journal *Revista Multicolor* and Borges's first translation of Oscar Wilde's "The Happy Prince," which appeared in the Buenos Aires newspaper *El País* (1910).

Special thanks go to Romy Sutherland for her support and generous willingness to read, discuss, and improve countless versions of the manuscript.

Alberto Cordero and Christopher Maurer are responsible for many improvements in this book. As in previous works, I have relied on their frank, constructive observations; and I write in the hope of meeting their exacting standards.

This book is dedicated to Christopher Maurer as a token of my admiration for his contributions as literary critic and translator.

Introduction

Immortals have, generally, another destiny. The details of their feelings or thoughts tend to vanish or lie invisibly in their work.

—*Jorge Luis Borges*

On September 5, 1953, the author of *Fictions* and *The Aleph* wrote a letter to settle the final details of a lecture he would deliver on the Kabbalah. Almost as an afterthought, Jorge Luis Borges offers biographical information requested by his host. After indicating his birth in Buenos Aires in 1899, he introduces himself as the translator of Franz Kafka, Virginia Woolf, William Faulkner, and Henri Michaux.[1] The note continues with other aspects of his literary activities, but Borges puts forward his translations before mentioning any of the titles that established his renown as a towering figure of contemporary literature.

Borges is best known as a spellbinding fabulist whose literary works often require the creative complicity of his readers—not merely their suspension of disbelief—to produce the sense that a window has been opened onto singular worlds of fiction with a logic of their own. He disconcerts and beguiles with the same conceits. His preposterous situations and impossible objects have the air of the credible, and his characters, usually unendearing and sometimes endowed with extraordinary attributes, are intriguing, if not outright compelling. Borges writes with such aplomb and understated confidence, that he has persuaded readers as demanding as George

Steiner, Umberto Eco, and Harold Bloom, that they are entering a literary world of momentous significance. Borges is also one of the greatest Latin American poets of the twentieth century. He has shaped an unmistakable lyrical persona who oscillates between the uncanny aperçu and the disarming confession, while producing lines that have enriched the Spanish language. The recent publication of his *Selected Non-Fictions* (edited by Eliot Weinberger and splendidly translated by Weinberger, Esther Allen, and Suzanne Jill Levine) revealed to an English reading public that Borges is also one of the most engaging essayists of modern literature. For the Hispanic world Borges's contributions must also include his major anthologies and the collections of translated novels he edited: he introduced fantastic and detective fiction to Spanish American readers, as well as the first Spanish versions of contemporary novelists such as James Joyce, Joseph Conrad, Virginia Woolf, and William Faulkner. Borges wrote a book on Buddhism, as well as eventful essays on the Kabbalah and Chinese literature, and is also responsible for the first history of Old English and Germanic literatures written in the Spanish language. As the critic José Miguel Oviedo has noted, "Borges incorporated a literary culture almost alien to Spanish American literature and that, thanks to him, is now a part of its tradition."[2] His influence on the distinguished Mexican writer Salvador Elizondo makes the point, but Elizondo is not the only major Latin American who embarked on a life of letters after reading Borges.[3] His paramount influence on contemporary Latin American fiction—acknowledged by Carlos Fuentes, Mario Vargas Llosa, Gabriel García Márquez, Octavio Paz, and many others—would itself warrant a book-length treatment.[4] Borges must also be reckoned a central writer in the context of Argentine literature. Many of his writings require a deep knowledge of the local context, and in seminal essays and anthologies on national themes, he played a decisive role in shaping the contemporary understanding of Argentine literary history. Moreover, he was also a beloved professor of English literature at the University of Buenos Aires, a dazzling conversationalist, and an enthralling lecturer.

Notwithstanding his achievement as fabulist, poet, essayist, editor, anthologist, and specialist of English and Argentine literature, Borges committed no injustice to himself by foregrounding his translations. Indeed, translation played a major role in every one of his literary endeavors, and it was his conviction that some of the most cherished pleasures of literature become available only after a work has passed through many hands and undergone many changes. In his presentation of himself as a translator, one senses the reserved pride of a powerful literary mind able to appropriate and transform what is presumably already present without seemingly changing anything.

Borges might have projected his delight in the secret achievement of translation onto some of his most memorable characters: Jaromir Hladík, who was offered a miraculous instant that lasts the time required to finish a play no one will ever read; or the protagonist of "Tlön, Uqbar, Orbis Tertius," who translates a Spanish version of Sir Thomas Browne's *Urn Burial* not intended for publication; or Tzinacan, who deciphers the highest mystery of his religion and chooses to let it die with him; or Pierre Menard, who writes a few pages of prose syntactically identical with passages from *Don Quixote*. Borges's testy narrator hails Menard's *Don Quixote* as a masterpiece and calls it an "invisible work," that is, an unnoticed achievement overshadowed and obscured by another work it has surpassed. Moved by that hyperbole, George Steiner calls Borges's story "the most acute, most concentrated commentary anyone has offered on the business of translation."[5] In his consideration of Borges, Steiner argues that "a true translator knows his labor belongs 'to oblivion' (inevitably, each generation retranslates), or 'to the other one,' his occasion, begetter, and precedent shadow."[6] In his own essays, Borges was fond of celebrating unnoticed literary achievements he called *secret* or *invisible*. In the preface to his translation of Stevenson's *Fables,* for example, Borges calls the work "a brief and secret masterpiece."[7]

The purpose of this book is to demonstrate that translation, not as a loose metaphor for influence or intertextuality, but as a process whereby a writer remodels one sequence of words into another, is central to Borges's reflections on writing and to his contribution to literature. It is well known that Borges was a translator, but this activity has been considered a minor aspect—a mere curiosity—of his literary achievement. In an essay that played a significant role in his reception, Paul de Man lamented that Borges, a brilliant writer and translator of American literature, was not better known in the United States: "Although he has been writing poems, stories, and critical essays of the highest quality since 1923, the Argentine writer Jorge Luis Borges is still much better known in Latin America than in the U.S. For the translator of John Peale Bishop, Hart Crane, E.E. Cummings, William Faulkner, Edgar Lee Masters, Robert Penn Warren, and Wallace Stevens, this neglect is somewhat unfair."[8] Since de Man wrote this article in 1964, Borges has become universally acknowledged as a central figure of twentieth-century literature, but his work as translator is still considered a marginal aspect of his curriculum.

Translation, however, is inseparable from the fiber of those works once so little known in the United States and now so widely received. As Roger Callois pointed out some time ago, *The Universal History of Infamy*, Borges's first book of prose fiction, includes a series of stories that are actually loose translations of nonfictional texts depicting the lives of criminals and outlaws.[9] Callois noticed that Borges recreated and transformed his originals at will. This clue has been ignored in the vast amount of literary criticism devoted to Borges's most celebrated works. And yet Borges's translations, and his reflections on translation, are invariably at the core of his creative process. Borges once wrote that the "feelings or thoughts [of great writers] tend to vanish or lie invisibly in their work."[10] The purpose of this book is to make visible Borges's creativity as translator.

Borges wrote famously that "no problem is as consubstantial to literature and its modest mystery as the one posed by translation." One could add that no activity, other than reading, has been more central to his creative process than translation.[11] There is no better vantage point from which to appreciate his creation and recreation of literature.

My approach was anticipated by Jaime Alazraki when he argued,

in a seminal article, that Borges's most characteristic literary practice lies in creative recreation of works he read.[12] I was also encouraged in my work by the scholarship of Ronald Christ, John T. Irwin,
and Daniel Balderston. They have deftly unearthed rich layers of
reference and allusion.[13] And I would like to praise the brilliant work
of Michel Lafon who has demonstrated how relentlessly Borges rewrote and copied ideas, sentences, and entire passages from his own
writings as he fashioned new ones.[14] In this study I share the belief
that contextual approaches enhance our understanding of Borges's
writing.[15]

My work is intended to analyze the significance of translation
in Borges, an area that has not been explored, either systematically
or with much clarity. To date, the most significant contribution to
the study of Borges and translation is a chapter from Annick Louis's
sedulously researched *Jorge Luis Borges: Oeuvres et manœuvres,* in
which she offers an impressive account of Borges's views on translation. Louis demonstrates convincingly that, for Borges, a translation is not inherently inferior to its original, but she is mistaken in
attributing to Borges the view that it is impossible to "establish a
hierarchy between the two."[16] Louis is not interested in making aesthetic value judgments in her literary analysis, but Borges was in
his. Depending on the specific case, he at times favored a translation over its original, other times an original over its translation,
and he was often interested in weighing their relative merits, aesthetic and otherwise. Louis is one of the few literary critics to
notice that Borges sometimes corrected his own translations from
publication to publication, but she does not indicate that in his translations Borges often corrected the originals and that those corrections bear on the gestation of his most celebrated literary works.

The main purpose of this book is to offer an account of the role
translation played in Borges's creative process. The connections I
will draw between Borges's practice as a translator and his writings
do not hinge on any radical epistemological assumptions.[17] Borges's
fictional world, which has engaged both deconstructionists and ana-
lytical philosophers alike, is hospitable to a variety of approaches.
Not all of his stories are philosophical, but even in those that are,

Borges's literary contributions are not contingent on his philosophical coherence or even on his appeal to philosophers of different persuasions, but rather, as Juan Nuño has urged, on his genius for transforming "the most schematic and stiff of philosophical topics into animated tales, and vivid descriptions of fantastic worlds."[18] Indeed, Borges was fundamentally a fabulist.[19]

My purpose, therefore, is not to examine the metaphysical content of Borges's writings nor to indicate that his literary world has affinities or discordances with this or that philosophical, political, or cultural approach to literature. I offer an unapologetically literary study of Borges's engagements with the works he transformed. I am not interested in confirming the global tenants of any literary theory with examples drawn from the Borges canon, but in underscoring the pivotal role translation plays in the gestation of his literary world.

Borges was interested in translation as a means of enhancing a work because the work mattered more to him than its author. Since my objective is to offer insights into Borges's art, I am most interested in translation as it informs his ideas about literature and his creative process. My method, therefore, differs sharply from Borges's. For Borges translation was a means to enrich a literary work or a literary idea. For me translation provides a way of understanding his oeuvre.

I take guidance here, as I have in previous works, from Richard Wollheim's recommendation that the scrutiny of a literary work ought to include an attempt to reconstruct the creative process. A work of art is, at least in part, the result of a problem-solving operation that can often be mapped: works of art show traces of design, error, changes of intention, and accident. The inevitable rewriting of previous works of art in any individual work is also central to Wollheim's doctrine of criticism as retrieval: "[The artist] will assemble his elements in ways that self-consciously react against, or overtly presuppose, arrangements that have already been tried out within the tradition."[20] Wollheim's approach complements Gombrich's suggestion that the study of a work of art should pay as much attention to the repertoire of the artist as to the finished product.

To understand the possibilities and the choices involved in the creation of a painting, for example, Gombrich would recommend the study of the artist's palette.

Translation figures prominently in Borges's palette. A significant number of his literary works can be read as solutions to problems resolved in the process of translation or as responses to works he translated. One can trace many of his artistic decisions to the changes he made to works he translated and to the ways in which he incorporated his translations, or his ideas about translation, into the fabric of his fictions. In short, Borges's translations offer insights into his creative process, and into the workings of his imgaination.

Harold Bloom said of Shakespeare that his own powerful imagination erased the status of his antecedents as influences. Rather than "erase" the status of his antecedents as influences, Borges often reorients and sometimes deflates them. In some cases the deficiencies, gaps, and unfulfilled potentialities in the writers he translated were not recognized until Borges engaged with their works. Some of the fictional possibilities Borges foregrounds in his involvements with the work of others may have been available to the writers whose works he translated, and some of them may not have been. Either way, Borges does not leave the majority of his precursors untouched the way most writers do when rewriting aspects of literary works that inspired them. When, for instance, he incorporated his recreation of Poe's "The Purloined Letter" as an ingredient in his own story "La muerte y la brújula" ("Death and the Compass"). Borges shows by example that Poe never combined detective fiction, a genre he invented, with the fantastic, a genre he mastered.[21] Borges is not just rewriting Poe; he is underscoring a possibility in Poe's writings that Poe never explored.

Borges's transformations amount to a critical practice that, at its most productive, invites readers of literature to reconsider their views about the writers with which Borges engaged himself. According to Borges's own doctrine of literary influence (generously acknowledged by Harold Bloom), a new work of literature invents its precursors, preparing future readers to identify features that could not have been recognized when the work was written, as when

Melville's "Bartleby the Scrivener," which Borges translated, is re-read as Kafkaesque.

This book is intended to make a literary rather than a biographical statement about Borges, but it will draw on some aspects of his personal and intellectual biography that offer insights into his views and methods with respect to translation.[22] Borges's mature views on translation came together in the 1930s (remaining fairly constant ever since), when he abandoned two positions he had considered seriously and in some cases defended vehemently. The first is the idea that literature is fundamentally autobiographical and that its ultimate significance is lost on those who ignore the circumstances of individual authors. The second, which he sometimes related to the first, is the view that literature is the expression of a nationality or a national character. Borges was so embarrassed by these and other views he held in the 1920s—and perhaps also by the baroque language in which he expressed them—that he refused to reissue his first three books of essays in which he had held those views in good steed.[23] His friends reported that over the years he would buy any copies of those books he could find in order to destroy them.

From Borges's early period he salvaged his metaphysical bent—or at least the certainty that metaphysics offered him rich literary possibilities—and many of his literary preferences, including his passion for Walt Whitman and his admiration for Sir Thomas Browne, even as he reconsidered their significance. The experience of reevaluating his interpretations of writers he continued to cherish may have had a role to play in the skepticism he developed with respect to interpretation: his belief that interpretation is a secondary, sometimes even an irrelevant practice that can be happily forsaken by those who truly appreciate literature without subterfuges. Given a choice, he preferred to discuss literary effects rather than the meaning of literary works; and he could not countenance any talk about literary theory that did not address the craft of writing.

Borges never abandoned altogether the view that personal circumstances can be a relevant factor in the discussion of a literary work, but since the 1930s the individuality of the writer played an ever-diminishing role in his observations on literature, especially when compared to the impersonal and collective factors of the literary experience. In this context Borges developed a view on translation in which an original work does not harbor an advantage over a translation. The work, for Borges, became a collective enterprise that carries more weight than the input of any individual author, reader, or translator. It is also in this context that Borges developed a way of writing fiction informed by his own approach to translation: a way of writing that willfully adopts, transforms, and adapts the works of others.[24]

There is yet a third period in Borges's life that must be addressed in the discussion of those aspects of his biography that have a bearing on his views and methods of translation. That period can be dated from 1960, when he lost his ability to read due to a congenital eye disease that led progressively to his blindness. From the 1960s until the end of his life, he could no longer correct manuscripts, drafts, or proofs by himself, and required assistance in the writing process. Before losing his sight, he had collaborated on many translations, but after the 1960s collaboration became a necessity. He also began to compose shorter pieces of prose and poetry in his mind. As he continued to stress the impersonal aspects of literature, he became increasingly interested in sharpening his literary receptivity to such an extent that he felt more comfortable speaking of himself as a reader than as a writer. And yet, his output as a writer was prolific; he continued to publish an impressive number of essays, poems, narrative fictions, and translations. In fact, the last major book he published in his lifetime was a translation of Snorri Sturluson's *Prose Edda*, a work in which Borges was at the height of his powers. In his translation he transformed the single most important source of Nordic mythology imbuing it with his most enduring literary concerns.

TRANSLATION LOOMS so large in Borges's work that an exhaustive treatment is neither possible nor desirable in a short book whose aim is to stress its central role in Borges's craft, a role not yet fully grasped or even acknowledged in the massive body of scholarship devoted to his writings. Of the several essays on Borges's translations, the more instructive ones appreciate stylistic features in the language of those works. But the standard view that Borges wrote faithful translations that sometimes improved the style of the originals needs correction. Some of Borges's translations are faithful but many are not, and the idea that Borges "required of a translator a rigorous identification with the original," expressed by many critics with the intention of honoring him, is both mistaken and unintentionally misleading. For Borges translation was a creative process.[25] Even though Nestor Ibarra never developed the idea with textual analysis, he made plain the pertinence of translation for Borges better than anybody else: "Here is a man of letters interested in the problem of translation, and when he has two admirable works in front of him, one inspired by the other, all he finds is the happy opportunity to reshape his eternal mask."[26]

My analysis of Borges's translations will show that his strategies as a creative writer have much in common with his methods as a translator but that the two overlapping writing practices are not co-extensive. As a creative writer and as a translator, Borges took many liberties in his transformations of other literary works, but his translations remain identifiable reflections of the originals while the literary works he signed as his own are not that at all. His translations transform his originals into drafts that precede them; his own literary works transform his readings into a repertoire of possibilities in which his own translations, and his views about translation, play a decisive role.

In this book I will describe Borges's views on translation, his practice as translator, and the pivotal role of translation in his creative process. For heuristic reasons I will treat these topics in three separate chapters whose themes will sometimes overlap. Chapter 1 is an account of Borges's ideas about translation, which amount to an original contribution to literary theory and criticism. Chapter 2 studies Borges's methods as a translator by analyzing a number of his versions from poetry and narrative fiction in which he took liberties as he translated the originals. Chapter 3 explores the role of translation in some of his most important works of narrative fiction. I will discuss translation as a literary theme in Borges's fictions, especially because many of his principal literary characters are translators and many of his stories are presented as imagined translations. I will also analyze a number of Borges's translations in the gestation and construction of his literary world.

Along the way we will visit many of Borges's fictions, poems, essays, conferences, interviews, and letters and explore numerous real and apocryphal translations that inform his approach to literature. I underscore the richness of the topic for readers of Borges whose own views and interpretations might be enhanced or refined by the knowledge that translation played a central role in his literary concerns and in the very content of his literary works. I see translation as more central to Borges's literature than the celebrated labyrinths, mirrors, tigers, and encyclopedias that abound in his literary world.

NOTE: In many essays where Borges compared translations from languages other than Spanish, the Argentine writer would actually quote his Spanish versions as if they were originals. Often, he would say that he was "copying" rather than "quoting" to indicate that he was offering a Spanish text of a foreign work. Borges justified his procedure in as much as the features he wanted to underscore in his comparisons were not affected by the transfer of one language to another. Borges was also fond of comparing translations, in this manner, of works he could not read in the original. He wrote several essays, for example, in which he compared Homeric translations from English in his Spanish "copies." In chapter 1 I will explain the notion of "copying" in the context of my account of his views on translation.

In the sections of this book comparing Borges's translations into Spanish from English, I will offer my own English versions of Borges's translations in the body of the work and will include Borges's Spanish versions in the endnotes. In my comparisons of Borges's translations from foreign languages (German, French, Italian, and Old Norse), I will also include the foreign language originals in the endnotes. The majority of the transformations that I highlight involve elisions or interpolations rather than linguistic differences between languages. It is quite possible to appreciate, in my English versions, the aspects of Borges's translations that I will discuss in this book. Scholars who may be interested in checking the foreign language originals, or readers who know any of the foreign languages involved, can look to the endnotes for all of the originals.

Finally, I would like to stress that this book is not intended to be a comprehensive review of all of Borges's translations, or of the significance of translation in each of his creative works where it plays a role. My purpose is to underscore the significance of translation in Borges's oeuvre, rather than to offer an exhaustive treatment of this rich topic. It is my hope that many more discussions of Borges's writings will take note of his translations and of his ideas with respect to the practice of translation as an approach to literary creation.

Invisible Work

CHAPTER I

Borges on Translation

It must be visible, or invisible,
Invisible or visible or both.
—Wallace Stevens

Borges affirmed, in earnest, that an original can be unfaithful to a translation. He vehemently objected to claims that certain translations he admired are "true to the original" and derided the presuppositions of purists for whom all translations are necessarily deceitful in one way or another. Borges would often protest, with various degrees of irony, against the assumption—ingrained in the Italian adage *traduttore traditore*—that a translator is a traitor to an original. He referred to it alternatively as a superstition or pun. For Borges the Italian expression, unfairly prejudiced in favor of the original, is an erroneous generalization that conflates difference with treachery. The idea that literary translations are inherently inferior to their originals is, for Borges, based on the false assumption that some works of literature must be assumed definitive. But for Borges, no such thing as a definitive work exists, and therefore, a translator's inevitable transformation of the original is not necessarily to the detriment of the work. Difference, for Borges, is not a sufficient criterion for the superiority of the original.

Those who demand that a translated text be different from the original and yet reproduce the original's every nuance and detail assume that a work of literature has some sort of religious or legal status, as if a literary work were like the Bible, a sacred text dictated to "copyists by the Holy Spirit."[1] Those for whom an original work has the status of scripture might assume that the alteration of a single detail of the literary work (such as the numerical value that the kabbalists attribute to every Hebrew letter) is akin to mutilating a binding clause in a legal document. In a sense they would hold the literary translator up to an impossible, misleading standard. A translation cannot be identical to its original and claim to be a translation, and the differences between a translation and its original are not necessarily betrayals. A legal clause is not mutilated when a translator finds appropriate equivalencies for the sake of judicial clarity; and the literary qualities of a work are not mutilated when a translator modifies the original to reproduce artistic effects that would otherwise be lost. For Borges, condemning a literary translation because it is not identical to the original is as unfair as condemning the translation of a contract because its equivalencies are not literary.

A translator rewrites a sequence of words with a different sequence of words. The unavoidable changes that any translation presents vis-à-vis its original are, in and of themselves, insufficient grounds for claiming a translation is either dishonest or inferior to the original. Borges was certain that a translation could enrich or surpass an original and that one of the most fertile of all literary experiences is a comparative survey of the versions of a work. Borges thought of the original as a text produced not by a superior being but by a fallible human, a text laden with possibilities and potentialities, attainments and failures. Borges, for whom a translation "is a variation one is justified in attempting,"[2] would have few scruples about editing the original as he translated. A good translator, according to him, might choose to treat the original as a good writer treats a draft of a work in progress. In fact, for Borges, the translators of a work may be more beneficial to the work than its author, not because they have a superior literary sense but because their lack of vested interest in the text as it was published makes them more effective as editors: "It is far easier to forgo someone else's vanities than one's own."[3] According to Borges translators should be willing to cut, add, and transform for the sake of the work. The process can be as endless in a translation as in the creation of an original. In the preface to his translation of Paul Valéry's "Le Cemetière Marin," Nestor Ibarra makes a comment that Borges would appreciate: "my translation is infinitely perfectible, since it is the first."[4] Ibarra, who appears as a character in Borges's fictional world, was also one of his first translators into French. In his translations of Borges's stories and poems Ibarra took many liberties welcomed by his old friend.

Borges, who admired Ibarra's translation of Paul Valéry more than the original, might endorse the claim that the first translation of a work can be thought of as a starting point for further improvements, but he might add that the potential to ameliorate a draft should not be taken as an argument against publication, because correcting drafts is a never ending process. Borges was fond of quoting Alfonso Reyes, who would say, "We publish because otherwise we would spend our lives going over our drafts."[5] That being said, Borges would often make changes to existing published works when they were reprinted. Thanks to Jean Pierre Bernès's remarkable French Pléiade edition of Borges's *Oeuvre*—the first extensive account of Borges's transformations of his own works (offering rich bibliographical information indicating the original publication of many works)—we can begin to appreciate the full extent of his revisions.[6] Just as Borges revised his original works, including the contents of his books, from edition to edition, he also revised some of his own translations when published in new contexts.

The Translatable and Untranslatable

Borges knew it could be difficult to transfer the meaning of each word of an original in translation and did not think it desirable to do so when translating a work of literature ("literal translations are not literary").[7] He recognized that in translation some aspects of an original will disappear, but he did not consider those losses necessarily undesirable. He knew that it might be impossible to render a text with the same grammatical qualities, rhythms, and rhymes and that it might be miraculous to find identical meanings, connotations, and associations when one substitutes one word for another. Borges acknowledged the commonplace idea that "a good poem is always untranslatable," if by *translate* one means to replicate the original, maintaining all characteristics and nuances.[8] It is also untranslatable if what matters in poetry "is essentially in the intonation, in a certain way of breathing a phrase."[9] Borges became increasingly interested, especially after 1960 when he lost his sight, in poetic lines that provoked emotional effects in him, even before he understood their meaning, on account of the connotations and even the arbitrary associations of words. In some cases, as in Quevedo's famous line "Y su epitafio, la sangrienta luna" (literally, "and his epitaph, the bloody moon"), Borges felt that the power of a poetic line can be impoverished by its immediate context or by interpretation.[10] One of the compensations for his blindness was his memorized anthology of poetic lines, in several languages, which he considered "unique and eternal," lines which, in or out of context, gave him a joy that had more to do with associations than with meanings,[11] for example Gerard Manley Hopkins's line "Mastering me God, giver of breath and bread." If translators aim to convey the approximate sense of that which is untranslatable, their works "are a means and a stimulus to bring the reader close to the original."[12]

Borges would differentiate between what he called "the language of ideas" and "the language of emotions." He maintained that in literary translation ideas raise no significant difficulties, while emotions suggested by words raise problems that are almost insurmountable. Certain works, therefore, afford pleasures lost in translation. A writer like Shakespeare cannot be successfully translated into a foreign language, even into modern English, because "in an English that is not Shakespeare's many things would be lost." But with regard to the translation of ideas, he could feel deeply affected by a production of *Macbeth* in a horrible translation, with bad actors, and misguided scenery.[13] Umberto Eco utilizes a similar dichotomy to compare the contributions of Borges to those of Joyce ("the two contemporary authors I have most loved and who most influenced me.")[14] Eco calls Borges a "delirious archivist" whose own experimentations, as opposed to those of Joyce, take place at the level of ideas, not language. Whereas Joyce treated language as a "jeu de massacre," Borges played with ideas, "letting words insinuate new and unexpected horizons."[15] According to Eco, Borges is at his most conservative in his own writing when it comes to the organization of sounds in literature, and at his most experimental when it comes to ideas. Eco's insight can be applied to Borges's views on translation, with the caveat that for Borges a text is untranslatable not because it is conventional or experimental at the level of language but because its conjunction of cadences and associations are not transferable. Borges would often compare two literal versions of the same text and argue that the emotion of one was lost in the other: "A cadence is akin to the cipher of an emotion. Two lines may be conceptually identical but not emotionally; intellectually they may be the same, but not emotively."[16]

In his commentary on Salas Subirat's translation of Joyce's *Ulysses*, a novel he considered failed, tedious, and chaotic, Borges insists on its moments of "verbal perfection." At times Borges referred to *Ulysses* as an almost impossible challenge to a translator, by which he meant it would be impossible to render all of Joyce's verbal experiments into any other language.[17] On other occasions he denied that the novel was untranslatable, recommending that it be used as a pretext for the creation of another work. For Borges some works of literature are more translatable than others, but no work of literature is untranslatable in principle, because a translator can always take the necessary liberties to achieve what any creative writer should strive for: a convincing work of literature. As a reader of literature Borges seeks a hedonistic response that involves either perceptual pleasures, as with his response to Joyce's language, or mind-enhancing satisfactions, as with his response to a Shakespeare play in a poor translation.[18] Borges was famous for encouraging his students of English literature at the University of Buenos Aires to read what gave them pleasure and to avoid what did not. It is not necessary, however, to scratch too deeply beneath his hedonistic pronouncements— and sometimes not necessary to scratch at all—to notice that his own judgments about the merits of a translation involve an interplay of relativistic and objectivistic criteria that also inform his general views about literature as an art. Borges is a relativist in as much as he delights in the liberties a translator can take in transforming one text into another. But he is an objectivist in as much as he rejects some translations when those liberties do not produce a text that meets his aesthetic standards. As an objectivist Borges was persuaded that the cadences and arbitrary associations of words in certain combinations warrant the claim of "verbal perfection," and that some literary works are more successful than others in producing literary effects. As a relativist, he endorsed transformations and misprisions, and did not mind if ideas and other aspects of an original were either eliminated or transformed in translation. His objectivistic and relativistic standards converge in his conviction that original works do not have, in principle, any advantage over translations from the perspective of their literary merits.

Borges does not rule out the unlikely eventuality that a translator might be able to reproduce all the relevant features that characterize a particular work; and at the same time, he recognizes that the most concentrated efforts of a poet, exploiting the unique possibilities of a particular language, may be impossible to translate. However, those linguistic aspects that cannot be reproduced in translation do not cause Borges any more anxiety than the fact that a paraphrase is never identical with its original. In general one paraphrases to underscore certain features of a text while ignoring others, and one generally translates to underscore certain aspects of an original while downplaying others. All the same, an "untranslatable" text remains "translatable" for Borges because it is always "possible to recreate the work, to take the text as a pretext."[19] Where the cadences of the original are lost, the translator may be able to find new cadences that did not exist in the original. In short, for Borges, the poetry of ideas can always be translated in such a way that the original and the translation amount to the "same" text, and the poetry of emotions can be translated also, as a recreation: "[Poetry] can always be translated as long as the translator forgoes either scientific or philological precision."[20]

Ultimately, for Borges, the decision as to whether a text is translatable or untranslatable depends not on theoretical but on practical considerations: on whether a translator is able to recreate the text in such a way that it produces a gratifying literary effect. Borges made many general observations about the practice of translation, but he limited judgment on whether a particular work was translatable or untranslatable to his examination of specific cases:

I believe Benedetto Croce held that a poem is untranslatable, but that it can be recreated in another language. In good logic, it would suffice to have a single well-translated line to refute his assertion. Everything depends on what one means by "well translated." As for myself, I am a nominalist. I defy abstract affirmations and I prefer to concentrate on particular cases.[21]

Borges agrees with those who claim that "each language has its own possibilities and impossibilities" but does not draw the inference that a translator is doomed to failure.[22] On the contrary, he affirms that the differences between languages and modes of expression offer multiple possibilities to a translator whose aim is to recreate the original.

In his insightful commentary on the short story "La busca de Averroes" ("Averroës' Search"), Marcelo Abadi summarizes Borges's view that for "a man of letters it is not so terrible to make a mistake in a translation, and it is not so dramatic that there are no strict correspondences between languages."[23] In fact, for Borges the "mistakes" of a translator or the lack of strict correspondences between languages can favor as much as they can play against any particular translation, or any section of a translation. In the case of poetic lines like those of Quevedo and Hopkins quoted above, it makes no sense for Borges to fault a translator for failing to render what cannot be rendered. But such moments of literary concentration are rare in the work of any poet, and they are not the sole province of an original. Indeed, a translation may sparkle in passages where the original falls short. Borges would agree with George Steiner's contention that a translation can tap into potentialities unrealized in the original, precisely because the linguistic differences or incompatibilities between two modes of expression may bring forth aspects of the work that would be obscured in the language of the original. In a 1934 essay on the forthcoming English translation of *Don Segundo Sombra* (Argentina's most celebrated novel about the life of the gaucho), Borges indicated that he was able to observe clearly what he had not noticed in the Spanish original, that the Argentine novel is intimately related to Mark Twain's *Huckleberry Finn:* "Going through the English version of *Don Segundo*, I have continually perceived the gravitational pull and the accents of another essential book of our America: Mark Twain's *Huckleberry Finn*."[24] Borges says he examined the translation with Adelina del Carril (Güiraldes's widow) in galley proofs. He attributes the English translation of *Don Segundo Sombra* to a collaborative effort between Federico de Onís, a celebrated professor of Hispanic studies, and Waldo Frank, the American essayist and novelist who had friendly relations with Borges's literary circle in Buenos Aires.[25] Borges says that Onís produced a version that eliminated the localisms of the text and that Waldo Frank transformed the draft into a work of literature. Borges's account may be a fabrication or a mistake since the translation, which includes a prologue by Waldo Frank, was not signed by Federico de Onís but by his wife Harriet de Onís, the author of many important translations into English from both Spanish and Portuguese, including Borges's story "La escritura del dios" ("The Writing of the God") published in *Labyrinths*. Borges does not indicate whether he assisted those responsible for the English version after reading the proofs, but his observation about the affinities between *Huckleberry Finn* and *Don Segundo Sombra* was taken up by Waldo Frank in his introduction when the novel was published in New York in 1935: "*Don Segundo Sombra* occupies in Argentine letters a place not unrelated to that of *Huckleberry Finn* in ours."[26] Years later Borges feigned that the original comparison between the American and the Argentine novels was Waldo Frank's, not his own. He wrote that Frank "established an identical parallelism between *Don Segundo Sombra* and *Huck Finn*."[27] Since Borges may have assisted in the translation, one wonders if he discovered the affinities between Mark Twain's novel and Güiraldes's as he was reading the galley proofs, or whether he was responsible for suggesting the connections between them in the first place.[28] Be that as it may, the point worth stressing is that for Borges, as for Steiner, a translation can bring to light aspects of a work that may be lost on a reader of an original.[29] But Borges would go further than Steiner. As far as he was concerned, a translator can also interpolate his own inventions and excise passages that could have been rendered with ease. A translator can produce an unfaithful work that surpasses the original precisely because it is unfaithful. This is so because a translator can correct mistakes and inconsistencies of a text and edit sections that may obscure an aspect of the work that might be worth foregrounding.

Even if it were possible to do the impossible and produce a translation that captured all the meanings, connotations, and effects of the original, Borges might not prefer it to a translation that modifies it. Even Virgil and Dante, poets Borges greatly admired perhaps more than any others, are susceptible to improvement. Borges was fond of those translators who "thought of Homer as the greatest of poets [but] knew he was human . . . and could therefore reshape his words."[30] For Borges, there are no perfect originals, any more than there can be perfect translations or rough drafts. A translator, therefore, should not be faithful to an imperfect text, but to a perfectible work. Why should a translator find equivalents for what Borges has called the "idiocies of the text" when these may hamper the very effects the text would otherwise produce? Why should a translator forgo those possibilities and potentialities in a text that the author of the original neglected out of carelessness or lack of vision? Borges's answer to these questions is so unequivocal that he included it verbatim in several of his essays on translation: "To assume that every recombination of elements is necessarily inferior to its original form is to assume that a draft nine is necessarily inferior to draft H—for there can only be drafts. The concept of the 'definitive text' corresponds only to religion or exhaustion."[31] Borges's claim that a translation necessarily involves a transformation with regards to the original is hardly controversial, but some may want to draw the line where Borges encourages translators to take liberties and call such work a "loose translation," an "adaptation," or an "imitation." These considerations, however, are not pressing ones for Borges. He was as cavalier with unconventional views regarding a translator's liberties as he was with plagiarism.

In his general views on literature, the work is more important than the writer: "An artist cares about the perfectibility of the work, and not the fact that it may have originated from himself or from others."[32] It matters little to Borges that his views on translation may be a justification for plagiarism: "If the work improves, why not? Why not make it a collective project?"[33] In *El oro de las tigres*

(The Gold of the Tigers) Borges observes after recalling, with admiration and even an air of nostalgia, that Spanish poets in the sixteenth and seventeenth centuries willfully copied texts from Latin poets: "Our concept of plagiarism is, without a doubt, less literary than commercial."[34] In discussing the similarities between Borges's Haikus and those of the old Japanese masters, María Kodama points out that repetition of certain lines from one poet by another—a common practice in Borges's own poetry—was not considered an imperfection: "No one thought that repetition was plagiarism, no one thought in terms of personal vanity."[35] Borges was persuaded that the vicissitudes of the translation process can generate literary works to be cherished for their collective, impersonal, ongoing qualities.

Alexander Coleman has suggested that Borges's bent towards impersonality and anonymity in literature is informed by T. S. Eliot's famous essay, "Tradition and the Individual Talent."[36] Eliot dismisses the need of those literary critics who stress the individuality of a writer as a "prejudice" that should be overcome to see literature as a collective enterprise, where the old speaks through the new and the new reorients the significance of the old: "What happens when a new work of art is created is something that happens simultaneously to all the works of art which preceded it."[37]

Borges admired "Tradition and the Individual Talent," and his views on translation can be read as a compliment to Eliot's ideas on the depersonalization of literature. Borges's own skepticism about individuality or personality in literature informs his notion of a perfectible work, his endorsement of the liberties a translator might take, and his suggestion that contradictory versions of the same work can be equally valid. Borges's views on translation are also underwritten by a claim, which Harold Bloom has held even more forcefully, that ours is a belated age for the creation of original works of literature.

On many occasions Borges affirmed that after three thousand years of literary production it is highly unlikely that contemporary writers can generate new or original ideas. There is a sense, therefore, in which translation, in one way or another, is an element of any literary work of the recent past. Borges had highly developed scruples with regards to a translation that impoverishes the work on artistic grounds but no qualms about a translation that transforms a previous translation, provided, of course, that he could approve the results. In fact, Borges rewrote his own translations of the same work, and might have stepped over the line into what some may consider plagiarism. Once, for example, he signed as his own a translation of Chesterton's "The Honour of Israel Gow," which amounts to a corrected version of a previous translation published by his good friend Alfonso Reyes.[38]

Borges not only maintained that a new translation can be an improvement over a previous one; he also thought that the chronological precedence of an original with respect to a translation is no guarantee of the literary primacy of the original: "I am not one of those who mystically prejudge that every translation is inferior to the original. Many times I have confirmed, or I have been able to suspect, the exact opposite."[39] Borges was more impressed by Schopenhauer's translation of Baltazar Gracian's *A Pocket Oracle* than by the original because it avoids the original's fastidious word games that obfuscate "the ideas it proposes."[40] And he preferred De Quincey's translation of Lessing's *Laocöon* for its superior "urbanity and eloquence."[41] He considered Baudelaire a superior poet to Stefan George but maintained that George was "a far more skillful craftsman."[42] He therefore was more partial to George's *Blümen des Böse* than he was to the original *Fleurs du mal*. Borges preferred Dante in the original but Cervantes in an English translation. He remembers, perhaps in jest, that *Don Quixote* seemed to him like a "bad translation" the first time he read it in Spanish.[43]

On the Translation of His Own Works

On the one hand, Borges disapproved of certain German translations of his own works as excessively literal, relying too heavily on the authority of the dictionary ("dictionaries are misleading"). Borges thought lexicons should serve to enliven, rather than dictate, a translator's choices.[44] On the other hand, he applauded several French and English translations which deviated from his originals. He often insisted that translations resulting from the intelligent or inspired taking of liberties improved his originals. Indeed, some of the freest translations of his own works were written with his collaboration or approval.

Borges collaborated with Norman Thomas di Giovanni in the English translations of at least four books. Di Giovanni reported on the nature of their approach: "We agree that the text should not be approached as a sacred object but as a tool, allowing us, whenever we feel the need, to add or subtract from it, to depart from it, or even, on rare occasions, to improve it."[45] Carter Wheelock considers that in their translations "Borges and di Giovanni have created a situation as ambiguous and subtle as one of Borges's tales."[46] Wheelock argues that the translation simplifies Borges's elaborate language of the 1940s and 1950s according to Borges's inclination, in the 1970s, "toward the simple and straightforward."[47] He also recognizes that the translators decided to take into account that their readership is a much wider audience than the original audience, readers who could ascertain many more of the contextual references, particularly those that pertain to the Argentine context. Wheelock is not disturbed by the losses that these translating procedures entail because, among other reasons, the translations can be thought of as independent versions that will not erase the perception that Borges's originals are "full of involutions and nuances heavily dependent on a particular vocabulary, often shockingly ill-fitting, ambiguous, or otherwise strange."[48]

Others, however, have been more critical. Matthew Howard considers that the collaboration between di Giovanni and Borges has "left a troubling legacy for Borges's readers and critics," in as much as they took many liberties with the originals.[49] Although Howard, like Wheelock, is willing to consider the translations as an intended self-recreation by Borges and appreciates di Giovanni's attempt to render the Argentine allusions clear to North American readers, his general assessment is fraught with suspicions about the results and even about di Giovanni's literary competence. The translation of Borges's poetry into French by Nestor Ibarra has been equally deplored by some distinguished critics and translators. One of the sharpest rejections of Ibarra's translation is found in an essay in which Albert Bensoussan argues that all the significant translations into French of Borges's main poems, including those by Nestor Ibarra and Roger Callois, are lamentable. He takes issue with Callois's literal translation but is especially disconcerted by Ibarra's work. Bensoussan, a distinguished translator himself, is aware that Borges gave Ibarra full license to translate his poems as he saw fit and knows that Borges wrote a preface with praise and gratitude; and yet, he considers Ibarra's translations to be dishonest transpositions that take unwarranted liberties with the original.[50]

However, Borges, in fact, encouraged Ibarra to take those liberties and collaborated with di Giovanni's transformations of his own works. In each case he considered the end result to be a collective work. In the preface to Ibarra's translation he reiterated his idea that the work takes supremacy over the author and that, in principle, a translation ought not be judged negatively if it deviates from the original. And Borges also regrets that "no one likes to celebrate those pages whose paternity is uncertain. The same goes for translations of poetry. We want to admire the poet, not the translator, and this scruple, or this prejudice, has favored the literal version."[51]

The issue at hand is not a simple one. Borges himself argued in favor of literary practices that were collective and impersonal and often expressed skepticism with respect to the individuality of any author, including himself. And yet, Wheelock, Bensoussan, and others have a valid point to make when they express serious reservations in their assessments of translations that transform or mollify the uniqueness or idiosyncrasies of Borges's literary genius, even when the gestures appear to be in the spirit of views that Borges himself held or in terms of the very conceits Borges was fond of practicing. My intention is not to make value judgments about Borges's views on translation—since I am interested in understanding them as they shed light on his practices as a masterful creative translator—but it is important to recognize that the reception of his work, for decades, has faced a dilemma: one can accept Borges's views about the impersonality of literature and thus downplay the significance of his personal genius, or downplay the significance of his literary views in order to appreciate his genius.[52]

In a seminal work on the reception of Spanish American literature in France (and the international reception of Borges owes much to French interest in his work), Sylvia Molloy castigates Ibarra for presenting Borges to the French public with Borgesian tactics and procedures that confused unsuspecting readers about Borges's individuality: "If Ibarra was keen on mystifying his reader, he could not have been more successful. . . . One would have preferred an introduction, perhaps less brilliant, but one which would have given, to the extent possible, a better articulated image of the writer."[53] Molloy seems to suggest that once Borges's readers recognize the Borgesian conflation of fiction and fact they can enjoy it, but she also suggests that there is something misleading about the Borgesian game when it is not clear that it is being played.

But whether or not Borges was a willing accomplice in the mystification of his own works, he would invariably and enthusiastically express his preference for the translations that took liberties with, or corrected, his originals. In this regard, di Giovanni once reported that a university professor complained that a translation of a Borges short story had corrected an inconsistency. The professor would have preferred that the translation conserve the inconsistency, as he considered it a charming Borgesian touch. As di Giovanni recalled the matter: "Borges was mildly angered; first of all, he found nothing charming in the slip, and, secondly, he feels that he has the right to shape and alter his work as he sees fit. One of the great luxuries of working with Borges is that he's interested only in making things better and not in defending a text."[54]

An original text offers a translator opportunities precisely because an equivalent word may have different connotations and arbitrary associations in the language or in the linguistic modalities of the translator. Borges also conjectured that one of the possible advantages of a translation over an original is its likelihood to eschew aspects of a work involving historical or linguistic idiosyncrasies that have little to do with why the work is worth reading in the first place. That is why Borges would at times recommend to young writers that they read great works of literature in translation rather than in the original: "It is better to study the classics in translation to appreciate the substantive and to avoid the accidental."[55]

A translator—like a writer correcting a draft—often cuts, adds, and reorganizes a text to produce a work that improves on rougher sketches. For Borges, therefore, translation from one language to another is a special case of rewriting a draft that does not differ, in principle, from the transformation of a text in the same language, from one dialect or one modality to another. It may be easier, for example, to translate a journalistic article from French into English than to modernize Chaucer or Shakespeare into any modern language, including English.

In Borges's earliest statement about translation—a short article he published in 1926—he argued that translation exists fundamentally in two forms, a literal and a periphrastic:

> I suppose that there are two types of translation. One involves literality, and the other periphrasis. The first corresponds to the Romantic mind-set, and the second one to the classicists. I would like to reason through this affirmation to diminish its paradoxical air. Classicist are interested in the work of art, but never the artist. They believe in absolute perfection and they seek it. They disdain localisms, rarities, and contingencies. . . . Conversely, Romantics never look for the work of art, they look for the man. And the man (as is well known) is not intemporal nor archetypal. He is John Doe, not Bill Smith. He owns a climate, a body, the propensity to do this rather than that, or to do nothing at all. He has a present, a past, a future, and even a death that is all his own. Watch out if you touch a single one of the words he ever wrote![56]

In the retrospective light of his later essays on translation, informed by his views on the impersonality of literature, some critics interpret the two options Borges offers as alternatives to which he gives equal weight. Notwithstanding his ironic tone, however, in 1926 he was more skeptical about the option he attributes to the "classicists." In the 1920s Borges sometimes maintained that literature was the direct expression of an individuality. This view, which he was soon to abandon, is consistent with the "Romantic" approach to translation, which he seems to favor in this essay: "That reverence of the self, of the irreplaceable human differentiation justifies the literal translation." And yet, Borges's preference is not categorical.

He recognizes that for texts of the past, it may not be possible to capture the individual who produced them, and to that extent recreations are inevitable. To the extent, however, that the reconstruction of the individual who created the text is no longer possible, translation of ancient works becomes "a game of variants."

By the 1930s Borges had abandoned the view that literature is strictly autobiographical, and he no longer discussed the problem of translation in terms of classicist or Romantic mind-sets. That being said, the 1926 essay expresses a view about language, inspired by his readings of Novalis, that would have a lasting significance in Borges's general ideas about both literature and translation. Borges cites a fragment in which the German Romantic poet affirms that words have singular meanings *(eingentümliche Bedeutungen)*, connotations *(Nebenbedeutungen)*, and arbitrary associations *(willkürlichen Bedeutungen)*.[57] This distinction informed a picture that would remain a constant in Borges's discussions of language, literature, and translation: that in the passage of time it becomes increasingly difficult to determine the connotations and arbitrary associations of written language that has come down to us from the past.

From the 1930s onward Borges continued to think of language in terms of meanings, connotations, and arbitrary associations. This view determined how he examined the vicissitudes of a text over the course of time: the meanings of words survive while connotations and associations change, even across languages and modes of expressions, because the same words may have different connotations for different language communities separated by space or time. For instance, Borges thought that certain Argentine poetry would be lost on contemporary Chileans because the same words in the same language suggest different meanings in the two contexts. He also believed that the transformations of a language, its accidental developments over time, could either improve or impoverish a work as the connotations and arbitrary associations of words evolve, even as general meanings are maintained. Borges would often indicate that meanings, concepts, and ideas are easier to transfer from one mode of expression to another than are connotations and associations, where emotions play a greater role.

His disdain for translations that supposedly capture the veracity of an original whose theme is foreign or distant also held over from the 1926 essay into future essays on translation. In an idea he expands in his famous essay "El escritor argentino y la tradición" (the Argentine writer and tradition) Borges claims that to capture the "foreign" elements of the original, the translator must necessarily distort: foreign elements are self-evident, require no description in their original context, but when they are explained in a translation, the translation distorts the original. It upsets Borges that the preface of Doctor Madrus's translation of the *Arabian Nights* includes the indication "literal and complete," when he believes it resembles the luxuriant style of Oscar Wilde's *The Portrait of Dorian Gray*. Thus, for example, the original "They arrived at a column of black stone, in which a man was buried up to his armpits" is transformed by Madrus into "One evening the caravan came to a column of black stone to which a strange being was chained, only half of whose body could be seen, for the other half was buried in the ground."[58] Borges likens Madrus's role as translator to the graphic artist charged with illustrating a novel or short story: the artist includes details not necessarily mentioned in the work. Borges does not object, in principle, to the practice of adding details to a work of literature, but it disturbs him when the claim of "complete veracity" is made of any translation that expands the original to produce effects of strangeness or local color: "The announced purpose of veracity turns the translator into an impostor, since in order to maintain the strangeness of what he is translating, he is obliged to express local color, to make the raw rawer, to turn sweetness into syrup, and to emphasize the lot until it becomes a lie."[59]

Borges's insights intriguingly coincide with those of some analytic philosophers who follow Quine by claiming that any given text can have an indefinite number of valid and even contradictory translations. Borges was fond of demonstrating the difficulties of transforming a simple Spanish text into another one. He once offered two different Spanish versions of the first lines of Argentina's most famous poem, José Hernández's *Martín Fierro:* "Aquí me pongo a cantar / al compás de la vigüela" (Here I begin to sing / to the rhythm of my guitar). Borges's first translation is intended to be drawn-out, but literal: "In the very place where I find myself, I am beginning to sing with my guitar."[60] His second translation takes a liberty with respect to the original: "Here, with my fraternal guitar, I begin to sing."[61] Borges compares his two translations, and concludes that the second and less accurate one is the better. The first "so ridiculous, and sluggish! is almost literal."[62] Subtle as always, Borges did not mean to reject the literal translation outright, but only the justification of those who might prefer it on the grounds that a writer's text constitutes his uniqueness.

In the 1920s Borges had already identified the benefits of a translation that takes liberties.[63] In the 1930s his views on translation coalesced. He vindicated the right of a translator to swerve away from the original and to interpolate, and he formulated a definition of translation he would continue to restate for decades to come: *translation is a long experimental game of chance played with omissions and emphasis.*[64] In his incisive definition Borges recognizes that translation involves choice, chance, and experimentation. For Borges, the incommensurability of any two languages, or even two modes of expression within the same language, provides stimulating challenges to the literary translator, who must choose between registering the singularities of an original work and eliminating the details that obscure its general effects. A literal translation can sometimes generate ridiculous results, but it can also spawn strange and wondrous surprises. Borges's views on translation percolated into his fictions as well. In "La lotería en Babilonia" ("The Lottery in Babylon"), for example, no two books are alike because "the scribes make a secret oath to cut, interpolate, and alter."[65] Borges first formulated his definition of translation in a sustained reflection on a famous polemic between Matthew Arnold and Francis E. Newman.

The Arnold-Newman Discussion

In 1856, after many years of work, Francis Newman published his English version of Homer's *Iliad*. The distinguished professor from the University of London had set out to produce a faithful and literal translation that would capture every linguistic detail and all of the Homeric peculiarities to such a degree that it would be possible for a contemporary reader to comprehend the Greek world. Once his task was accomplished he announced, with a sense of satisfaction and pride, that his *Iliad* would be the model for any future English translation of classical Greek, excepting, perhaps, the case of Pindar.

It did not take long for the reputation of his *Iliad* to suffer a damaging blow. Bringing to bear his prestige as an Oxford professor and admired poet, Matthew Arnold announced he would offer not one but a series of lectures to demonstrate that Newman's *Iliad* was a dismal failure. Arnold recognized Newman's erudition and his command of Ancient Greek, but argued that a good translation requires an attribute Newman lacked: the literary sensibility of a good poet who knows when to edit and modify anything in the original that may obscure the general effects of a work. Newman's approach might be of some use to a certain kind of reader interested in every detail of a text, but it constitutes a recipe tainted with the odd and uncouth. No translator of Homer can respect every detail of a work if the purpose is to recreate the original so that an English reader of the translation would experience the same effects as a reader of ancient Greek.

According to Arnold, Homer expressed his ideas with clarity; his Greek is plain, direct, and rapid. Newman's translation, on the other hand, is slow, rough, and confusing. Rather than reproducing the general effects of Homer's *Iliad*, Newman's translation registers the considerable linguistic incompatibilities between English and ancient Greek. Newman's literal translation abounds in grammatical constructions that strike any English reader as strange, when it should have flowed with the clarity of Homer's Greek. He rendered sentence structures from the Greek that do not exist in English, when he should have found English equivalents to reproduce the effects of the original.

Homer, for example, uses the double epithet, a common construction of ancient Greek unavailable in standard English usage. For instance, the translation of two consecutive adjectives can produce curious effects in English that are quite commonplace in the original. With this, and many other examples, Arnold concluded that a good translator must sacrifice linguistic fidelity to reproduce the effects of a work.

Newman was hurt and affected by Arnold's lectures. He accused his fellow Hellenist of bad faith and wrote an entire book to acquit himself of the poet's objections. The so-called "strange English constructions," so discordant to Arnold, were inevitable because they reflect Homer's peculiarities. A Homeric translation ought to sound strange to a contemporary reader because ancient Greek is as foreign to an Englishman of the nineteenth century as the ancient world itself. Had he eliminated the peculiarities of ancient Greek, including the double epithets and other constructions Arnold disliked, he would not have captured the essence of Homer. One would be glossing over substantive differences between the world of the ancient Greeks and that of modern England if one's translation of Homer read as if written by a contemporary.

The famous polemic between Newman and Arnold inspired Borges's most important observations about the task of producing a new literary version of a preexistent work. In numerous essays and interviews spanning his lifetime, Borges referred to the Arnold-Newman debate as a beautiful exchange or lively and intelligent discussion.[66] Most literary critics who have glossed Borges's take on the Arnold-Newman controversy have assumed that the Argentine writer is simply summarizing the views of the two British professors, but that is misleading. When Borges discussed the controversy, he did it selectively. He did not credit Newman's aspiration to offer a window onto the ancient world for a modern reader, nor Arnold's attempt to recreate, in English, the same effects that a contemporary sensitive reader would have experienced with the original. Borges ignores Newman's concerns regarding the reconstruction of the Greek world and focuses on his literal method. He also ignores Arnold's insistence on the effects that an ancient work might have on a contemporary who understands Greek and focuses, instead, on the effects of the work without giving the original any special status, ignoring, in fact, the original altogether. Borges shrewdly side-steps the most serious incompatibilities between the two Hellenists so that their irreconcilable differences appear to involve matters of preference.

In Borges's personal synthesis the two Hellenists represent the two main options available to a translator: either a literal translation that strives to register all the singularities of a work, or a recreation that eliminates the details, obscuring the work's general effects. A bad literal translation can produce curious and even ridiculous effects, and a recreation can be more faithful to an original than a literal translation. This, of course, was Arnold's main objection to Newman's translation. Borges, however, does not assume that the effects of a literal translation are necessarily objectionable, because they can enrich and even revitalize a language: "The paradox is—and of course, 'paradox' means something true that at first appearance is false—that if you are out for strangeness, if you want, let's say to astonish the reader, you can do that by being literal. [Literal translations can create] something that is not in the original."[67]

Borges proclaims that some of the greatest resources available to English speakers came precisely from the unexpected and astonishing effects produced by the approach Arnold objected to in his critique of Newman. Borges accepted Arnold's description of Newman's procedure as the encounter between two distinct modes of expression, but he qualified the negative value judgment: "If Matthew Arnold had looked closely into his Bible [and Arnold had recommended to Newman that one might want to approach the translation of Homer with the model of a biblical translation] he might have seen that the English Bible is full of literal translations and that . . . the great beauty of the English Bible lies in those literal translations."[68] Had the powerful biblical phrase "Tower of Strength" been translated according to Arnold's approach it should have produced something akin to the drab "a firm stronghold," and the "Song of songs" would lose its poetry had it been translated more faithfully as "the highest song" or "the best song." Borges corrects Arnold by commenting that "it might be said that literal translations make not only, as Matthew Arnold pointed out, for uncouthness and oddity, but also for strangeness and beauty."[69]

The positions of Arnold and Newman are, of course, mutually exclusive, but Borges found merits in each of them: "Newman favored the literal mode that retains all verbal singularities. Arnold, on the other hand, favored the severe elimination of distracting details. The latter produces sound uniformities, and the former produces unexpected surprises."

Informed by his reflections on Newman and Arnold, Borges developed a doctrine of translation that does not favor a priori the views of one or the other as he characterizes them but, rather, appreciates both as options. In short, he relativizes their views. A translator has to decide whether to cut or alter effects in the original. According to Borges, a translation can take place in a single language, and it is possible to copy a text from one language to another. If whatever one would like to say about the English phrase "the black water" could also be said about the Spanish "el agua negra," Borges would say that the Spanish is a copy of the English.

In his famous essay "The Homeric Versions" Borges compares six versions of a passage from the *Odyssey* in his own Spanish "copies." Eliot Weinberger restores the original English texts in his superb English translation of Borges's essay. Borges's procedure and Weinberger's restoration are both justified. The aspects Borges underscores in his comparisons do not involve linguistic differences between English and Spanish but other considerations, such as the reverential manner of one version, the luxuriant language of another, the lyric tone of one versus the oratorical tone of another, the visual emphasis of one versus the more factual emphasis of another, the spectacular versus the sedate features of another.

A translation, as opposed to a copy, suggests a transformation that may surpass the original. One of Borges's favorite literary practices was to compare a translation to an original and to judge the translation and the original on equal footing, as two versions of the same work. Borges argued that the ideal arbiter of a translation is the unlikely reader who can resist the almost inevitable prejudice in favor of the original: "If we did not know which was the original and which the translation, we could judge them fairly,"[70] which is to say that the best judge of a translation is the unprejudiced reader. In this spirit he sometimes underscored the benefits of ignoring the original language of repeatedly translated works: "The *Odyssey*, thanks to my opportune ignorance of Greek, is an international bookshelf of works in prose and verse."[71] Borges expressed his hope "that someday a translation will be considered as something in itself."[72]

In his prologue to Nestor Ibarra's translation of Paul Valéry's "Le Cimetière marin," Borges criticizes several lines of the original with the argument Arnold deployed to censure Newman's literal translation. "Le changement des rives en rumeur" (the changing of riverbanks in rumor), according to Borges, leaves much to be desired when compared to "La pérdida en rumor de la rivera" (the loss of rumor from the riverbank). According to Borges, Ibarra's line is not superior merely because it sounds better than Valéry's; it is superior because it supposedly captures, more effectively than its French counterpart, Valéry's poetic vision: "To insist on the contrary with too much faith is to renege on Valéry's poetic vision in favor of the temporal individual who formulated it."[73]

Borges held that not even San Juan de la Cruz, "the greatest . . . of Spanish poets," was beyond improvement.[74] Borges preferred Roy Campbell's "When all the house was hushed" over San Juan's "Estando ya mi casa sosegada" (when my house was at rest): "Here we have the word 'all,' which gives a sense of space, of expanse, to the line. And then the gentle English word 'hushed.' 'Hushed' seems to give us somehow the very music of silence."[75] "Music of silence," to the Spanish reader, is an English translation of San Juan de la Cruz's stunning paradox "música callada," which in a more literal translation would be "silent music." Even as he compared many translations to their originals, Borges insisted that the aesthetic value of a translation does not depend on its relationship to the original. Borges would often recommend the reading of translations, as with Juan de Jauregui's Spanish version of Lucan's *Pharsalia*, which are "completely unfaithful and very beautiful."[76]

A good translation can be unfaithful to the original as with FitzGerald's *Rubáiyat*, but it can also be more faithful to the "vision" of the work than the original, as Borges insists is the case for Nestor Ibarra's translation of Paul Valéry. The *Concise Oxford Dictionary of Quotations* offers as its only entry for Borges a comment on a translation: "The original is unfaithful to the translation." The context of this quotation is his analysis of Henley's English translation of William Beckford's *Vathek*. Borges thinks that the French original is unfaithful to the translation because it was rendered with sloppy haste, whereas the English version was crafted with thoughtful care and attention to detail.[77]

The translations Borges condemned with greatest vehemence are those he called spoiled versions of admirable works. In his indignant review of poet León Felipe's Spanish version of Whitman's "Song of Myself," Borges offers his "copies" of Whitman (which he quotes in Spanish as if they were verses by Whitman) to condemn Felipe's translation. The following transcribes, in English, a fragment of Borges's review. In the original all of the quotations appear in Spanish including the Whitman quotation, which Borges presents not as a translation but as an equivalent to the original in order to contrast it to Felipe's translation, which Borges considers a dismal failure (the original Spanish texts of Borges's "copy" and of Felipe's "translation" are both in the endnote):

Whitman writes ("Song of Myself"):
    Walt Whitman, a cosmos, from Manhattan the son
    Turbulent, carnal, sensual, eating, drinking, engendering. . . .

Felipe "translates" (Canto a mí mismo):
    I am Walt Whitman
    A Cosmos. Look at me!
    The son of Manhattan.
    Turbulent, strong, sensual;
    I eat, drink, and engender. . . .

The transformation is notorious; from the psalm-like voice "of Walt Whitman" to the spoiled little cries of an Andalusian deep song.[78]

Borges was especially interested in the destiny of the translation of ancient literature.[79] In "The Homeric Versions" he observes that

the events of the *Iliad* and the *Odyssey* "survive completely" while
the connotations of Homer's language have been lost: "The present
state of [Homer's] works is like a complex equation that represents
the precise relations of unknown quantities. There is no possible
greater richness for the translator."[80] Borges understands, therefore,
why there are so many translations of Homer, "all of them sincere,
genuine, and divergent." To make his point Borges examines a
strange Homeric adjective. He offers a few examples including the
following: "those rich young men who drink the *black* waters of
the Aesepus" (my emphasis). Borges knows that the waters of the
River are probably not "black." Some translators whom Arnold
might have praised omitted the adjective. Others defend the inclu-
sion. Alexander Pope believed such adjectives had a liturgical function the translator ought to retain; and Remy de Gourmont thought
they must have had an enchantment that has been lost to us. Borges offers another conjecture: "They may have been to the Greeks
what prepositions are to us: modest and obligatory sounds that usage requires and upon which no originality may be exercised." In
the sentence regarding the young men who drink the black waters
of a river, "black" could correspond to the word "transparent." Borges might have been amused to note that Samuel Butler's translation of the same passage reads, "the limpid waters of the Aesepus,"
while Navarro's celebrated Spanish translation says the exact opposite: "the muddy waters of the Aesepus."[81]

On the Arabian Nights

In one of his many discussions of the *Arabian Nights,* Borges
celebrated the chain of translations that brought the stories from
"the Hindostan to Persia, from Persia to Arabia, from Arabia to
Egypt, growing and multiplying itself."[82] After the text was set in
the fourteenth Century in Egypt, the copyists supplemented the collection with new stories. Borges applauded the cunning of Antoine
Galland who continued the practice by enriching the original with
new tales of his own invention (or from oral tradition), such as the
stories of Aladdin. Borges also admired Richard Burton for includ-

ing personal interpolations when he translated the *Arabian Nights*.
Borges secretly participated in the process of transforming Arabian
stories. He recreated a translation by Galland and invented a story
he attributed to Burton.[83]

Borges's most sustained and boldest essay on translation is "The
Translators of the *Thousand and One Nights*."[84] Not only a comparison of the various translators of the *Arabian Nights,* the essay
presents a number of his views on translation heretofore not fully
articulated. If in other essays Borges maintained that an original and
its translations were variations on a theme, no text being a priori
superior to any other, in "The Translators" Borges declares that
translators often translate against one another. To understand why
some translator adopted one approach over another, it might be useful, Borges argues, to know against whom the translator was translating. Harold Bloom has called Borges "a great theorist of poetic
influence."[85] Bloom's own doctrine of "the anxiety of influence"
has its acknowledged antecedent in ideas Borges first developed in
his meditations on translation, years before he wrote his seminal essay
"Kafka y sus precursores" (Kafka and his precursors).[86]

In his essay on the *Arabian Nights* Borges also contends that a
translator has the option to interpolate passages into a text not in
the original. He coins the term "buenas apocrifidades," which Esther
Allen improves with the phrase "fine apocrypha," to refer to the
fortunate additions with which a translator can supplement the original.[87] As an example, Borges was fond of quoting Chaucer's translation of the latin phrase "Ars longa, vita brevis" as "the lyf so short,
the craft so long to learn." Borges approves of the transformation:
"[Chaucer] gave the line a kind of wistful music not to be found in
the original."[88]

Borges approves not only of small apocryphal changes, but even
of major ones and holds that the more successful the apocryphal
entry, the more it becomes inexorably linked to our notion of the
work. As an example, he offers Galland's interpolated stories in his
eighteen-century translation of the *Arabian Nights*. Borges lists a
number of specific examples to make his point that to exclude
Galland's interpolations would now be taken as an amputation of

the work, which for contemporary readers should include "the stories of Aladdin; the Forty Thieves; Prince Ahmad and the Fairy Peri-Banu; Abu al-Hassan, the Sleeper and the Walker; the night adventure of Caliph Harun al-Rashid; and the two sisters who envied their younger sister."[89]

Borges maintained that some interpolations in a translation may leave the content of a work untouched because they are implicit, yet unstated, in the original. He felt, for example, that his short story "El fin" ("The End") is not so much a continuation of José Hernández's *Martín Fierro* as an explicit account of a story that can be deduced from the original. Borges insists that other than an incidental character "nothing or almost nothing is my invention."[90] In the original the gaucho Martín Fierro kills a man and later defeats a vengeful relative of the victim in a verbal duel that diffuses the revenge; in Borges's story the vengeful relative kills Fierro.[91] One of Borges's tours de force, as a translator, is his interpolation of a paragraph in his translation of Sir Thomas Browne's *Urn-Burial.*[92] The protagonist of the story "La memoria de Shakespeare" ("Shakespeare's Memory") argues at length that an interpolation in an eighteenth-century critical edition of an unnamed work by Shakespeare has become an "undeniable part of the canon."[93]

Some translations become anachronistic as the meaning of words change. Language shifts may work for or against translations, just as they might for original works.[94] In one of Borges's many reflections on Shakespeare he wonders if some of the bard's images have been improved by the history of the language. He illustrates his point with a quotation about Christ in Israel: "Over whose acres walk'd those blessed feet, / Which, fourteen hundred years ago, / were nail'd, / For our advantage, on the bitter cross."[95] Borges speculates that the word "advantage" ("a word which in a sense is not very beautiful but sounds like the right word") may have had sharper theological connotations in the seventeenth century when it could have meant "salvation." If so, "perhaps the line wasn't as beautiful as it is today. Nowadays, the word advantage comes with a sharp surprise. I am grateful to Shakespeare, but, for all we know, maybe time has bettered the text."[96]

Just as shifts in language can have positive or negative effects on a work or on its translations, so, too, distortions by a translator can have positive or negative effects. Borges prefers Galland's distortion when he translates a tryst between a princess and "one of the lowliest servants" over Richard Burton's distasteful rendering of the same text as "a black cook of loathsome aspect and found with kitchen grease and grime."

Borges thinks it is legitimate to "mutilate" an original if one has good reason to do so. Thus, for example, he considers it fitting to downplay the sexual content of the *Arabian Nights* in order to underscore its magical aspects, but inappropriate to do so to uphold a Puritan worldview. He therefore approves of the discreet ways in which Galland suggests aspects made explicit in the original, as with the euphemism "to receive in her bed" to describe an erotic encounter. He deplores, however, the "convolutions and occultations" of Edward Lane when avoiding the word "hermaphrodite" by replacing it with "mixed species," and when erasing the sexual practices in a harem by replacing a sentence describing a king's conjugal visits with a comment on his impartiality.

If Lane erased the erotic context of the original, which Galland had insinuated into his translation, Richard Burton reinstated them with exaggerated vigor. Borges disapproves of Burton's sexual amplifications in the *Arabian Nights* as a deliberate provocation to attract attention and to establish his reputation as an Arabist conversant with the intimacies of the Orient. In the case of the *Arabian Nights,* Borges urges, the "disinfected" versions are actually a restoration of a primal text. The tales were versions of ancient love stories, not obscene but "impassioned and sad." Borges defends the "disinfected" versions with another argument: "An evasion of the original's erotic opportunities is not an unpardonable sin in the sight of the Lord when the primary aim is to emphasize the atmosphere of magic."[97] Borges uses the theme of the unintended restoration of an original in his own stories, as when Herman Soergel in "Shakespeare's Memory" expresses his admiration for Chapman's Homeric translations because they "bring English back—without his realizing it—to its Anglo-Saxon origin (Ursprung)."[98]

Just as a literal translation that transforms the meanings of the original can produce surprises, Borges does not exclude the possible benefits of carelessness that can produce "involuntary good results." Borges contends that Lane achieved this in his translation: "At times [his] lack of sensibility serves him well, for it allows him to include commonplace words in a noble paragraph, with involuntary results. The most rewarding example of such a cooperation of heterogeneous words must be: 'And in this palace is the last information respecting the lords collected in the dust.'"[99] In a passage prefiguring a major theme of "Pierre Menard, Author of the Quixote" and his essay "Kafka and His Precursors." Borges argues that expectations can play a consequential role in the reception of a translation: "I have sometimes suspected that the radical distinction between poetry and prose lies in the very different expectations of readers: poetry presupposes an intensity that is not tolerated in prose. Something similar happens with Burton's work: it has a preordained prestige with which no other Arabist has ever been able to compete. The attractions of the forbidden are rightfully his."[100] So, too, does the intended audience affect a translation: "[the original audience of the tale was] roguish, prone to exaggeration, illiterate, infinitely suspicious of the present and credulous of remote marvels. [Burton's club of subscribers on the other hand] were the respectable men of the West End, well equipped for disdain and erudition but not for belly laughs or terror."[101]

Borges prefers a translator who falsifies to a translator who claims to capture the veracity of the original. He admires Doctor Madrus's proliferous translation of the *Arabian Nights* because of its infidelities: "To celebrate Madrus's fidelity is to leave out the soul of Madrus, to ignore Madrus entirely. It is his infidelity, his happy and creative infidelity, that must matter to us."[102] Of all the translations of the *Arabian Nights,* the one Borges dislikes more than any other is Enno Littman's, the one he believes is the most faithful. Borges disapproves of Littman's version because it is the one that least engages with literature. All of the more unfaithful translations Borges prefers "can only be conceived *in the wake of literature.*"[103] To translate in the wake of literature is to enter into a dialogue with re-

sources fashioned by others, as when Burton engages his translation with English literature, or Madrus with the literature of France.
According to Borges, Littman's dry accuracy sidesteps literary considerations:

> In some way, the almost inexhaustible process of English is
> adumbrated in Burton—John Donne's hard obscenity, the
> gigantic vocabularies of Shakespeare and Cyril Tourneur,
> Swinburne's affinity for the archaic, the crass erudition of the
> authors of 17th-century chapbooks, the energy and impreci-
> sion, the love of tempests and magic. In Madrus's laughing
> paragraphs, *Salammbô* and La Fontaine, the *Mannequin d'osier*,
> and the *ballets russes* all coexist. In Littmann, who like Wash-
> ington cannot tell a lie, there is nothing but the probity of
> Germany. This is so little, so very little. The commerce be-
> tween Germany and the *Nights* should have produced some-
> thing more.[104]

Nestor Ibarra echoed this idea in one of the prefaces to his translations of Borges: "During that ephemeral possession of a text (and
to some degree of an author) which takes place in the process of
translating, we engage much more than our ideas about translation,
literature, aesthetics, and almost everything else."[105] Borges prefers
the "contaminated" translations if their approach to literature is
worthwhile. And as he laments the "uninspired frankness" of Littman's translation, he wonders what Kafka would have created had
he translated the *Arabian Nights:* "What wouldn't a man do, a
Kafka, if he organized and accentuated these games, if he refash-
ioned them according to the German distortion, the *Unheimlichkeit*
of Germany?"[106]

Borges's Doctrine of Translation

As with many other topics that engaged him, Borges never wrote
a fully elaborated treatise on translation. In his observations about
literary matters he was inclined more toward the scrutiny of par-

ticular cases than toward theoretical considerations. He preferred
the pertinent and sometimes surprising aperçu to the general abstraction. That being said, his views on translation remained fairly
constant after the 1930s, and it would be possible to construe an
approach, even a doctrine, on the basis of his general observations.[107]
Borges wrote several essays in which he outlined the parameters of
the practice of literary translation, and offered specific criteria to
discuss the results.

The view of translation most akin to his, although Borges did
not accept all its implications, is that of Novalis, whose fragments
Borges translated on several occasions. In "Pierre Menard, Author
of the Quixote," the narrator indicates that Menard's project to produce a text identical to Cervantes's novel was inspired by "that philological fragment of Novalis . . . that outlines the theme of a total
identification with a given author."[108] Novalis's fragment is worth
quoting in full: "I show I have understood a writer only when I
can act in his spirit, when I, without diminishing his individuality,
can translate him and change many things."[109] Borges shared Novalis's idea that a translator is allowed to transform the original, but
would not hold a translator to the demand that he or she should
merge with a writer's spirit or individuality. Borges's indifference
to those aspects of Novalis's view is illustrated in "Pierre Menard,
Author of the Quixote," when Menard considers becoming one with
Cervantes and rejects the option as too simple: "[the enterprise is
not difficult], it would suffice to be immortal to finish it."[110] Once
he rejects the idea of becoming spiritually one with Cervantes,
Menard decides to continue with his project of producing a work
that would be identical to pages found in *Don Quixote* but to continue as himself, not as Cervantes.

In short, when Borges wrote "Pierre Menard," he was not interested—as he might have been in the 1920s—in Novalis's Romantic
ideas about the individuality of a poet, but he fully endorsed the
view that a translator could reshape and improve an original. Borges also shared Novalis's view that the beauty of literature, even of
poetry, is not necessarily lost in translation. As Kristin Pfefferkorn
has indicated: "According to Novalis, if the translator is a conjurer,

so too is the poet. And if there is artistry in one, so there is in the other."[111] For Novalis, a translator may surpass the original by expressing the idea of the work, or perhaps its ideal, with greater success. Borges did not share the view that the translator was beholden to the spirit of the author, to a specific ideal, or to the essence of the work;[112] but he was in full agreement with a notion Novalis expressed in a letter in which he congratulated Schlegel for surpassing Shakespeare in his translations of the plays: "To translate is to produce literature, just as the writing of one's own work is—and it is more difficult, more rare. In the end all literature is translation."[113] And even though Novalis himself did not connect his views about translation with his idea that words have meanings, connotations, and arbitrary associations, Borges did. Borges argued that in the passage of time the meanings, connotations, and associations of words can change to such a degree as to justify repeated translations of the same work, as well as translations of translations.

In summary, for Borges a translation is not the transfer of a text from one language to another. It is a transformation of a text into another. The appreciation of a literary work, for Borges, can be enriched by translation, provided that the reader avoids the prejudice of assuming the original is the best version of the work. Judging a translation involves the scrutiny of two or more versions of the same work on equal terms.

One can translate within the same language, and one can copy from one language to another. Borges would call a text a "copy" if the most pertinent observations to be made about it could also be made of the original. In contrast, a "version" is a text with relevant differences with respect to either the original or another translation of the same work. For Borges, a literal translation attempts to maintain all the details of the original, but changes the emphasis (understood as meanings, connotations, associations, and effects of the work). A "recreation," on the other hand, omits many details to conserve the emphasis of the work, and it may add interpolations. Since a "copy" maintains both the details and the emphasis that matter in a discussion of a work, most translations, especially prose translations, include some measure of "copying." A faithful translation, for Borges, retains the meanings and effects of the work, whereas an unfaithful translation changes them. A literal translation that changes the emphasis of the work is therefore unfaithful, as opposed to a recreation, which conserves them.

A translation can be more faithful to the work of literature than the original when the original fails to fulfill its own potentialities and latencies. A translation is also faithful when it contains the same idiosyncrasies as the original. It is unfaithful when it does not contain the same idiosyncrasies, when it contains elements of strangeness not present in the original, when it lacks the verbal oddities of the original, or when an irregularity appears that was not in the original. A translator may provide cuts and interpolations that may or may not be unfaithful to an original; such cuts and interpolations may actually restore a text to a form that preceded the original at an earlier stage in the genealogy of the work, or they may succeed in drawing out possibilities latent in the original, even if those possibilities transform it.

A translation, for Borges, should be evaluated with the same criteria applicable to any work of literature. A literal translation or a recreation, faithful or unfaithful, can be successful or unsuccessful, depending on the results. And Borges could be hard on the results of a translation when they did not meet his literary standards. Borges did not hesitate to condemn certain translations as dull or inadequate when he felt their originals were of literary interest. He has called such translations "defamations" of a work of art even when more faithful than other versions.

Borges recognizes that circumstances or historical considerations bear on the process of translation, or on the reception of a translated work. He thinks, however, that we are burdened by our historical sense. Borges acknowledges that avoiding historical or circumstantial considerations entirely may simply be impossible, but his bias is in favor of bracketing those considerations in the hope that translations may attain the same status as original works of literature.

Borges's essays on translation are beginning to receive the attention they deserve—which places them next to those of Walter

Benjamin, Ezra Pound, and George Steiner—as among the most vigorous contemporary approaches to the literary version. Borges did not offer strict guidelines for translating, and, as Willis Barnstone has underscored, Borges's favorite word to indicate the choices, judgments, and discriminations of a translator was "preference."[114] That being said, Borges did develop his views on the alternatives available to a translator, and those guidelines amount to a loose methodology for literary translation open to and even encouraging of transformations and modifications.[115] He sometimes expressed restraint in modifying an original to avoid hostile reactions, and he also expressed his envy of those translators of classical texts who enjoy the right to transform an original with a freedom not available to a translator of contemporary works. The barriers against transforming a contemporary work are not only legal; they also involve the understandable reservations of readers who prefer a rough approximation to a creative recreation.

Borges's definition of translation as a combination of emphasis and omissions is not isolated from his general views about literature and art: "Time accumulates experiences on the artist, as it does with all men. By force of omissions and emphasis, of memory and forgetfulness, time combines some of those experiences and thus it elaborates the work of art."[116] Borges's idea that the imperfections of memory make imagination possible is a theme of some of his fictions, such as "Funes el memorioso" ("Funes, the Memorious"). It is also an element he introduced surreptitiously into his own translations. In his version of Kipling's " 'The Finest Story in the World' " Borges includes a passage that tellingly corrects Kipling.

(Kipling)
   I had just discovered the entire principle upon which our half-memory falsely called imagination is based.

(Borges)
   In that instant I had discovered the principles of the imperfect memory which is called imagination.[117]

In Kipling's version the frustrations of the writer attempting to approximate the faulty memory of a man unaware he has lived previous lives are expressed in the assertion that a broken memory is "falsely called imagination." In Borges's version imperfect memory is called imagination, presented not as falsity but as a positive fact one can discover. The positive effects of the imperfect memory have Nietzschean connotations akin to the potentially positive effects of the translation process as practiced by Borges, that is, transformations of originals shaped and reshaped until they gain a life of their own, until the old and the new become variations on a theme.

CHAPTER 2

Borges as Translator

*Admirals, soldiers, statesmen, moved her not at all. But
the very thought of a great writer stirred her to such a
pitch of belief that she almost believed him to be invisible.*

—Virginia Woolf

One of Borges's first literary exercises, as a seven-year-old boy, was a translation of sorts.[1] He filled a notebook with transcriptions of Greco-Roman myths in the charmingly clumsy English of a gifted child learning to write in a foreign language.[2] In his version of the Minotaur and the Labyrinth, a theme that would inspire some of his most famous pages, the young Borges retains several names in Spanish, as if he felt a special affection for their sound in the language in which he first heard them, even as their stories could be transposed into a language he was learning (before he had mastered its grammar or spelling):

> When Theseo was young, his father went to another country and was made king, liveing nothing to his son but his sword and sandles. One day his mother gave him the sandles and sword. So he went in serch, in serch of his father. Soon he went there, and soon find himself in his father's castle. There have had been a war in Creta and Thepas, and Creta was victory, Dedalo made a great laberinto, on which live the moster called minotauro.[3]

The versions are not mere transcriptions. At this tender age they already include personal additions such as a touching lament in his version of Acteon's death: "Oh Action, why did you went to look at Diana?"

Borges learned early that the vicissitudes of a translation are subject to the accidents of language. In his first published work—a translation of Oscar Wilde's "The Happy Prince" published in a Buenos Aires newspaper in 1910—we find such a surprise.[4] In the original a male swallow loves a fickle female reed-bird. Borges translates swallow as "la golondrina," using the female article "la," which does not determine the gender of the bird as there is no masculine alternative for the word. It would, however, sound awkward and technical in Spanish to use the female article to refer to a male swallow and would be poetically unsound. Spanish poetry invariably represents swallows as female. The young Borges transforms Wilde's male swallow into a female swallow, and the female reed-bird into a male bird. Whatever his reasons, and we shall examine some possibilities below, the young Borges imposes in his translation a set of connotations—regarding the friendship of the Happy Prince and the swallow and their shared kiss—that distinguishes the translation, where the swallow is female, from the original, where it is male.

BORGES DISCUSSED Wilde's children's stories in the prologue to a 1966 illustrated edition containing "The Happy Prince." The book circulated in Latin America in a collection of classics for young people, including modified versions of *Don Quixote, The Odyssey, The Divine Comedy, Robinson Crusoe,* and the stories of Shakespeare's plays. Borges's observations on the pitfalls of translating Wilde may have been lost on most young readers, for whom the collection was intended: "[Wilde] gravely assured his friends he had conceived one of his tales in black and silver, and yet the French translation had come out blue and rose." Borges proceeds to quote Wilde's own remark about "a change that reveals the greater capacity of the English language [than the French] to express somber tonalities."[5] Borges alerts his readers to the layers of meaning in Wilde's tales: "At first we let ourselves go with the plot, we then feel the pleasantry, the tenderness, the jest, the delicate play of contrasts, and finally perhaps the secret irony."[6] Borges concludes his prologue praising Wilde's "perennial youth, and the splendor of his malicious innocence."[7]

A Spanish version of "The Happy Prince," included in the volume with Borges's prologue but not translated by him, renders the tenderness of the original but not its "secret irony" or "malicious innocence." In the sanitized translation the veiled love story between the two male protagonists is eradicated by transforming the male swallow of the original into a female swallow.[8] Even the earnest declaration "you must kiss me on the lips, for I love you" is rendered more playfully as "it is better that you kiss me on the lips because I like you very much."[9]

Borges's translation, forty-five years earlier, would have been somewhat more suited to his prologue. In his version the love declaration is a command, even more forceful than in Wilde's original: "kiss me on the lips, because I love you."[10] But, as noted earlier, Borges's version, like the translation for young readers of 1966, transforms the male swallow into a female bird, and thus censures the possible homoerotic suggestions of the original. In both versions a fickle female becomes a male cad. The gender change in Borges's translation, as with the young reader's version, requires a number of other accommodations: in both Spanish versions, the fickle female reed-bird, who toyed with the feelings of the swallow, becomes a male bird, translated as "junco," a literal translation of the Spanish word for *reed* and a male-gendered Spanish word. In Borges's version the swallows constitute a group of cheerful adolescent girl-friends ("amigas") rather than a colorless group of "friends" as in the original. The "most beautiful Reed" in the original becomes "a very pretty junco" in Borges's version (or "the most handsome of the juncos" in the more masculine version for young readers).[11] The original's "he felt lonely and began to tire of his lady-love" becomes "she felt lonely and began to tire of her boyfriend *[novio]*" in Borges's version, (or "she felt lonely and had begun to get bored with her beau" in the version for young readers).[12]

It is possible that Borges felt reluctant to translate "swallow" as a male bird because the gendered word "golondrina" in Spanish carries female connotations, especially in the wake of Gustavo Adolfo

Becquer's migrating "golondrinas," which left an indelible trace on the Spanish language. It is also possible that Borges changed the gender of his birds in order to downplay the love relationship between the two male characters. It is more likely, however, that he drew on a preexisting Spanish version that had already made that switch in order to eliminate the homoerotic undertones of the tale.[13] Be that as it may, the young translator would learn lessons from the exercise. He experienced first hand that it is sometimes possible, and perhaps required by the language, to undertake such daring transformations in a translation as changing the gender of a principal character and that such transformations have ripple effects, as the translator accommodates the change with other alterations.[14]

Borges felt proud that his first publication was a translation and continued translating for the rest of his life. Most of his translations were from works published in English, but he also translated from German, French, Italian, Anglo-Saxon, and Old Norse (which he learned while losing his sight in the 1950s). Borges's translations include Herman Melville's "Bartleby the Scrivener," Viginia Woolf's *Orlando*, William Faulkner's *The Wild Palms*, Ralph Waldo Emerson's *Representative Men*, Carlyle's *Heroes and Hero Worship*, Robert Louis Stevenson's *Fables*, and Henri Michaux's *Un barbare en Asie*. In some cases, as in his translation of Walt Whitman's *Leaves of Grass*, or in his version of Angelus Silesius's *Cherubinischem Wandersmann*, Borges compressed the original to create a self-contained work he did not call a selection. His last major publication was Snorri Sturluson's *Gylfaginning* (the literary section of the *Prose Edda*), which he translated as *Gylfy's Hallucination*. He translated many short stories by Franz Kafka, Herman Melville, Jack London, Chesterton, Edgar Allan Poe, Villiers de l'Isle Adam, Guillaume Apollinaire, Nathaniel Hawthorne, and Rudyard Kipling, and poems by, among others, Wilhelm Klemm, André Gide, Wallace Stevens, Langston Hughes, and Herman Hesse. He also translated essays and chapters from books including a section of Sir Thomas Browne's *Urn-Burial*, and hundreds of passages from works he quoted in his anthologies and essays.

For Borges translation was both a private affair and a gregarious activity shared with some of his closest companions. He translated

many works alone, but years before losing his sight he also collaborated, and assisted others, in translation projects. Amongst his
most valued partners in the process were his mother, doña Leonor
Acevedo de Borges; his closest literary collaborator and good friend,
Adolfo Bioy Casares; the poet and editor Roberto Alifano; and his
wife, María Kodama.[15] Like Ezra Pound and many others, Borges
would sometimes translate works whose originals appeared in languages he did not know by drawing on other translations, as when
he reworked fragments of Chinese literature from German and English sources. But even in cases where he could read the original
work, he often consulted other translations. He sometimes signed
translations as his own that were actually corrected versions of other
translations, and he evidently also corrected translations by others
in books and anthologies he edited.

Borges's translations of novels tend to be literal, even as he ad-
justs the nuances of the original; María Elena Bravo has observed
this in his version of Faulkner's *The Wild Palms* and Frances Aparicio
in his version of Virginia Woolf's *Orlando*.[16] Borges himself provides a précis of his work with Woolf's novel:

> [In translating *Orlando*] I have felt what I always feel when I
> have to translate or to write. I have felt the conviction of my
> incompetence, and at the same time, I have felt that I could
> somehow resolve those apparently insoluble difficulties. As
> far as the book by Virginia Woolf, I thought at first I would
> simplify the style. Then I realized that that would falsify it,
> and so I opted for an almost literal translation. Of course,
> for reasons of euphony I sometimes have to invert the word-
> order, or change one word for another. But in general, I think
> the translation is rather faithful, in as much as a translation
> from English can be faithful in Spanish, since the two lan-
> guages differ so profoundly, each having different virtues and
> defects.[17]

A careful stylist in her own translation, Suzanne Jill Levine has
pointed out that Borges's translation of *Orlando* "is linguistically

more succinct than the original."[18] Indeed, Borges's penchant to cut redundancies, to substitute synonyms for word repetition, and to compress are still evident in the longer translations. Some also include other slight modifications in content, not just style, that are decidedly Borgesian. His translation of *Orlando,* for example, includes a labyrinth where the original does not use the word; and in *The Wild Palms* he removes the sections pertaining to an abortion, which may have offended his sensibilities or those of his mother, with whom he often collaborated in his longer translations. If Borges was more conservative in his translations of novels, modifying style and adding Borgesian touches in the content here and there, he was adventurous in his translations of many other works.

German Expressionism

Borges's family moved to Geneva in 1914 for a short period of time, which was extended five years on account of the First World War. As Emir Rodríguez Monegal put it, the family was "trapped in Switzerland."[19] This was a period of intellectual discovery and effervescence. He learned French to attend a French lycée; and he taught himself German to read German literature and philosophy. He discovered Schopenhauer, Carlyle, Whitman, Chesterton, Kafka, Flaubert, and many other writers he would revisit for decades to come. This is also a period in which he first encountered Jewish culture, which would inspire future writings.[20] He read Heinrich Heine (he remembered crying once able to read Heine's poetry in German without a dictionary), Gustav Meyrink's *Der Golem,* and the writings of Martin Buber.

This was also the period in which he developed his interest in Chinese literature and philosophy ("Towards 1916 I resolved to study oriental literatures").[21] Borges recalled the sobering, and perhaps liberating, experience of his first encounters with Chinese literature in translation. It puzzled him that the very same Chinese sentence could be rendered in one version as "Someone who has been condemned to death is not afraid to walk along a precipice because he has renounced to live," and in another as "The servants destroy works of art in order not to have to judge their splendors and their failings."[22] The bewilderment he felt confronting incompatible translations of the same original work in a language he did not know became a source of joy, as he confidently found his own way about literature.

During his years in Geneva, Borges resumed active translating. He translated a story by Meyrink that he might have revised in a 1938 publication, and he began a translation he never published of Martin Buber's *Die Legende des Baalschem*.[23] He worked on a brief section of the book called "Jerusalem," Buber's version of a mystical Jewish story featuring the founder of Hassidism, Baal Shem Tov, mentioned in "Death and the Compass" and in other Borgesian stories and essays. The original evokes a strong religious piety and not the magical and linguistic aspects of the Kabbalah Borges cherished.[24] In the unpublished translation Borges downplays the pious aspects of the tale in which the apparent harshness of God is a shield for a love his people are not yet ready to bear. He transforms the notion of "affliction" (Heimsuchung) in the original to that of "temptation" (tentación), and he substitutes language underscoring weariness for the original's vocabulary charged with a sense of death looming over the ruins of Jerusalem and with the vain and mystical search to reach the city.[25] In his translation Borges appears to shy away from the more pious elements of the original, but he does not offer an alternative version that is both sound and Borgesian. Perhaps this explains why he never published it. All the same, the translation is evidence of an interest in Jewish themes early on in his literary development.

The most visible result of his literary discoveries during his stay in Geneva was his interest in and practice of German expressionistic poetry, which he began to publish after his family moved from Geneva to Madrid in 1919.[26] Borges was, as Linda S. Meier has indicated,

> practically single-handedly responsible for bringing Expressionism, the reigning avant-garde movement in Germany from 1910 to 1933, to the attention of the Spanish-speaking

world. . . . Out of a total of five articles concerning Expressionism which appeared in Spain in 1920 and 1921, four belong to Borges, not to mention the later essay 'Acerca del expresionismo' which he included in *Inquisiciones*.[27]

Borges's efforts to disseminate the poetry of German Expressionism were applauded by luminaries of Spain's literary milieu, including Rafael Cansinos-Assens and Ramón Gómez de la Serna.[28] In the introduction to his "Anthology of Expressionism" for the Spanish literary journal *Grecia* in August 1920, Borges defined the movement as an attempt to elevate the reality of the senses and emotions into what he called an "ultra-reality." In his characteristically dense, sometimes impenetrable style of the period, Borges pronounced that "[Expressionism's] main source is constituted by that athletic and Cyclopean vision that comes from Whitman's rhythms and the plurality of his poetry."[29] Borges sent copies of the journal, along with his translations, to some of the authors themselves. He was thrilled when Wilhelm Klemm responded "with a letter in the style of Whitman and a book of poems with a personal inscription," as he reported excitedly to his dear friend Maurice Abramowicz.[30]

Borges's encounter with Whitman and with German Expressionism, while his family was safely trapped in Switzerland during the First World War, led to a literary vision best summarized by Emir Rodríguez Monegal: "He could not help feeling the impact of those poems that violently attacked war and proclaimed the need for all men to unite in a universal brotherhood."[31] This vision informs both his essays on the Expressionist movement, and his translations. Many of the poems Borges translated were a protest against war. José Luis Vega, in his meticulous analysis of Ernst Stadler's "Der Aufbruch" (the outbreak), one of the Expressionist poems Borges translated, labels differences between Borges's translation and the original as errors and distortions.[32] Vega attributes the discrepancies to what he considers Borges's "insecurities with his ability with the source language."[33] It is true that Borges's German was not as fluent as his English or French when he translated the Expressionist poems and that he may have made mistakes in comprehension, but some of his

changes were clearly intentional. In his translation of "Der Aufbruch," Borges modifies a line to change an emphasis in the poem.

(Stadler)
> To strip reality from the body as one would the dusty armor
> of a knight.[34]

(Borges)
> To strip naked the reality of the body as from a dusty uni-
> form.[35]

Borges's translation distorts the original but underscores his concerns about World War I (Stadler wrote the original in 1912, before
the war) by transforming the armor of the original into the uniform of his version. The change also gives more credence than the
original to Borges's claim that "the war did not create expressionism, but justified it."[36] Borges's version, with more force than the
original, seems to prefigure the war with prophetic force, calling
attention to the uniforms of contemporary soldiers at the expense
of knightly armor. The change of uniform for armor also indicates
Borges's dislike of the picturesque evocations of symbolist poetry
as practiced in Spain and Spanish America.

In some cases Borges's changes produce effects different from
the original. In his translation of Kurt Heynicke's "Hinter der Front"
(behind the front line), Borges effects a significant shift.[37] The poem,
contrasting the silent death of bystanders with that of the warriors,
concludes with the word "Abend" (evening), which Borges renders
as "twilight."[38] The original stresses the respite of a given day of
war, while Borges's translation suggests, perhaps, the Germanic notion of apocalyptic termination.

In his compressed version of Wilhelm Klemm's "Schlacht an der
Marne" (battle of the Marne), Borges introduces his personal
vocabulary into the poem. Where Klemm writes "Zwei kolossale
Stunden rollen sich auf zu Minuten" (two colossal hours turn into
minutes)[39], accelerating time, Borges instead slows time, as if underscoring the horror or stunned confusion of the war, which induces
the sense that time is moving at an excruciating pace ("Two infinite hours unfold in minutes"). Borges "corrected" other aspects

of Klemm's poem, as in the following excerpt that treats the raging
of war:

(Klemm)
    The battery raises its lion's voice
    Six times in the land. The grenades howl.
    Silence. Faraway the fire of the infantry simmers.
    For days, for weeks.[40]

(Borges)
    The battery raises its lion's voice
    One and six times. Silence.
    Faraway the infantry is boiling.
    For days. Also for weeks.[41]

Borges's version is shorter and produces a slightly different effect.
In Klemm's original, hand-thrown grenades follow the batteries of
tanks, and in the wake of silence one perceives the infantry's displacements. In Borges's version the onslaught of the infantry is more
focused and threatening. He cuts the hurling of grenades by human hands, which would signal the arrival of the infantry. In Borges's
version one feels the infantry's imminent onslaught, which follows
the bombing that has prepared their arrival. In the original, somewhat in contrast, the infantry has moved away, the immediate danger has passed, but war remains an imminent threat.

    Borges not only transformed the poems he translated; he modi-
fied some of his own translations. The language of his second rendition of a poem by Alfred Vagts, for example, is more direct:

(first version)
    A cloud, a cranium without a lower jaw, smoothes the field
        gnawed with craters.
    · · · · · · · · · · ·
    The gas grenades explode like a punctured intestine,
    The proboscis of the carts limit their horizon to a minimum
        of existence.[42]

(second version)
   A large black storm cloud [nubarrón], a skull without a
   jawbone, smoothes the field gnawed with craters.
   . . . .
   The gas grenades explode like a punctured intestine,
   The snouts of the carts limit their horizon to a minimum of
   existence.[43]

The second version turns the cloud of the first into a "black storm,"
which better prepares the reader for the image of a large skull sweep-
ing across the field of battle. The substitute of "snouts" for "proboscis" makes the image of tanks as elephants more direct. Borges's
transformations of the German expressionist poems are modest, but
they offer an inkling of more daring translations to come, especially
after the 1930s, once he had developed the unconventional views
on translation that offer a window into the creative process of the
literary works for which he is best known. Borges's encounter with
Walt Whitman offers illuminating insights into his development as
writer and translator.

Whitman and the Translation of Poetry

   Although the most visible contribution Borges made to literary
culture after he left Geneva was his dissemination of German Expressionism in the Spanish-speaking world, a more profound discovery for him was the poetry of Walt Whitman. In his "Autobiographical Essay" Borges remembers coming across Whitman in 1915,
when he read a poem translated into German by Johannes Schlaf.[44]
Soon after his discovery he acquired his own English version of
Leaves of Grass, which he read with passion. For many years he would
say that for him Whitman was synonymous with poetry. His excite-
ment for Whitman did not diminish even as he was eagerly absorb-
ing other currents of world literature. In a letter to Maurice Abramowicz dated 1919, he writes of his fervor over German Expressionism,
but he adds that for him "the master continues to be Whitman."[45]
   One of Borges's most consequential translations is his version
of Whitman's *Leaves of Grass*, which had been announced as a forth-

coming publication as early as 1927. It was only in 1969 that the book appeared in print. In the long interim, however, Borges developed a lively and evolving relationship with the poet he so enthusiastically admired. His earliest publication inspired by his engagements with Whitman was not a translation or an essay but "Himno al mar" ("Hymn of the Sea") (1919), his first published poem, which appeared in the journal *Grecia*.[46] He referred to it in a letter to Abramowicz as one of "my first Whitmanian attempts."[47] Carlos Cortínez has indicated the exact passages from Whitman that inspired the poem and explains its significance in the context of Borges's future poetry.[48] "Hymn" evinces a number of features Borges considered quintessential in Whitman, including the first person collective voice, what he once called "the vast respiration" of the Whitman's verse,[49] a sense of the erotic, and the exuberance of enumeration; but the poem also includes a pessimistic undertone informed, perhaps, by Borges's simultaneous engagements with German expressionism:

> Brother, Father, Lover! . . .
> I enter the great garden of your waters and swim far away
>   from the earth.
> . . . .
> The waves come in with a fragile crest of foam,
> Fleeing towards failure. Towards the coast,
> with its reddish peaks,
> with its geometric houses,
> with its toy palm trees,
> that have become livid and absurd, like rigid memories!
> I am with you, Sea. And my body extended like a bow
> fighting against your impetuous muscles.[50]

Borges condemned his early poetry as shoddy imitations of Whitman, and yet in "El otro" ("The Other"), a short story from *The Book of Sand*, he seems to allude obliquely to this early poem with rueful fondness or irony, as if it were a poem by Whitman himself. In the fantastic story in which an old Borges meets his younger double, they discuss the significance of a poem ostensibly written by Whitman in which an apparent sexual encounter by the sea is belied by hints that it never took place:

> I remember that brief piece in which Whitman remembers a night shared with a loved one by the sea, in which he was truly happy.
> "Yes Whitman sang that song," I observed, "because he desired her and it did not happen. The poem gains when we guess that it is the manifestation of a desire, and not the story of a fact."[51]

The story attributes this unnamed poem to Whitman, but it could be a description of Borges's "Hymn to the Sea" where the line "Fleeing towards failure" belies the depiction of ecstasy. In the story, the young and the old Borges have little in common except their love of Whitman, although they appreciate different qualities of the American poet. The exchange between the older and the younger Borges reflects a profound reorientation in Borges's understanding of a poet he cherished above and beyond his different interpretations of *Leaves of Grass*.

Borges underwent several considerable changes in his aesthetic and political views through the 1920s. In his literary biography Emir Rodríguez Monegal notes that Borges became a fervent nationalist after returning to Buenos Aires with his family from their long stay in Geneva and Madrid: "The young Borges did everything he could to become a patriotic bard."[52] In the 1920s Borges was proud of his allegiance to Argentina. Some have characterized him during this period as a populist.[53] But in the 1930s he did an about face. What seemed a virtue now became a vice ("the most incorrigible Argentine vice is nationalism").[54] If only because of his rejection of nationalism, it is understandable that Borges repudiated his three books of essays expressing his most chauvinistic ideas, as well as a number of xenophobic poems he excised from future editions of his first books of poems.[55] But Borges experienced other substantive changes that account for the repudiation of those early works, which were written in highly stylized baroque language—using learned loanwords and Latinate syntax—in a haughty and self-satisfied pitch that bears little resemblance to what José Miguel Oviedo has called the unpretentious, affable, "serene, and cordial tone" characteristic of Borges's essays of later periods.[56] Borges went on to reject not only his style but also the substance of some of his most fundamental ideas about literature. Borges would modify in important ways his views on life and literature that he developed in the 1920s. At that time he had expressed a thought he would later reject, that all literature is autobiographical: "I can state my literary credo as the religious man states his: it is mine to the extent that I believe it, not because it was invented by me. I believe that it is universal, even in those who would like to contradict it. This is my postulation: in the final analysis all literature is autobiographical."[57] As he made this declaration, during his most nationalistic period, Borges was preparing a translation of Walt Whitman's *Leaves of Grass*. In February 1927 the literary journal *Martín Fierro* published an anonymous note titled "A New Version of Walt Whitman" to announce Borges's forthcoming translation. It sung the praises of his methods:

> Jorge Luis Borges is currently working on a translation of *Leaves of Grass*. It is an important enterprise, to render the compact production of Whitman into our language; and it is of particular interest to accomplish this task according to Borges's design: to produce such a close fit with the original and its author's innovative conception that the reader will be in contact with the most genuine Whitman and his informal style down to his vocabulary in the *argot,* or low-brow English, of the United States. We only know one other translation of Whitman, that by Mr. A. Vasseur, which certainly does not measure up to those standards.[58]

This translation was not published and, judging from the surviving fragments, it would have been notably different from the one he did finally publish in 1969, particularly with regard to his credo about literature as autobiography, a view he relinquished in favor of the view that literature is a collective, almost impersonal enterprise, as explained in chapter 1. It is possible that his reconsideration of

Whitman itself played a part in his skepticism about those who stress "individuality" in their literary assessments.

It is likely that Borges's evolving interpretations of Whitman dissuaded him from publishing his early version of *Leaves of Grass* in 1927. By 1969 Borges had long abandoned the view that Whitman's poetic voice is an autobiographical expression in any strict sense. Borges had developed a richer and more nuanced view of the matter, that the persona in Whitman's poetry and the individual who wrote the poems bear a complex relationship with each other and with the "reader" of the poem—a relationship that is hardly autobiographical:

> When Walt Whitman began, he thought of his own life. He thought of having been born in Long Island, but he thought that this isn't enough: I should have been born all over America. Then he created this very strange character, Walt Whitman, not to be taken for the writer of the book. . . . He attempted a very daring experiment, the most daring and the most successful experiment in all literature as far as I know. The experiment was this. The central character would be called after the author, Walt Whitman, but he was, firstly, Walt Whitman the human being, the very unhappy man who wrote *Leaves of Grass.* Then a magnification, or transmogrification of that Walt Whitman, called Walt Whitman, who was not the real Whitman at all, or at least not the Whitman his contemporaries knew, but a divine vagabond. . . . And since this person has to be a trinity—for he thought of it as a trinity—he introduced a third person. That third person is the reader. So Walt Whitman is compounded of Walt Whitman the man, of Walt Whitman the myth, and also the reader, because he thought of the reader as being also the hero of the book.[59]

One can detect a trace in the shift from Borges's less nuanced approach to the autobiographical qualities of literature, to this more sophisticated view in his correction of a 1929 newspaper article he wrote about Whitman, which reappeared in *Discusión* in 1932.[60] In the newpaper article Borges considers Whitman a model for his own ideal of becoming a national poet: "I am thinking that Whitman's destiny—a very, very human being, simplified by the alien vision of a mere giant—is an abbreviated symbol of his country."[61] Once Borges cast aside both nationalism and the notion of a transparent autobiographical significance of literature, he transformed this passage. In the 1932 version the phrase characterizing Whitman as a "very, very human being" (hombre humanísimo) becomes "a man of many inventions" (hombre de muchas invenciones).[62]

In the introductory note to his 1969 translation of *Leaves of Grass*, Borges hopes that someday it might be possible to "translate and recreate [Whitman] with total liberty," but since Whitman's language is too well-known to Spanish readers, Borges opted for a compromise, to "oscillate between a personal interpretation and a resigned rigor."[63] He calls his translation an interpretative recreation. A few critics have already compared Borges's translation to the original, but they have not noticed Borges's work as a recreator. Carmen Valero Garcés discusses many stylistic differences between the original and Borges's version.[64] Since she considers many of the differences to be deficiencies, she calls it an imperfect translation that, nevertheless, captures many essential aspects of Whitman. Frances Aparicio has a more positive assessment of the translation, which she considers faithful and "rigorously literal."[65]

It is possible to examine how Borges grew more confident, more assertive of his own voice in translating Whitman by comparing fragments of the 1920s translation work on *Leaves of Grass* to the 1969 publication. In the poem "Once I Pass'd through a Populous City," Whitman's poetic voice recalls a passionate encounter with a woman he met casually and left and then remembers the woman as if she were present: "I see her close beside me with silent lips sad and tremulous." Borges's earlier translation is quite close, with one important modification: in Borges's version the woman is not "sad" but "hurt" (dolida) in anticipation that she will be abandoned. The version is somewhat less narcissistic than Whitman's original, where the woman detains the man "for love of me." In Borges's 1927 version he is detained "for love."

In Borges's 1969 version the alterations are more dramatic. Whitman's original and Borges's 1927 translation conclude with the following two lines, constituting a single sentence:

(Whitman)
   Again she holds me by the hand, I must not go,
   I see her close beside me with silent lips sad and tremulous.[66]

(Borges)
   Again she holds me by the hand, I must not go,
   I see her close beside me with silent lips, hurt and
      tremulous.

In the 1969 translation the two lines become two independent sentences. In fact, the second sentence is separated from the first by a line space. The effect is significant:

(Borges 1969)
   Again she holds me by the hand, she does not want me to go.

   I see her once again by my side with silent lips sad and
      trembling.[67]

In Whitman's poem the woman retains him; he thinks he must not go and therefore remains and observes her. In Borges's 1969 version, Whitman's "I must not go" and the following comma are changed to "she does not want me to go" followed by a period. Rather than Whitman's continuation with "I see her" following the comma, Borges offers "Vuelvo a verla," which can mean either "I turn and see her" or "I see her once again." By adding the word "again" in the last line, Borges breaks the continuous series of actions of the original, in which she holds him, he stays, he looks at her. In Borges's 1969 version the final line is a new event; she holds him by the hand and asks him to stay, but he turns away from her, or stops looking at her. Then he looks at her once again.
   There is yet another possible reading of Borges's translation—

an interpretation consistent with his inclination toward cyclical themes in his own poetry. Borges's fondness for the cycle justifies Saúl Yurkievich's characterization of Borges as "the circular poet," in an essay which helped to situate Borges as one of the central figures of contemporary Latin American poetry.[68] From this perspective one could read a transforming effect into Borges's choice of the verb "volver," an effect absent in Whitman's original. Whereas Whitman created the illusion of reliving an event in the past, it is possible to read Borges's version as a regression. In Whitman a vivid remembrance evokes a real presence. In the "circular" interpretation the lyrical voice also remembers having felt the woman's presence in the past, creating an infinite regress of leaving, remembering, feeling presence, leaving again, remembering again, and so on. Had the final line of the translation read "In my human flesh, eternity keeps recurring," the poem would have been circular without a doubt, but that line is from one of his own many poems with cyclical themes.[69]

Borges used Whitman's conceit of a poem being realized in the process of reading in many of his poems, some of which bear the word "cyclical" in their titles. But he also introduced cyclical themes in more subtle ways that evoke other aspects of Whitman. In his version of those poems in *Leaves of Grass* in which the lyrical voice anticipates the presence of a future reader, Borges tends to depersonalize Whitman's poetic voice. Thus, Borges renders Whitman's "To conclude, I announce what comes after me" as "To conclude, I announce what will come afterwards."[70] In the poem "Full of Life Now," Whitman invokes those who will read him in the future and says,

> When you read these I that was visible am become invisible,
> Now it is you, compact, visible, realizing my poems, seeking
>   me,
> Fancying how happy you were if I could be with you and
>   become your comrade;
> Be it as if I were with you. (Be not too certain but I am now
>   with you.)[71]

Borges modifies the poem somewhat. He simplifies the grammar of the first line and transforms the search for Whitman's self, through the reading of the poem, to a search for the poem itself. Accordingly, the presence of the poem is more certain than the poet in Borges's version:

> When you read them [my songs], I that was visible will be invisible,
> Now it is you, concrete, visible, who reads them, who seeks them,
> Fancying how happy you would be if I were by your side and were your friend;
> Be as happy as if I were by your side. (Do not be too sure that I am not with you).

Borges used and adapted Whitmanesque interjections by the poetic voice of an implied writer directed to an implied reader in many poems and short stories. In "To Whoever May Be Reading Me," Borges offers an inversion of the theme of the writer who may be present with the reader, by exploring the mortality of the "invulnerable" reader who happens to be reading the poem. The poem begins with the line: "You are invulnerable," and ends with the idea that in reading the poem "in some way you are already dead."[72] The poem "G. A. Bürger" is another variation on the theme. Here a poet has been meditating on Bürger, a nineteenth-century German poet from Göttingen with whom he feels affinities (and whose name resembles Borges's own). As the poem concludes, Borges's lyrical voice expresses the idea that the dead poet is actually writing as he is finishing the last lines of the poem, or perhaps even as the reader is reading them: "Bürger is alone, and now / precisely now, he files a few poetic lines."[73]

To read Borges's version of "Once I Pass'd through a Populous City" as a cyclical poem is to assume a consistency with other transformations in his translation of *Leaves of Grass*. In the section titled "Children of Adam," for example, there is a poem called "Ages and Ages Returning at Intervals," which Borges translates as "Ciclicamente vuelvo al cabo de largas edades"[74] (cyclically I return at the end of long ages.) The idea of a recurring experience is clearly in Whitman's title, but Borges's title evokes Nietzsche's notion of "eternal return."

Our reading of Borges's translations of some poems by Whitman as cyclical fits with other translations in which Borges unambiguously interpolates cyclical themes. In his translation of a Herman Hesse poem, for example, Borges transforms the intimation of a specific religious experience, perhaps reincarnation, into powerful suggestions of the eternal return. The conceit of the original involves the substitution of the veils of worldly perception for a Godly dress. The poem opens with the image of the veils falling: "Again I see the veils go down, / and the familiar becomes unfamiliar."[75] In the original the first person poetic voice, the familiar, becomes unfamiliar. In Borges's version, the first person singular voice becomes a plural voice for which the notions of the intimate and the eternal are dissolving: "Once again in front of my eyes, there are descending veils. / What is most intimate and eternal, moves away from us."[76] In the original, there are intimations of "earlier births" and, perhaps, of future ones: "From earlier births / distant presentiments are flashing."[77] In Borges's version the intimation is of cyclical time: "I have the presentiment of something vague, something vague and remote / that comes to me from lives, from previous cycles."[78] Hesse's poem ends with the image of a Godly garment woven from the shattered threads of the previous experience: "From torn threads is woven a new and more beautiful garment of God."[79] Borges's version involves a possible allusion to writing, which replaces the specific reference to God in the original: "The plot unravels, and the Inspiration weaves, / more ungraspable and beautiful, its renewed finery."[80]

The changes in this Hesse poem were not accidental, and the five poems Borges translated with Roberto Alifano are all personal recreations. The poem "Irgendwo" (somewhere) begins in the original with the line "I wander [irr ich] through the desert of life, glowing," which Borges translates as "Blind, I cross the desert of life."[81] In Borges's version the word "blind" carries a double meaning not present in the original: the poetic voice is blind in that it does not know where it is going, but "blind" can simultaneously be read as an allusion to Borges's own blindness.

Borges also transforms a love poem by Hesse into a metaphysical poem offering literary allusions not found in the original. Both Hesse's original and Borges's version begin with the conceit of a lover's dark world in the loved one's absence. Hesse follows with,

> That you know a golden mean
> in the turbulence [dem Getribe] of life,
> made you and your love
> for me a good spirit.[82]

Borges transforms the original:

> That in this world of chaos and death
> you reveal the true path to me
> and be my shepherd and my Virgil
> by the light of your love that will be a star.[83]

Hesse's poem concludes with the notion that the woman's love will be life's core of goodness ("Lebens süssen Kern"). In Borges's version her immense love will instruct him "to perceive the primordial sources."[84] Hesse's love poem in Borges's pen becomes a salute to Dante. His references to Virgil and to the stars, absent in the original, can be read as allusions to the *Paradiso*.[85]

Borges's transformations of Hesse, or of Whitman, are not limited to metaphysical themes. As Fernando Alegría has pointed out, Borges transforms some of Whitman's poems of homoerotic love into poems of heterosexual love. In a poem that reads, "I am satisfied, I dance, laugh, sing: / as the hugging and loving bed-fellow sleeps at my side," Borges makes the "bedfellow" an unambiguous feminine character.[86] Borges does not delete all references to homoeroticism in the collection. He includes several poems in which a man is in love with another man. My own conjecture is that Borges did not mean to ignore the homoerotic contents of Whitman's poetry but to explore, in Whitman's voice, various types of erotic experience. Alegría has argued that in his translation of Whitman, Borges felt freer to explore erotic themes he avoided in his own poetry. According to Alegría, "It is quite possible that no Hispanic translator has ever equaled Borges in his masterful versions of Whitman's ambiguous sexual poems."

Borges's translation of Whitman involves a selection from a larger work *(Leaves of Grass)*, but it reads like a coherent whole. He used the same approach in his subtle version of the *Cheribunischer Wandersmann* (1675), a mystical work by Johannes Scheffler (1624–1677), who assumed the name Angelus Silesius after his conversion from Protestantism to Catholicism. Borges's book, translated in collaboration with María Kodama, is a bilingual edition, Spanish with the German original, of 101 rhymed couplets that Borges translates into short aphorisms in unrhymed poetic prose.

Borges states that his version is "an aid for the good comprehension of the text."[87] The translation, however, like his translation of Whitman's *Leaves of Grass*, oscillates between a literal and personal recreation. The original is a lyrical meditation on the relationship between man and God. In the original, man has being and access to divinity by God's grace. God's being is self-contained and yet diminished without the loving attention of his human creature, superior to the angels because free to behold or ignore his creator.[88] Time, for Silesius, is therefore more noble than eternity. In time man makes the choice to love or not to love his God. Borges, who wrote essays on the refutation of time, might have been more interested in Silesius's meditations on the relationship between time and eternity in themselves than in the contradictions through which the mystic attempts to approach God. In his translation Borges nuances Silesius's search, and ultimate attainment, of God as expressed with images from the natural world, including such flowers as the rose, lily, and tulip and such animals as sheep, eagles, and doves. Of these Borges only translates the couplets involving the rose, a recurrent symbol—in his own poems, short stories, and essays—of the unattainable for which literature can be a consoling compensation. Consider one of Borges's preferred lines in the writings of Silesius:

"The rose is without why, it blooms because it blooms."[89] As a text by Borges the line can be interpreted, as Adelheid Hanke-Schefer has done, as a meditation on "being without cause or end," a notion Borges used, occasionally to discuss his aspirations as a writer.[90] Once, when asked to indicate his greatest literary ambition, Borges responded, "to write a book, a chapter, a page, a paragraph that is everything for all men . . . that is the rose without why, the platonic and intemporal rose of Silesius's *Querubinsicher Wandermann*."[91] In the context of Silesius's religiosity, however, the "rose without why" is not a metaphor for literary ideals but an affirmation of God's presence and perfection in nature.

In Borges's translation, the relationship between man and God is one of parity. This is not the case in the original, where God's experience of himself would be diminished without man but where God is also presented as man's superior. Borges does not translate any of the poems with themes such as baptism, sin, or those addressing the redemptive power of Christ. His work as translator, but also as editor, is marked by a post-Schopenhauerian sensibility in which the human being gains a certain parity, codependency, or even superiority with regard to God.

Some couplets from Borges's translation of Angelus Silesius can be interpreted differently depending on whether one thinks of the author or the translator. There are, however, also texts in his translation of Angelus Silesius that Borges transformed. The following couplet by Silesius holds that God would be diminished without man; Borges's translation presents God as superfluous without man:

(Silesius)

Man is the Highest Thing

Nothing appears to me to be too high; I am the highest
    thing,
because God without me is diminished in size.[92]

(Borges)

The Highest Is Man

Nothing seems high to me. I am the highest.
God is nothing without me.[93]

Rather than affirming humanity's highest place in the order of creation, so high that God would be diminished without man, Borges's
translation reads almost as a precursor to the Nietzschean negation
of the divine. The couplet titled "Gott schaut man mit Gelassenheit,"
which can be translated as "one sees God with composure," is transformed by Borges as "We see God with abandonment":

(Silesius)

One sees God with Composure

The Angel looks at God with cheerful eyes
I however, even with more happiness, since I can leave
      God.[94]

(Borges)

We see God with Abandonment

The angel looks at God with serene eyes.
I see him much better if I can abandon him.[95]

Borges's change of cheerful eyes to "serene" and the elimination of
"happiness," coupled with the notion of abandonment, transforms
Silesius's original from the joyful contemplation of God by a being
who has the freedom to turn away from his creator, to the sobering
suggestion that man can abandon God.

   Borges also changes the dynamic of the place ("Der Ort") in
Creation, which must be forsaken to experience eternity, into a more
radical Schopenhaurian notion that space and time are both prod-

ucts of the will. In the original, "there is a place" will be replaced in the future by eternity. In Borges's translation, space, time, and eternity are simultaneous:

(Silesius)

The Place Is in You

You are not in the place, the place is in you.
If you were to get rid of it, eternity would already be here.[96]

(Borges)

Space Itself Is in You

Space is in you. You are not in space.
Reject it. Eternity is already here.[97]

The final couplet of the book, which Borges had quoted in German concluding the essay "A New Refutation of Time," suggests a relationship between being and writing:

(Silesius)

Conclusion

Friend, it is enough. In case you want to read more,
therefore, go and become the writing as well as the being.[98]

(Borges)

Conclusion

Enough, friend. If you want to go on reading
become the book and its stuff.[99]

In the original the relationship between writing and being involves the word of God and man; in Borges's version it entails the dissolution of being into literature.

Poe

As with his translations from verse, in his translations of narrative fiction Borges does not hesitate to omit details, cut sections, or change emphases to recreate an original. Borges revered Poe's "The Purloined Letter" as one of the most accomplished stories in the genre of detective fiction and, yet, did not hesitate to enact any number of daring adjustments of style and content when translating it with Adolfo Bioy Casares for *Los mejores cuentos policiales* (1943), an anthology of detective fiction.

Borges venerated Poe's imagination but disparaged his writing skills. He often said that Poe is a writer that one enjoys when remembering his tales, not while reading them in English. Borges praised Baudelaire for vastly improving the style of Poe's tales in his French version, and he energetically enacted stylistic alterations in his translations of "The Purloined Letter" and "The Facts in the Case of M. Valdemar," which he also translated.[100] He eagerly looked for synonyms to translate around Poe's repetitions and deleted sections he considered superfluous. Compare a passage from "The Purloined Letter" with Borges's version:

(Poe)
"Perhaps it is the very simplicity of the thing which puts you at fault," said my friend.
"What nonsense you *do* talk!" replied the Prefect, laughing heartily.
"Perhaps the mystery is a little too plain," said Dupin.
"Oh, good heavens! who ever heard of such an idea?"
"A little *too* self-evident."
"Ha! ha! ha!—ha! ha! ha!—ho! ho! ho!" roared our visitor, profoundly amused, "oh, Dupin, you will be the death of me yet!"
"And what, after all, *is* the matter at hand?"

(Borges)
>   "Perhaps the mystery is too simple," said Dupin
>   "What is the mystery?" I asked.[101]

In this passage Borges not only simplifies but eliminates the notion
of the mystery being "too self-evident," an elision consistent with
his creative recreation of the tale.

Borges compresses Poe's verbose periphrasis to the essential core.
Consider the following fragment: "It is clearly inferred . . . from
the non-appearance of certain results which would at once arise from
its passing *out* of the robber's possession—that is to say, from his
employing it as he must design in the end to employ it." Borges
simplifies: "We know it . . . from the nature of the document, and
from the fact that certain results would have arisen if the document
were not in possession of the robber."[102]

Borges also sharpens some of Poe's points. Before his demon-
stration that it is relevant to the case that the thief is a poet, Dupin
discusses a mathematical equation to show that the thief's being a
mathematician is also irrelevant:

> I never yet encountered the mere mathematician who . . . did
> not clandestinely hold it as a point of his faith that $x^2 + px$
> was absolutely and unconditionally equal to q. Say to [a math-
> ematician] by way of experiment, if you please that you be-
> lieve occasions may occur where $x^2 + px$ is not altogether
> equal to q, and, having made him understand what you mean,
> get out of his reach as speedily as convenient, for, beyond
> doubt, he will endeavor to knock you down. I mean to say
> . . . that if the Minister had been no more than a mathemati-
> cian [the Prefect] would have solved the mystery.

Borges's Dupin puts the matter more succinctly:

> I have not met an algebrist who would not profess as a clan-
> destine point of faith that $(a + b)^2$ is unconditionally equal
> to $a^2 + 2ab + b^2$. Say to one of these gentlemen that in cer-

tain occasions $(a + b)^2$ may sometimes not be strictly equal to $a^2 + 2ab + b^2$, and before you finish your sentence run away so he will not destroy you. . . . [103]

Borges's version is more elegant. A fundamental theorem of algebra is more likely to be a "point of faith" than Poe's arbitrary equation with one variable and two constants. Borges's stylistic changes are minor, however, compared to his modifications of content.

In the story, Minister D. steals a woman's letter before her very eyes. She cannot call attention to the theft because she wishes to hide the existence of the letter from another person present as the theft takes place. In Poe's original the owner of the letter is probably the Queen of France. Poe identifies the thief as a "Minister D." but does not indicate the purpose of the theft. Perhaps the letter contains evidence of illegitimate love or political intrigue, information that must be kept secret for the common good, or any number of other possibilities.

Poe is clear that the owner of the letter is a woman, but Borges deliberately obfuscates the character's gender. In Borges's version the content of the letter may indeed compromise a lady, but the owner of the letter is not necessarily a woman. In the original the prefect of the Parisian police tells Dupin that he has information "from a very high quarter" regarding the theft of an important letter. Borges translates "a very high quarter" as "un alto funcionario" (a highly placed male functionary from the royal house).[104] The usage of the word "funcionario," suggesting the anachronistic idea of a civil servant, is not a casual one. It also appears in the original, albeit in a different context. Poe uses the word "functionary" several times in the story to refer to the prefect. Each time Poe does so, Borges substitutes "prefect" for "functionary." Borges choses to use the term "funcionario" to refer to the individual who informs the prefect of the letter's theft. Borges, therefore, invents a character who does not exist in the original, "the functionary." In his version, a male functionary, not a female as in the original, informs the prefect of police about the theft.

In the original version a woman is alone in her room reading a letter. She is interrupted by another person who enters the room and from whom she wishes to conceal the missive. Minister D. enters, notices the letter, and steals it with the woman's knowledge but unbeknownst to the person who entered the room. In the original both the reader of the letter and the unnamed person who enters the room are referred to as an "exalted personage." The woman then confides in the prefect of police, Monsieur G., who consults with Auguste Dupin and with the narrator of the story.

Borges's version involves more characters. The owner of the letter is not necessarily a woman; in fact, it may well be that the recipient of the letter is the character Borges invented, the "functionary," that is to say, the man who communicates to the prefect of police that the letter was stolen from the royal quarters. The letter may indeed compromise a lady, but Borges is judiciously establishing an ambiguity not in the original: the letter belongs either to a man who is involved romantically or politically with a woman of importance, or it belongs to the woman herself. When discussing "The Purloined Letter" Borges specified that his "functionary" is a male "politician": "In his story 'The Purloined Letter' Poe presents a politician who has been robbed of a very important letter."[105] This statement by Borges is consistent with his own translation of the story, but not with the original.

In Borges's translation the victim of the theft could be a man, as per Borges's own interpretation of the story, or a woman, as per the splendid ambiguity in his text. In his version the indication that a woman of stature could be compromised by the contents of the letter and, therefore, that she may have been the victim of the theft in the first place is not offered until the very last paragraphs of the story, when Dupin expresses his political solidarity with the "compromised lady" (Borges) ("lady concerned" [Poe]).[106] Even if the victim of the theft is a woman in Borges's version, his translation differs from Poe's original in that there the reader knows unambiguously from the outset that the victim of the theft is female.

Borges creates this ambiguity of gender, where Poe does not, by eliminating all feminine articles and personal pronouns indicating the feminine gender of the thief's victim. Instead, he refers to the character with Spanish words such as "persona" or "víctima,"

words with the grammatically feminine ending but that do not indicate the gender of the individuals to whom they are applied; Borges also refers once to the victim as "el dueño" (the owner), in context a word grammatically masculine but gender nonspecific. Borges
is also thorough in eliminating all clues suggesting the woman's
noble status.

Compare a text of the original with Borges's translation. In Poe's
version the illustrious personage, unannounced, enters the room of
the woman reading the letter:

(Poe)

> The document in question—a letter, to be frank—had been
> received by the personage robbed while alone in the royal
> boudoir. During its perusal she was suddenly interrupted by
> the entrance of the other exalted personage from whom es-
> pecially it was her wish to conceal it. After a hurried and vain
> endeavor to thrust it into a drawer, she was forced to place
> it, open as it was upon a table.

(Borges)

> The document—a letter to be frank—was received by the vic-
> tim of the possible blackmail, while alone in the royal quar-
> ters. Almost immediately, a second individual from whom the
> first individual especially wanted to hide the letter, entered.
> The individual in question barely had enough time to leave
> it, open as it was upon a table.[107]

In Borges's version the individual who receives the letter is not
referred to with the personal pronoun *she*. *Ella* in Spanish would
have indicated her gender as in the English version. The substitution of "habitación real" (royal quarters) for "boudoir" erases another indication as to the character's gender. "Boudoir," a French
word used in English and Spanish, would have indicated that the
place of the theft was the salon or private room of a woman. The
translation suggests that the theft took place in a less intimate place
of the royal palace. Borges's version eliminates the word "exalted,"
erasing another clue that—in Poe's version—the character could be

the Queen of France. Borges also adds a phrase: "the victim of the possible blackmail."[108] The word *blackmail* ("chantaje") is not in the original, and although the reader might surmise that blackmail could be involved in the theft of the letter, Poe designed to keep the use of the letter ambiguous. For example, he uses the word "employment" to refer to the possible use of the letter: "It is clear . . . that the letter is still in the possession of the minister, since it is this possession, and not any employment of the letter, which bestows the power. With the employment the power departs."[109] Borges exchanges the ambiguous notion of "employment" for the notion of "sale": "It is evident . . . that the letter is still in the possession of the minister: in that possession lies his power. Once the letter is sold, his power ends."[110] In the original the purpose of the theft involves political motivations. The prefect indicates that the letter has "been wielded for political purposes."[111] Borges omits this statement to remain consistent with the suggestion that the letter was used for the purposes of financial extortion.

The implications of Borges's modifications are hardly trivial. They reorient the focus of the story from the circumstances of the victim to the relationship between the detective and the thief. What matters in Borges's story is the interplay between two minds trying to outwit each other in their attempts to anticipate the other's thought process, while aware that the other is doing the same. Borges downplays the sections in which Poe's Dupin, the prototype of Sherlock Holmes and other famous literary detectives, indicates that he solves the crime by not overlooking the obvious and emphasizes the significance of understanding the mind of an opponent to solve a mystery. To this end Borges eliminates three long passages of the original, in which Dupin insists that the solution to the mystery unfolds on "account of its being so *very* self-evident."[112]

In Borges's story several aspects hovering in the background of the original move to the foreground: both the detective and thief are French poets; they have had an encounter in Vienna in which one was humiliated by the other; their current confrontation offers the opportunity for the loser of the previous encounter to humiliate the winner; they may have further encounters in the future; and, finally, they leave literary clues for each other to indicate that one of them—and nobody else—has triumphed over the other. In chapter 3 we will see that Borges's transformation of Poe's story played a crucial role in the gestation of "La muerte y la brújula" ("Death and the Compass"), one of Borges's signature tales, in which the criminal and the detective play a game similar to the one played by Dupin and the minister, with kabbalistic rather than literary clues.

Reyes and Chesterton

At times Borges edited the work of other translators while leaving his distinctive mark on their texts, on occasion even signing his own name to such a work. Borges and Adolfo Bioy Casares admired Alfonso Reyes's translations of Chesterton to such an extent that they corrected and republished one of them as their own.[113] Borges sent a letter, cosigned with Bioy Casares, to request discretely that Reyes allow them to publish his translation of Chesterton's "Honour of Israel Gow" for their anthology of detective fiction. In his response Reyes does not oppose their initiative, although he intimates that the rights of the translation belong to the estate of his editor:

México. D. F., November 17, 1943
Sr. don Jorge Luis Borges
Dear Jorge Luis and Adolfo:

Thanks for your letter dated October 23. . . . Israel Gow is honored. Let us hope the estate of Calleja does not object because it was their property. Do not forget to send me your anthology of detective fiction. I am following your writings when I can. I always remember you and I am very fond of you both.

(A.R.)[114]

True to his literary tendencies, Borges did not simply publish Reyes's translation in its original form. He restored, for example, the original title of "The Honour of Israel Gow," which Reyes had translated as "The Honesty of Israel Gow." Whereas Reyes retained every sentence of the original, making minor shifts of nuance and emphasis, Borges and Bioy Casares excised and cropped.

The greatest mystery of Chesterton's story involves a bewildering clue. On a table, several objects lay

> arranged at intervals; objects about as inexplicable as any objects could be. One looked like a small heap of glittering broken glass. Another looked like a high heap of brown dust. A third appeared to be a plain stick of wood.

On the table in Reyes's translation lay

> several objects forming separate lumps, objects as inexplicable as they are inconsonant. One little lump appeared to contain the fragments of a broken glass. Another was a heap of brown dust. The third object was a walking-stick.[115]

The same passage in Borges's modifications becomes

> several objects as inexplicable as they are inconsonant. One appeared to be a little lump of broken glass. The other was a lump of brown powder. The third object was a walking-stick.[116]

In the original the objects are "as inexplicable as any objects could be," highlighting the strangeness of each. Reyes modifies this phrase to "as inexplicable as they are inconsonant," calling attention to the lack of commonalties among the objects, which is precisely what needs to be underscored to produce the sense of mystery the story requires. Reyes could have used the word *marrón* to translate "brown" but chooses "moreno," which in Mexico suggests a brownish skin color. Borges accepts Reyes's suggestion but uses "pardo" the equivalent of *moreno* in Argentine speech. Reyes calls the third object a "walking-stick," whereas Chesterton, at this juncture, called it simply a "stick," identifying it more clearly as a "walking stick" only after the mystery is revealed. Reyes refers to the three objects as "montones" (heaps), whereas Chesterton uses the word "heap," once for the broken glass and again for the brown dust. Borges corrects the inconsistency in Reyes's version and restores it to the original. Reyes added a comma in the sentence that describes the second object, calling more attention to it than to the other objects. Borges restores the original by eliminating the comma.

These various alterations make evident Borges's care in comparing Reyes's translation to Chesterton's original in fashioning his own version. But it is also clear that Borges took liberties to ensure that the story would conform to his own view that Chesterton's genius lay in his ability to present inexplicable situations that, even once demystified with a prosaic explanation, continue to disconcert. Borges composed beautiful pages about those stories in which Chesterton presents a mystery and offers a demoniacal explanation that is finally corrected by a mundane fact overlooked by all concerned. Father Brown, Chesterton's most famous detective, "wants to explain an inexplicable fact with reason." The word "inexplicable" in Chesterton is used to suggest the presence of a fantastic element. Borges at times lamented Chesterton's mundane explanation of his tales' irrational elements because, for Borges, they had a force and life of their own. Borges was fascinated by those stories of Chesterton's that suggest the presence of invisible men, man-eating dolls, empty corridors where frightening creatures are "seen" by a variety of people, including father Brown when he thinks he has seen the devil himself. For each of these occurrences, and many others, Chesterton offers a logical explanation that had been hidden by a mistaken perception of a fact or wrong inference. But Borges did not appreciate the explanations. In fact, he felt that Chesterton's best fictions were those that confounded their author's intentions, namely, those stories where the fantastic element convinces to the point that the mundane explanation feels somehow inadequate. Borges's reading of Chesterton illuminates one of his own extraordinary achievements: the combination of the fantastic with the detective genre.

In the translation of "The Honour of Israel Gow" Borges cuts Chesterton's interjections, once the mystery is resolved, that downplay the uncanniness of the story by stressing the psychological oddness of the characters. All the apparently inexplicable objects in question were once embedded in gold, which Israel Gow removed after he inherited the gold of the family he had served for many years. Chesterton follows this revelation with an image of collective relief: "The garden seemed to brighten, the grass to grow gayer in the strengthening sun, as the crazy truth was told." Borges deletes this sentence and other suggestions that shift the focus from the uncanniness of the evidence to the psychology of its characters.

When Reyes read the anthology of detective fiction, he congratulated Borges and Bioy Casares for their transformation of his translation: "I have been delighted to see the story by Chesterton transformed with an independent esthetic entity by its accidental translators. As a connoisseur, I have appreciated the fine touches."[117]

Translating Names and Titles

Some of Borges's changes affected subtle elements rather than global aspects of the stories he translated. Borges, who wrote himself into many of his fictions, helps Edgar Allen Poe do the same. In his translation of Poe's "The Facts in the Case of M. Valdemar," Borges refers to the mesmerizer who narrates the story as Poe. And, poignantly, for our purposes, M. Valdemar (a Spanish name with the French qualifier "M." in Poe's version and "Monsieur" in Borges's) was, as Poe makes clear, the Polish translator of *Wallenstein* and of *Gargantua,* under the pen name Issachar Marx. The subtleties compound.

Another of Borges's customs is to change the titles of the stories he translated. His version of Jack London's "The Minions of Midas" is called "The Concentric Deaths," and his version of Nathaniel Hawthorne's "Mr. Higginbothom's Catastrophe" is titled "The Repeated Deaths."[118] Borges often alters titles that reveal the ending. His translation of Stevenson's "Something in It" is "There Is Nothing to These Stories" ("En esas historias no hay nada"). In Stevenson's tale, an antecedent, perhaps, to Borges's story "El etnógrafo" ("The Ethnographer"), a missionary scorns the fables of the "natives" he intends to convert to his own religion. The proselytizing priest hears a story about a certain potion offered to the dead in the netherworld before they are delivered to Miru, their god. The priest dies and, in the realm of the dead, refuses the potion. Then Miru decides to return him to life. The priest is no longer dismissive of the stories he has heard but, on returning to the realm of the living, takes refuge in equivocation: "Perhaps there is not much in it as I supposed; but there is something in it after all. Let me be glad of that."[119] Borges's version produces an effect different from the original's. Stevenson's tale suggests there is something to the otherworldly stories from the very beginning, from the title in fact, and this is confirmed at the end. In Borges's version the title suggests that the stories are superstitious nonsense. But this suggestion will be altered. The final line reiterates the idea, before underscoring a change of mind: "There is nothing to those stories, but there is something to them after all. That makes me happy." Borges's version, by contradicting its own title, appears somewhat less skeptical of the story's fantastic twist than the original.

Borges's Arabian Stories

Another practice of Borges as translator was to participate actively in the reception of literary works that have been transformed as they have been handed down in time, such as the tales from the *Arabian Nights*. As we have already observed in chapter 1, Borges was fond of celebrating the chain of translations that brought those stories from Hindostan to Egypt where copyists supplemented the collection with new stories. Borges applauded the cunning of Antoine Galland, who continued the practice by enriching the original with new tales. He also admired the interpolations of Richard Burton. And Borges joined both of them in transforming Arabian stories.

Borges rewrote a story from Galland's translation of the *Arabian Nights*, the original title of which is "The story of the Blind Man Baba-Abdalla" and which Borges translates as "The Story of Abdula, the Blind Beggar." Borges compresses the story in two significant ways: by virtually eliminating its long introduction, retaining only the essential fact that a Caliph encounters a beggar who asks to be slapped in the face after receiving his alms, and, more significantly, by eliminating from the conclusion the protracted narration of the beggar's feelings of religious guilt, the basis for the original story.

Borges changes the point of view of the revelation from the first person to the third and places that revelation at the beginning, not the end of the story:

(from Galland's conclusion)
I had to resolve to beg, and that is what I have been doing until the present; but, to expiate my crime against God, I impose upon myself the punishment of a slap in the face from every charitable person who would have compassion for my misery.[120]

(from Borges's introduction)
The blind beggar who had sworn he would not receive any alms unaccompanied by a slap in the face, told the Caliph the following story.

Borges recreated Galland's version of the tale by removing the religious moralizing of the man whose greed led to his blindness. In Borges's version the blind man seeks the contempt of others to atone for his guilt.[121] Borges's transformation resonates with the ethos of his own tale "La forma de la espada" ("The Shape of the Sword"), in which a traitor asks to be despised for his perfidiousness, more than with the French original, in which the protagonist suffers for his sins against God.

Borges also pretended to have translated Arabian stories that were actually of his own creation. Before publishing "Historia de los dos Reyes y de los dos laberintos" ("The Two Kings and the Two Labyrinths"), as his own short story, Borges had published the tale as "a translation" from Richard Burton's *The Land of Midian Revisited* (1879).[122] But even when "The Two Kings and the Two Labyrinths" appeared as an original work of his own in the 1952 edition of *El Aleph,* Borges wrote an explanatory postscript in which he indicates that it may, after all, be a translation of sorts. He writes that it is the kind of story copyists interpolated into the *Arabian Nights,* adding that Antoine Galland refused to translate this kind of tale in his French version of the tales.[123] In the story "The Two Kings and the Two Labyrinths" Borges emphasizes precisely those religious elements excised from his translation of Galland's version of "The story of the Blind Man Baba-Abdalla." The transformation is not frivolous and makes sense in context. Borges perhaps chose to eliminate the pious aspects from his translation of Galland's story because they are unrelated to the plot. In Borges's apocryphal Arabian story, on the contrary, the protagonist prays for divine intervention, and God responds.

The shift in moral tone in Borges's Arabian stories is also evident in his version of a medieval Spanish tale by Don Juan Manuel. The original is called "De lo que contesçió a un deán de Sanctiago con don Yllán, el grand maestro de Toledo" (on that which took place to a deacon of Santiago with don Illán, the grand master of Toledo), which Borges transformed into "El brujo postergado" (the postponed magician). Several critics who have analyzed Borges's version of the tale have argued that the only changes Borges made involved wording. Marta Ana Diz has set this misconception straight, pointing out that, even though Borges borrowed Don Juan Manuel's plot, his version differs so significantly from the original that one can rightfully consider them two different stories.

In both stories a deacon visits a magician to gain knowledge of his occult powers. The magician appears willing to oblige, but (without the knowledge of his guest) he conjures up the illusion that a few minutes are expanding into many days. The deacon believes, as does the reader, that he is ascending the hierarchy of the Catholic Church on his way to becoming the pope. At that moment the magician reveals the illusion and sends the deacon away from his home. While the deacon lived the illusion that he was gaining power and influence, he never offered a hint of gratitude to the magician.

As Diz points out, a major difference between the two stories is Borges's elimination of the moralizing elements of the original: "[The] moralizing elements move to the background so that magic can become the focus of the story. From a frustrated relationship between a master and a disciple in Don Juan's story, Borges's accomplished version dramatizes a relationship between enemies."[124] According to Diz, Don Juan Manuel's story is about a test, and Borges's story is about a trap. In Don Juan Manuel's version the magician offers the deacon many opportunities to fulfill his promise to repay him for his services, pointing out the deacon's mistakes and begging him to mend his ways. All of the magician's reproaches are eliminated from Borges's version. In Don Juan Manuel's story, the failure of an individual to pass a test exemplifies his moral shortcomings. In fact, the deacon's visit to a master of dark powers is itself suspect in the original.

In Diz's reading of Borges's version, the test is a perverse triumph of the magician over his guest. It is also possible to read Borges's version as the process whereby a magician tries to decide—without any of the moralizing or demonic connotations of the original story—whether or not an individual is worthy of becoming his disciple. Borges offers a variation on the theme in his story "La rosa de Parcelso" ("The Rose of Parcelsus"), in which a magician opts to conceal his magical powers from a skeptical disciple. The magician, in Borges's tale, prefers to gain the reputation of a charlatan than to reveal his secret knowledge to an unworthy soul.[125]

Kafka, the Fragment, and the Dream

Borges recreated many short stories he translated, but he also placed fragments of literal translations into his own works. In his "Poema conjectural" ("Conjectural Poem"), as is well known, Borges includes a literal translation of a line from canto 5 of Dante's *Purgatorio:* "Fleeing by foot, leaving a bloodstained trail."[126] The poem depicts an Argentine man killed in the civil wars following independence from Spain. Francisco Laprida, the protagonist, had wanted to be a man of letters, but his destiny was to die at the hands of gauchos he considered barbarians. The poem is not only an inverted allegory of Borges's nostalgia for a heroic age and a political commentary on the advent of Peronism but, more poignantly, his attempt to fill a gap in a passage from the *Divine Comedy.*[127] "Conjectural poem" can be read also as a brilliant complement to Dante's canto tale, which begins exactly at the moment where the poem ends: when a military man is losing his life from a wound to his throat.[128]

Borges also assembled new works of fiction based on his translations. For example, he created a story he attributed to Kafka, based on short fragments and aphorisms scattered in posthumously published volumes of Kafka's works, without indicating his procedure. Isolated, the short texts by Kafka are self-contained. Borges, however, creates a powerful story called "Four Reflections," based on four connected experiences: the first evokes the need to make virtue out of necessity; the second depicts the paradox of a mighty illusion of power that is underpinned by impotence; the third is a parable addressing the inevitability of defeat; and the final one is an almost humorous observation of the social scruples that preclude escaping misery through suicide.[129] Borges changes significantly the vocabulary of the third reflection, a parable about hunting dogs at rest on a patio but that will inevitably capture a fleeing deer in the forest. Borges substitutes a rabbit for the deer in Kafka's German text, perhaps to allude to a version of Zeno's paradox, the kind Borges often brought to bear when discussing Kafka.

Borges was able to emulate some of Kafka's literary resources, but he could not transfigure Kafka the way he transfigured most writers he translated.[130] At his most daring, Borges was able to alter subtly one of Kafka's innovative ideas. His translation of Kafka's "The Truth about Sancho Panza" involves a subtle, but consequential change in vocabulary. In the brief parable, Sancho Panza is depicted as a man haunted by a demon. To neutralize his demon, Sancho is assisted by many novels, especially romances of chivalry. Later, he names his demon "Don Quijote" and decides to follow him in his wanderings. To qualify the performance of Don Quijote's wildest dreams, Kafka uses the German adverb "haltlos" suggesting a lack of restraint. Borges translates "haltlos" as "desamparado" (forsaken), which suggests both abandonment and helplessness in Spanish. If Kafka's original highlights the wild adventures of the don in the first part of the novel, Borges's translation underscores the despair of Cervantes's protagonist in the second part, which he preferred.[131]

Sometimes Borges shifted the emphasis of a story by adapting its context. His version of Kakfa's "Die Sorge des Hausvaters" (the concerns of a family man) is titled "Odradek" in his *Book of Imaginary Beings*. The title is an invitation to read the text as a description of an impossible being, thereby underplaying the story's psychological and theological dimensions.

In his translations of shorter works, Borges at times took the kernel of a fragment out of context to create a distinct effect. He was fascinated, for example, by the ancient Chinese story of Chuang-Tzu, who dreams he is a butterfly but on waking must consider that he may be the butterfly's dream.[132] Many critics have noticed the importance of this tale for Borges, but to my knowledge no one has noticed that Borges significantly transformed the anecdote in several different translations. Borges fashioned his brief versions of the story from longer texts by Herbert Allen Giles and other nineteenth-century sinologists. He included versions of the story in anthologies and literary journals, recreated it in many poems and stories, and discussed it in numerous essays.[133] Borges first published a version of the fragment as a story in the *Anthology of Fantastic Literature* (1940), which he edited with Bioy Casares and Silvina Ocampo:

(from "Dream of the Butterfly" in *Anthology of Fantastic Literature*)
  Chuang-Tzu dreamt he was a butterfly. Upon awakening, he did not know if it was Tzu who had dreamt he was a butterfly or if he was a butterfly and was dreaming it was Tzu.[134]

In 1946 he published a new version of the story that he reprinted in *Cuentos breves y extraordinarios* (brief and extraordinay stories) (1955), an anthology of very short stories he edited with Adolfo Bioy Casares:[135]

(from "Chuang-Tzu's Dream" in *Cuentos Breves y Extraordinarios*)
  Chuang-Tzu dreamed he was a butterfly but did not know when he awoke if he was a man who had dreamt he was a butterfly or a butterfly who was now dreaming it was a man.[136]

A noticeable variant between the two versions is the title. The first version's title is ambiguous, signifying either a dream *about* a butterfly or a butterfly's dream. If the entire story is the butterfly's dream, the short text produces a vertiginous effect of regress because the dream of the butterfly begins with Chuang-Tzu dreaming he is a butterfly, awakening, and wondering whether he is Chuang-Tzu or the dream of a butterfly. In the second translation the title is unambiguous: "Chuang-Tzu's Dream." The second version of the little story is shorter (just one sentence), plainer, with no infinite regress, and it conserves the most significant conceit of the initial version: whether it is Chuang-Tzu who has dreamed he was a butterfly, or whether Chuang-Tzu is the butterfly's dream. Both versions are creative recreations.

Borges cites Herbert Allen Giles as his principal source for the story. In fact, when he includes it in the volume *Cuentos breves y extraordinarios,* Giles appears in the index as its author. That being said, Giles's text is not an original work but a translation, considerably longer than the text Borges attributes to him:

> Once upon a time, I, Chuang-Tzu, dreamt I was a butterfly, fluttering hither and thither, to all intents and purposes a butterfly. I was conscious only of following my fancies as a butterfly, and was unconscious of my individuality as a man. Suddenly, I awaked, and there I lay, myself again. Now I don't know whether I was then a man dreaming that I was a butterfly or whether I am now a butterfly dreaming that I am a man. Between a man and a butterfly there is necessarily a barrier. The transition is called Metempsychosis. Showing how one may appear to be either of two.[137]

Borges crops and curtails the sinologist's version in his literary renditions. He eliminates the first person voice, which gives preeminence to the man, in favor of a more impersonal third person narrative voice, and he suppresses the sentence indicating that during his dream Chuang-Tzu is oblivious of being Chuang-Tzu. Borges knows exactly what he is doing. In a different context, in his essay "A New Refutation of Time," he offers yet another translation of the anecdote, in which he includes the idea that in the dream Chuang-Tzu lost his sense of self when he dreamt he was a butterfly: "I dreamt I was a butterfly that was moving in the air and that knew nothing of Chuang-Tzu."[138] Borges quotes this sentence in his essay to reinforce his discussion of the "psycho-physical parallelism" between the two beings. The possibility that two distinct beings appear in each other's dreams is not excluded in the two versions Borges published as stories, but those versions are also open to other interpretations: they could be about a single being who does not know whether its life is a dream, or an allegory about the fragility of the imagination. Borges's two literary versions, as well as the version he included in his metaphysical essay, are related more closely to his own tales and poems of dreams within dreams than to a religious vision involving the mutation or transmutation of beings that might have informed the original Chinese tale. Many variations of this anecdote in Borges's fictions and poems resonate with his translation of a fragment by Novalis: "Dreams show us the malleability of our soul, its gift to penetrate any object, and to turn itself into it."[139]

The pervasiveness of dreams and dreams within dreams in Borges's fictional world has been noted by many critics including Jaime Alazraki, Saúl Yurkievich, and Teodosio Fernández.[140] Claudio César Montoto has pointed out that some major stories by Borges can even be read as complex dreams in the sense that their twists and turns might evoke the interventions of dreamers struggling with their dreams in the process of dreaming.[141] Drawing on one of the most venerable traditions of Hispanic literature, Borges often compared life as a dream one cannot control (and a source of literary ideas) to literature, a dream that can be shaped and reshaped not only by an individual but by generations. Alazraki has remarked that Borges's interest in Old Germanic literatures can be explained in part by the significance that dreams have in the ancient sagas. Teodosio Fernández has developed this point proposing that Borges's interest in the Nordic sagas is due to their dream-like qualities. He identifies several short stories in which Borges introduces elements from Icelandic sagas to imbue his stories with oneiric suggestions:

It is not hard to find links between his interests for those medieval literatures and stories such as "El espejo y la máscara" ("The Mirror and the Mask") "Undr," and "El disco" ("The Disk") from *The Book of Sand,* with its Nordic characters and Nordic atmosphere. The use of those possibilities culminates perhaps in "Ulrika." . . . The encounter between Ulrika and Jacier Otálora in the city of York, an encounter which—like in the old Scandinavian world—unfolds as if it had not taken place, as if it had transpired in a dream.[142]

The Prose Edda

Borges's version of Snorri Sturluson's *Prose Edda,*[143] his last major translation, can be read as the culmination of his explorations of the literary dream. The *Prose Edda* was written in Iceland in the early thirteenth century. According to François-Xavier Dillman it "constitutes the most complete, the most coherent, and the most intelligible compilation of Nordic mythology that has come down to us from the Scandinavian Middle Ages."[144] Borges would add, in his introduction to the saga, that Snorri's interest in Icelandic mythology was not religious but literary: "Snorri did not believe in the almost forgotten mythology, as he probably did not believe in Christianity either, but he was correct in judging that it was necessary to understand skaldic poetry" (the traditional Norse poetry of the Viking age).[145] In his *Antiguas literaturas germánicas* (1951), the first book published in Spanish treating old Germanic and Scandinavian literatures, Borges offers the following summary of the *Gylfaginning,* the *Prose Edda*'s central literary and mythological section:

> Gylfi is a Swedish King versed in the art of magic who takes up the form of an old man and arrives at the castle of the gods. He tells them his name is Gangleri and that he has come by the roads of the serpent, which means that he is lost. In the hall there are three gods in three seats one on top of the other; these seated gods are called High, Equally High, and

Third. Gangleri hears from their lips the story of the beginning and of the end of the world, according to the Voluspa.[146]

In his book on ancient Germanic literatures, Borges chose to interpret the *Gylfaginning* as a story about deceit. Nevertheless, he left
open a possibility that would become the major emphasis of his
translation, some thirty years later, that the core of the tale depicts
the dreamlike quality of life. According to Borges the entire work
may be "illusory; the gods have deceived the king, but they themselves are a deceit."[147]

In his translation of the Prose Edda, Borges concentrates on the
Gylfaginning, the most literary section of the Nordic masterpiece,
and he removes passages that diminish the original's most artistic
qualities. The excized sections include the introduction that brands
the saga as the bearer of an inferior pagan mythology superseded
by Christian doctrine. As he had done in his translations of Martin
Buber, the *Arabian Nights,* and "The Postponed Magician," (his
version of El Conde Lucanor's medieval Spanish tale), Borges removes divine elements from the original to emphasize magical aspects and dreamlike qualities of fiction.[148] He is also imaginative in
titling the work "Gylfi's Hallucination." The original Old Norse
"Gylfaginning" would have been translated more literally as "the
deluding of Gylfi," suggesting the tricks in the saga played on Gylfi
as well as on other unsuspecting heroes. But Borges's choice of "Hallucination" erases the divine flavor of the title, which underscores
the gods' ability to deceive mortals. A substitution of the notion of
"hallucination" for that of "deception" provided an orientation for
the meaning of Borges's translation. In his version the gods have
produced a hallucination for Gylfi, but they themselves may be a
hallucination.

Borges is shifting an action perpetrated by the gods into a personal experience partially induced by the gods. The systematic translation of deception into hallucination is at the core of Borges's version. For example, in the original the god Thor is deceived by the
magic of the god Utgarda-Loki. In Borges's version Utgarda-Loki
prepares a series of hallucinations that Thor will experience in a

castle. The original wording "I have tricked you with magical shape-changings" becomes "I planned a series of hallucinations for you."[149] In the original, Utgarda Loki explains the source of Thor's deception as his own fabrications and subsequently makes the castle disappear. Borges transforms the world into a dream that unfolds to Thor as another hallucination, hiding the realities that remain true in the realm of Utgarda-Loki. Thor's return to a reality that conceals another level of reality prefigures the end of the *Gylfaginning*, when the hall and the gods that Gangleri had encountered vanish into oblivion:

(Jesse Byock's literal translation)

Next Gangleri heard loud noises coming at him from all directions. He looked to one side, and when he looked back again he was then standing outside on a level plane. He could see no hall and no fortress. Now he left and traveled back home to his kingdom, where he told of the events that he had seen and what he had heard. And after him people passed these stories down from one to the other.

(Borges)

Gangleri heard loud noises all around him and when he looked he saw he was outdoors in open air and there was neither hall nor castle. Then he proceeded walking and returned to his kingdom and he told those things he had seen and heard, and after him people continued telling them."[150]

Whereas in the original Gylfi returns home to report on the experiences he had with the gods who deceived him; in Borges's version the protagonist appears to be returning to normality after experiencing an extraordinary hallucination, as one who awakes from a spectacular dream. The original is a tale of divine magic deceiving the human mind. Borges's version is a story of life as a dream.

Beyond this fundamental change Borges's translation offers many examples of his lyrical abilities at their most concentrated. The origi-

nal is composed of fifty-four distinct prose sections, many of which
are accompanied by skaldic poems that often serve as commentaries or summations. Borges translates the whole work in prose but
puts the poetic sections into italics as lyrics in prose. These lyrical
sections include inspired moments of poetic intensity, as in Borges's
"*Dark will be the shining of the sun*" for the original "The sunshine
becomes dark."[151] Borges changes the original in which the sun is
extinguishing to a powerful image where the sun is emitting darkness. Borges's lyrical intensity in his free version of the *Gylfaginning*
can be gleaned in comparison to versions by scholars translating the
Old Norse more literally. Take two examples:

(Byock)
    Loathsome are for me the mountains,
    I was not long there,
    only nine nights.
    The howling of wolves
    seemed ugly to me compared to
    the song of swans.

(Borges)
    Deserving of hate were the mountains for me. I was not in
       them for a long time; nine were the nights. Atrocious was
       the howling of wolves after the swan song.[152]

And

(Byock)
    I could not sleep
    on the beds of the sea
    for the screeching of the bird.
    That gull wakes me
    who comes from the wide sea
    each morning.

(Borges)

In the beaches of the ocean I was not able to sleep. I was troubled by the sea birds. They woke me every morning when they came from the ocean.[153]

Borges's transformations combine his erudition, his own lyricism, and his inclination to take liberties. Take for example the episode in which Gylfi arrives at Odin's home Valhalla, the hall of the slain, in the form of an old man. He observes "a hall so high that he could scarcely see over it. Golden shields covered its roof like shingles."[154] This passage is followed by a skaldic poem that has been translated faithfully by Jesse Byock:

(Byock)

On their backs they let shine,
when they were bombarded with stones,
hall shingles of Odin,
the men thinking wisely.

(Borges)

Over their shoulders, the skillful seamen transported the shingles of Odin's hall which they had polished with stones.[155]

To understand this passage it is important to realize that "a shingle of Odin's hall" is a kenning (or skaldic periphrasis) for a warrior's shield. This understanding increases one's admiration for the acute lyrical economy of Borges's translation. The stones that pelted their shields in battle become the stones that polished the shields of these heroes, suggesting not only their valor in battle but also their pride as tested warriors. Borges had already used the metaphor of polishing to express the passage of time in the story "The Man on the Threshold" ("El hombre en el umbral"), where he describes a very old man similarly: "Many years had reduced and polished him, like water polishes stone or generations polish men, to a sentence."[156] The elegant economy of the metaphor Borges added to his translation of the lyrical passage from the *Prose Edda* suggests a feeling for the Vikings' heroic way of life.

In this translation Borges does not always indicate, as in the original, the gender of his characters. For example, he eliminates the gender differences of the planets in a passage where he downplays sexual tensions to produce an effect of serenity. Notice that Borges in the following passage removes the male gender from the sun and the female gender from the moon:

(Byock)
> Sun did not know
> where she had her home.
> Moon did not know
> what strength he had.
> The stars did not know
> where their places were.
> This was before the earth was created.

(Borges)
> The sun did not know where its home was. The moon did not know its power. The stars did not know where they were. This was before the earth was made.[157]

In other sections Borges discovers ingenious solutions to deal with the differences between Spanish and Old Norse with respect to gendered words. In Germanic languages the sun is feminine and the moon masculine; the opposite is the case in Spanish. Borges uses the Old Norse word "Sól" as a proper name for a female sun, and the Old Norse word "Máni" as a proper name for a male moon.

Sections in the original read as if Borges is writing, or rewriting, his own tales. In the passage dealing with the origins of anthropomorphic life, a cow licks salty blocks of ice, either incurring or creating a being. In the original, "the hair of a man" appears on the first day, "a man's head" on the second, and "the whole man" on the third. In Borges's version, on the first day "hair" appears, on the second "a head," and on the third a "man." Borges's version is more ambiguous and suggestive than the original. The conceit of the creation of a being in the *Gylfaginning* is reminiscent of Borges's

"Las ruinas circulares" ("The Circular Ruins") in which a man dreams another man into existence, one body part at a time.

There are also sections of the *Prose Edda* that can be interpreted as corrections of other works he translated. A passage describing impossible objects reads as a correction of his own translation of "The Honour of Israel Gow," in the light of his critique of Chesterton's propensity to give prosaic explanations to his powerful uncanny inventions. Borges thought that the uncanniness of Chesterton's sequence of strange objects turned the prosaic explanation into bathos. In the *Prose Edda* the description of a sequence of impossible objects is followed by an equally uncanny explanation. Borges was so taken by this passage of the *Gylfaginning* that he translated it twice, once in 1951 in his book on old Germanic literatures and a second time in 1984 in the translation we have been discussing. It is instructive to compare the 1951 translation of the passage with the 1984 version on account of a few slight but significant modifications, the most important of which is the removal of the word "delusion" from the 1951 version, also systematically removed from other sections of the work to stress a dream-like atmosphere:

(Borges, 1951)

> It was constructed from six elements: the noise of a cat's footsteps, the beard of a woman, the roots of a mountain, the sinews of a bear, the breath of a fish, and the spittle of a bird. Though previously you had no knowledge of these matters, you can quickly see the proof that you have not been deluded; you will have noticed that a woman has no beard, a cat's movement makes no loud noise, and mountains have no roots. Truly, I say, all you have been told is equally reliable, although you will have no way to test some things.[158]

(Borges 1984)

> It was made of six things: the sound of the footstep of a cat, the beard of a woman, the root of a steep rugged rock, the sinews of a bear, the breath of a fish, and the spit of a bird.

And although you still don't understand this matter well, you will have the proof that I am not lying: you must have noticed that a woman does not have a beard and that a passing cat makes no noise and that there are no roots under rugged rocks. And, on my faith, everything I have told you is no less certain although there are some things you cannot put to the test.[159]

In the 1984 translation Borges interpolates into the *Prose Edda* a number of effects characteristically his own: experiments with the representation of time. In the original, for example, there is a passage addressing the agony of waiting experienced by a god. Borges transforms the passage evoking a theme he had explored elsewhere, namely, the contraction and expansion of time. The original ends with the suggestion that the waiting time of days has the feeling of months. Borges's version, in addition, suggests that each day feels longer than the previous one:

(Byock)
> Long is one night,
> Long is another.
> How will I suffer through three?
> Often a month seemed less to me
> Than half this waiting time.

(Borges)
> Long is one night, long is a second one. How will I do to wait for a third? There was a time in which one month would pass sooner than that first night.[160]

In another passage Borges transforms the tantalizing idea of a character living throughout the ages into the even more fantastic idea of a being who "lives simultaneously in all ages."[161] Borges's version of Snorri Sturluson's *Gylfaginning* is the last of his major publications. It is the culmination of his exploration of the literary dream. It is also a catalogue of his methods as translator, and its themes resonate with those he pursued throughout his literary career.

Borges's Method as Translator

Borges's main goal as a translator was to create a convincing work of literature. This principle is at play in his literal translations and recreations, as well as in his faithful and unfaithful ones. Setting aside stylistic issues (difficult or impossible to explore in a book such as this, directed to English-speaking readers), five stratagies cover the cases studied in this chapter. (1) Borges's most common practice as a translator was to remove what he once called the "padding" of a work: words and passages that seem redundant, superfluous, or inconsequential. (2) He removed textual distractions. This stratagem involves cutting part of the content of a literary work that might distract attention from another aspect Borges would prefer to highlight. (3) Borges often added a major or minor nuance not in the original: changing a title, for instance. (4) Borges sometimes rewrote a work in the light of another, as when he inscribes a post-Nietzschean sensibility to his translation of Angelus Silesius. (5) He sometimes included a literal translation of a work in one of his own works.

Borges's translations are often daring, but they remain identifiable with their originals: they are still versions of the same works even when they have acquired Borgesian touches. He reserved his most adventurous moves as translator to fashion some of his best known literary works. Borges's translation process, therefore, has been seminal in his work as creative writer.

CHAPTER 3

Translation in the Creative Process

In the end all literature is translation.

—Novalis

T he majority of Borges's short stories include at least one character who translates, and these characters are often the protagonists. Many of his fictions are presented as implied translations, many translated excerpts or fragments are inserted into the body of his writings, and many real and imagined translations play either hidden or transparent roles in the gestation or contents of his fictions.[1] Borges's translations offer illuminating insights into his creative process, and his general approach to translation is fundamental to our understanding of his art. Recognizing the significance of translation for Borges allows us to trace the creative practice underlying the invention of a brand of fantastic fiction that posits impossible objects and connects them with characters driven by unusual designs or endowed with extraordinary attributes (such as a perfect memory or immortality). Since Borges is best known as a writer of narrative fiction, the bulk of this chapter treats some of his best known tales in order to exemplify the different ways in which he integrated translation into his writings. The last few pages of the chapter will explore how his approach to translation has implications in his creative process with respect to works he did not translate, but treated as texts he did translate: as raw material he could adapt into the fabric of his fictions.

Our starting point is "Tlön, Uqbar, Orbis Tertius," considered by many his most ambitious and far-reaching story. It is a tale that combines his peculiar brand of fantastic literature, his panache for transforming philosophical ideas into literary themes, his interest in minor genres such as detective fiction and science fiction, his explorations of exotic worlds, his ironic humor, and his political and psychological anxieties. The story can be read as the translation of the universe as we know it into another universe which functions according to assumptions drawn from the speculations of philosophers who think the world is composed of perceptions rather than independent objects that our five senses can identify. But linguistic translation (as in the rewriting of a series of words into another) plays an even greater role.[2]

"Tlön, Uqbar, Orbis Tertius"

The protagonist of "Tlön, Uqbar, Orbis Tertius" uncovers, with the help of others, an extravagant conspiracy involving innumerable individuals who, over several generations, have been fashioning an alternative universe. The conspirators have produced a collective work, an encyclopedia, in which a universe called Tlön behaves according to a version of philosophical idealism. The story moves from the outlandish to the fantastic when the palpable universe, down to its physical laws, begins to transform itself into Tlön according to the designs of the conspirators. In this brave new world, the five senses are no longer coordinated, and nothing is necessarily identical to itself. One need only imagine an object for it to materialize, but the existence of objects is not continuous. Things disappear and are duplicated according to the vicissitudes of consciousness, memory, and the imagination.

To illustrate the peculiarities of Tlön, the narrator discusses the difficulties in translating a sentence from Tlön's *Ursprache*, the conjectural language (akin to our Indo-European) from which all other languages in Tlön can be deduced: "there is no word corresponding to the word 'moon,' but there is a verb which in English would be 'to moon' or 'to moonate.' 'The moon rose above the river' is *hlör u fang axaxaxas mlö*, or literally: 'upward behind the onstreaming mooned.'"[3] This phrase is an instance of Borges at his most magical. His comment on translation is both engagingly believable and useless for any serious attempt at reconstruction of Tlön's *Ursprache*. But that awkward-seeming translation shows an exquisite linguistic sense. It is intended to represent differentiated grammatical features the reader is in no position to identify. The reader must suspend disbelief to accept the existence of a language that corresponds to a world constituted of independent events rather than of independent objects, because Borges does not offer sufficient information to reconstruct such a world in the first place.

Borges cleverly conflates two different strands in his story: (1) a secret society's plot to imagine a universe that works according to the principles of a philosophical view akin to Bishop Berkeley's idealism, but without a god who would guarantee the continuity of objects or coordinate the experiences of the five senses; and (2) a universe working according to the same principles that slowly takes over our own. He is also superbly imaginative in presenting the transformation in transition, when visible effects of the conspiracy are becoming noticeable but before the obliteration of the world as we know it, that is to say, before our universe becomes unintelligible to Tlön.

In Borges's story the creation of the encyclopedia has a direct bearing on the radical transformation of the universe, but the change also requires the willing participation of many individuals. The idea that human beings can will the transformation of the physical universe is a wild fantasy inspired, perhaps, by Schopenhauer's conception of the world as will and representation.[4] Borges, however, does not and cannot offer a blueprint for a humanly willed transformation of the natural laws of the universe any more than he can give us the rules of Tlön's *Ursprache*, because he is creating the spellbinding illusion of an impossible world. Any coherent explanation of the transformation would undermine the fantasy Borges is creating and lay bare its extravagant premises. Borges's tale is persuasive because his characters take for granted the transformation he delineates, not because his readers can understand how it has taken place. Borges presents so persuasively both the conspiracy and the pathos of his protagonist as he struggles with the unbearable consequences of the transformation of his universe that his readers willingly accept the preposterous premises of his clever tale. The rewards for accepting this artifice are considerable because Borges manages to draw momentous consequences from his impossible world that have little bearing on its coherence.

The encyclopedia that transforms the universe—the imposition of a universal order concocted by some individuals and imposed upon others—has dire consequences that Borges invites his readers to consider as an allegory of totalitarianism. The narrator, initially fascinated by the attempt to imagine an alternative universe, is horrified by the change that is taking place and dismayed by the willingness of humanity to accept it. With bitter, understated irony the narrator explicitly compares the transformation of his universe to the rise of Nazism, anti-Semitism, and Stalinism: "Ten years ago any symmetry with the appearance of an order—dialectical materialism, anti-Semitism, Nazism—would enchant. Why not submit oneself to the meticulous and vast evidence of an ordered planet?"[5] The narrator's comment is consistent with Borges's fears, expressed in his political essays of the 1940s, that Fascism and Communism would gradually triumph and undermine individual freedom.[6]

The narrator protests stoically against a transformation he fears and abhors. While all the Indo-European languages are being replaced by languages based on Tlön's *Ursprache,* he decides to translate Sir Thomas Browne's *Urn-Burial* (or *Hydriotaphia*) into Spanish. He does not, however, intend to publish his translation; that would be pointless. Why publish the translation of a text of a disappearing language into another disappearing language in a world where humanity "enchanted, by the rigor of Tlön, is forgetting once and again" that Tlön is obliterating the known world?[7] Why publish anything in any of the languages suggested by the title of the story–Germanic (Tlön), Semitic (Uqbar), or Latinate (Orbis Tertius)?

There is no better commentary on Borges's story than his own translation, in collaboration with Adolfo Bioy Casares (who appears as a character in the story), of the fifth chapter of Sir Thomas Browne's *Urn-Burial,* where we focus on an interpolation not found in the original:

Many more facts have been buried in silence than registered, and the most copious volumes are but epitomes of what has taken place. The chronicle of time began with the night, and obscurity still serves it; some facts never see the light; many have been declared; many more have been devoured by the obscurity and the caverns of oblivion.[8]

Borges's interpolation underscores not only the fragility of memory, but the dark origin and conclusion of matters destined for oblivion. The interpolation is consistent with other changes he made to the *Urn-Burial* that resonate directly with the ethos of "Tlön, Uqbar, Orbis Tertius." The comment also results from many years of reflection on the work of Browne.

Borges first translated a long fragment of the fifth chapter of the *Urn-Burial* in an essay featured in *Inquisiciones* (1923). In the essay he expresses his admiration for the beauty of Browne's prose —an admiration he would maintain his entire life—but also for Browne's "paradoxical heroism," exemplified in his decision to persist in his speculations about beauty in response to a civil war that had broken out around him: "Browne was inspired by the paradoxical heroism with which he ignored the insolence of war, persisting in an endeavor of thought, placing his sights in a pure speculation of beauty."[9] To exemplify the meditative beauty of Browne's prose, Borges translates two fragments he appreciates. The first, from the *Religio Medici,* expresses Browne's distaste for national allegiances or prejudices (a sentiment that may have influenced Borges's own transformation from a fervent nationalist to a resigned cosmopolitan). The other is a long passage from the *Urn-Burial.*[10]

The long fragment from the *Urn-Burial* begins with "the iniquity of oblivion" and ends with Browne's affirmation of the nobility of humanity when humbly recognizing the vain illusion of those who seek everlasting fame and glory. Borges's translation carefully excises sections of the passage referring to the "sufficiency of Christian mortality" in Browne's original. In Borges's text humanity's humble acknowledgment of vanity and the affirmation of beauty over the inevitability of oblivion are not couched in terms of Christian redemption. The fragment contained within his 1923 essay is

an early draft of a full translation of the fifth chapter of *Urn-Burial,*
published in 1944, after "Tlön, Uqbar, Orbis Tertius" was already
in print.[11] Browne's affirmation of Christian salvation over the illu-
sions of wealth and power are transformed by Borges, in both the
1923 fragment and the 1944 translation, into the affirmation of
ephemeral beauty.

In the original Browne makes the poignant claim that "to be
nameless in worthy deeds, exceeds an infamous history,"[12] which
Borges subtly strengthens in his 1944 translation by turning "nameless" into "anonymous," and "exceeds" into "is worth more,"
emphasizing human choice in confronting an "infamous history."[13]
If Browne's *Urn-Burial* is a meditation on the stoic values rewarded
in the afterlife, Borges's translation articulates a quiet protest in the
face of obliteration.

The pathos of Borges's *Urn-Burial* translation, akin to that of
"Tlön, Uqbar, Orbis Tertius," is a recognition of the contingencies
of human history, and a silent disavowal of human vanity. Thus, the
story's narrator responds to the palpable transformation of the universe into Tlön by translating the *Urn-Burial,* a text in which Sir
Thomas Browne poignantly addresses the chimeras of those who
expect to subsist "in lasting monuments."

Shortly before writing "Tlön," Borges published an article to
express his outrage at the exclusion of Jewish authors, and other
writers who did not sympathize with the National Socialists, from
German literary life and from accounts of German literary history.
Borges found it obscene that in Germany the speeches of Hitler
and Goebbels were presented as literary models, while "Goethe,
Lessing, and Nietzsche have been distorted and mutilated." Borges
indicated in passing, that an equal disregard for culture had developed in Russia, whose revolution Borges considered "a generous
hope" that degenerated into a new version of Tsarism. The essay
concludes with an expression of his outrage at the German situation: "I find it insane to . . . perfect the criminal arts of barbarians."[14]

The triumph of Hitler, for Borges, represented the obliteration
of those aspects of German culture he most admired. He wrote
"Tlön, Uqbar, Orbis Tertius" in 1940, when he publicly deplored
the "indisputable truth . . . that the directors of the Third Reich

are procuring a universal empire, the conquest of the world." And
he decried, with bitter irony, the indifference of those who had not
yet taken a stand against National Socialism: "It is childish to be
impatient; Hitler's charity is ecumenical; in short (if the traitors and
Jews don't disrupt him) we will all enjoy the benefits of torture,
rape, and mass executions."[15] Borges's outrage against anti-Semitism
was not new. In 1934, when he was labeled a "Jew" by Argentine de-
tractors wanting to disparage his literature, he responded with an
article called "I, the Jew," in which he branded his critics as inquisi-
torial while expressing his identification with the Jewish people.[16]

Suzanne Jill Levine describes Borges's situation, as he was writing the story, with accuracy when she speaks of his "wartime alien-
ation from his fellow Argentines during those terrible years of WWII
when many of his friends were praising Hitler and National Socialism, and when he wrote some of his best fiction."[17] Indeed, as he
was writing "Tlön, Uqbar, Orbis Tertius," the Second World War
was raging, and in his journalistic essays Borges was condemning
Nazism with an argument paralleled by the plot of his story. Ideas
concocted by men can inflict deadly effects on humanity. Current
predicaments can result from philosophical speculations that take
on a life of their own, that impose themselves upon human affairs
many decades after first conceived. In his article, Borges argues that
the rise of German Nazism and Soviet Communism, two political
movements he despised, can be understood precisely in these terms.
To grapple with the implications of political events in the contemporary world, intellectuals require a vision that looks to ideas of the
past rather than to ideas of the present, whose effects, if any, will
only be felt in the future: "Political events derive from much older
theories, and often a great deal of time might elapse between the
formulation of a doctrine and its application. . . . Hitler, so horren-
dous with his public armies and secret spies, is a pleonasm of Carlyle
(1795–1881) or even J. G. Fichte (1762–1814); Lenin, a transcription
of Karl Marx. That is why the true intellectual refuses to take part
in contemporary debates: reality is anachronous."[18] Harold Bloom
falls into an unintentional Borgesian trap when he reads the postscript of the story dated 1947 as an addition to a story published in
1940. The 1947 postscript, like the prophetic epilogue to Borges's

complete works that summarizes an encyclopedia entry dated 2074, was a willful anachronism intended to surprise his contemporary readers. Bloom does, however, get to the heart of the matter, even if he does not realize that Borges wrote the story while the outcome of the Second World War was far from decided: "Borges, a skeptical visionary, charms us even as we accept his warning: reality caves in all too easily."[19]

In his final gesture, as reality is caving in, the narrator of "Tlön, Uqbar, Orbis Tertius" does not translate Browne's *Urn-Burial* into modern Spanish but, rather, in the style of Quevedo's seventeenth-century Spanish. Christopher Maurer offers insights regarding the significance of Quevedo in Borges's later poetry that shed light on the narrator's choice for his translation: "There is a certain stoic calm in Borges' later verse which I cannot help but associate with Quevedo. [Both] write of detachment from human passions and calmness in the face of death."[20] To exemplify Quevedo's presence in Borges's stoicism, Maurer discusses "Religio Medici," a poem from *El oro de los tigres (The Gold of the Tigers)* bearing the same title as a book by Browne. Maurer quotes a fragment of the poem before offering his persuasive gloss: " 'Defiéndete de mí [Defend yourself from me]. The words were spoken / By Montaigne and Browne and a Spaniard I forget.' That Spaniard was probably Quevedo: 'Desnúdate de mí [disrobe your self of me].' Certainly the idea is his." Borges's Quevedian stoicism found frequent reiteration in his work, including one of his later poems, a Haiku that reads: "The old man / continues to trace verses / for oblivion." If the "old man" were a translator, the poem would be a summation of "Tlön, Uqbar, Orbis Tertius" and of Borges's translation of Sir Thomas Browne's *Urn-Burial.*

The protagonist of "Tlön, Uqbar, Orbis Tertius" is one of a long series of Borgesian imagined scribes who translate and whose practice as translators has a bearing on the stories in which they appear.[21] In "Pierre Menard, Author of the Quixote," the catalogue of Menard's "visible work" includes several translations. Before embarking on his attempt to produce some pages identical to those that already appear in *Don Quijote,* therefore, Menard translates.[22] Menard's bibliography includes a French translation of a Spanish translation by Quevedo that ostensibly restores the original French.[23] Albert, the sinologist of "El jardin de sederos se bifurcan" ("The Garden of Forking Paths"), translates a vast work of Chinese literature by an ambitious man who relinquished political power in order to write it. James Nolan Ryan in "Tema del traidor y del héroe" ("Theme of the Traitor and the Hero") translates several Shakespeare plays into Gaelic, including *Julius Caesar*, which prefigures the events of the story. Hermann Soergel of "La memoria de Shakespeare" ("Shakespeare's Memory") translates one act of *Macbeth* but decides against translating the remainder of the play, arguing that German lacks the Latinisms he needs to produce a version that would satisfy him.[24] His reverse anticipates a more surprising failure—his inability to gain insights about Shakespeare's creative process—in the tale's fantastic twist, when he inherits the bard's memory. Soergel realizes that it is not Shakespeare's memory but his imagination that offers the key to his creativity. His genius consisted in translating the commonplace into the vivid: "Chance or destiny gave Shakespeare those terribly trivial things that every man knows; he knew how to transmute them into fables, into characters more vivid than the gray man who dreamed them, into lines that generations will not let go, into verbal music."[25]

Among Borges's translators of kabbalistic literature are Marcel Yarmolinsky, the victim of the first murder in "La muerte y la brújula" ("Death and the Compass"), and Jaromir Hladík of "Milagro secreto" ("The Secret Miracle"). They both translated the *Sepher Yezirah*. The kabbalistic book was especially important for Borges as a source of literary ideas, as Jaime Alazraki has indicated, because it is the first systematic formulation of the notion that the Hebrew alphabet's written characters constitute the foundation of Creation, and that God begat the cosmos combining them according to a secret order.[26] In "Death and the Compass" a translation of Yarmolinsky's book *History of the Sect of the Hasidim* gives Scharlach information he needs to lure Lönnrot into a trap. The fame of Nils Runeberg in "Tres versiones de Judas" ("Three Versions of Judas") depends, in part, on the translation of his works into German. In "La busca de Averroes" ("Averroës' Search") the Islamic philosopher cannot offer a translation of Aristotle's *Poetics* concomitant with modern versions because he does not realize that the words "drama" and "comedy" involve the dramatic arts. In a penetrating analysis of the story as, among other things, an essay on translation and language, Marcelo Abadi counterposes Borges's interest in a literary exploration of the barriers between languages and realities in the process of translation, on the one hand, with a more subtle theme, on the other hand, about the insignificance of such considerations in light of human suffering.[27]

Some of Borges's stories focus on characters frustrated by or distrustful of the translating process, for one reason or another. Among those characters who leave a translation unfinished is the above-mentioned Herman Soergel, and Gannon from "La otra muerte" ("The Other Death"). Gannon abandons his lyrical version of "The Past" because "Spanish literature is so tedious that Emerson becomes unnecessary."[28] There are also characters who refuse to translate material easily available to them. The American graduate student of anthropology in "El etnógrafo" ("The Ethnographer"), from *Elogio de la sombra (In Praise of Darkness)*, refuses to reveal the secret of the indigenous community where he has undertaken his field work, not because English is insufficient for the task ("I could spell it out in a hundred different and even contradictory ways"), but because Western science seems to him to be "a mere frivolity."

One of the most common openings of a Borges fiction is a short text by a narrator who introduces a translated manuscript constituting the body of the story. With this conceit Borges honors Cervantes's invention of an imagined Arab source that must be translated by an unreliable scribe so that the narrator of *Don Quixote* can write the story of the rueful knight. As in Cervantes, Borges's narrators are often not in a better position than the reader to understand the contents of the text they have decided to offer to a reading public. These many stories include clarifications regarding the kind of translation the narrator is presenting. In some cases the manuscript is described as a translation of a probable translation. In others, as in "Undr," it is presented as the translation of an interpolation in a translation:

I must warn the reader that the words that I translate will be searched for in vain in the *Libellus* (1615) by Adam of Bremen. . . . Lappenberg found them in a manuscript in the Bodleian at Oxford and judged them to be, given the number of circumstantial details, a late interpolation, but he published it, as a curiosity, in his *Analecta Germanica* (Leipzig 1894). The opinion of a mere Argentine amateur is worth little; let the reader judge them as he wishes. My Spanish version is not literal, but it is faithful.[29]

In "El informe de Brodie" ("Brodie's Report"), the narrator who introduces the story indicates that he discovered the manuscript signed by David Brodie in a volume of the Lane translation of the *Arabian Nights* (1840). The translating narrator, who believes the manuscript must have been written shortly after 1840, transposes some of the indigenous words of the source language into English-sounding words. He indicates that his translation is a literal one with two exceptions: he decided to eliminate biblical quotations as well as a passage about the sexual practices of the story's "apemen" (also called Yahoos), discretely rendered in the manuscript in Latin.

Any reader of Borges's tales is well advised not to dismiss as gratuitous any section that is the description of an imagined translation presented as the body of a story introduced by the story's narrator; each such section requires sustained analysis. The significance of this narrative strategy—structuring a story made up of a translator's note indicating the nature of an imagined translation that follows as the main body of the story—can be illustrated by analyzing Borges's "El inmortal" ("The Immortal"), a tale inspired perhaps by Virginia Woolf's *Orlando* (which Borges translated) in that its protagonist lives multiple lifetimes and experiences more than one self.

"The Immortal"

In the story a man drinks from the river of immortality and becomes an immortal. Hundreds of years later the same man drinks from a river of mortality to regain his mortality. The story is composed of three sections: an editorial introduction by the translator of a manuscript, the text of the manuscript itself, and a postscript commentary on the reception of the manuscript. The anonymous translator indicates that the manuscript was found in the copy of Alexander Pope's *Iliad*, once in the possession of a bookseller called Joseph Cartaphilus, whose name, an allusion to the wandering Jew, is a clue to associate this character with both the contemporary and ancient individuals mentioned in the manuscript. To differentiate him from the unnamed editor and translator of the manuscript and because the postscript indicates that the manuscript was attributed to him, I will refer to Cartaphilus as its author.

With the exception of the title, the Spanish in the story copies the original English, according to Borges's definition of a copy: a transparent rendering of a text from one language into another. Both the editor and Cartaphilus wrote in English, but the manuscript appears to Borges's readers in Spanish. Of greater significance is the note from the editor: "the original was written in English and abounds in Latinisms. The version we offer is a literal one."[30] The narrator certifies that his translation is literal, despite having rendered all the Latinisms in flowing contemporary English. He has not, however, extracted the Hellenisms that appear in the English manuscript as oddities. The note that indicates the nature of the translation is crucial. A translation of the Latin idiosyncrasies of the author's non-native English prose would add nothing to what the author claims about his own identity: that he was a Roman tribune. This is hardly the case, however, with the Hellenisms the translator chose to retain, for they suggest an acquaintance with a language the tribune did not know when he set out on his quest for immortality. Borges used a similar conceit in the introductory section of "La secta de los treinta" ("The Sect of the Thirty") describing the translated manuscript a narrator is publishing: "The original manuscript . . . is in Latin but a Hellenism here and there justifies the conjecture that it was translated from the Greek."[31]

To appreciate the significance of the Hellinisims in "The Immortal," one must slowly unravel Cartaphilus's fabulous autobiographical tale. He claims he was Marco Flavinio Rufo, a Roman who drank from the waters of the river of immortality. The highlights of his adventures are his encounter with Homer when the author of the *Odyssey*, also an immortal in the story, could barely remember the poems he had composed; the conflation of his own experiences with those of Homer; and his quest to regain his mortality, which, as the manuscript closes, the reader is assured has been achieved.

The text abounds in Homeric locutions, some of which are identical to those Borges has discussed in "Homeric Versions" and in other essays devoted to Homeric translations. An example is the epithet "black" (which Borges speculated could be an obligatory addition to certain Homeric words rather than a qualifying adjective). The translator copies "the black shadow," "the black pedestal," "black labyrinths," among other examples, because Cartaphilus writes them in his idiosyncratic English.

If the first clue to unravel the mysteries of the story is the presence of Hellenisms in the language of the manuscript, the second clue involves the concept of the "inexplicable," which has a specific connotation in the context of Borges's literary world— a gesture of his debt to Chesterton. Like Chesterton before him, Borges uses the word *inexplicable* to suggest the uncanny. Borges has used the adjective in his own stories but also in his translations, even when the adjective does not figure in the original. In his version of Herman Melville's "Bartleby" Borges translated "the unaccountable Bartleby" as "el inexplicable Bartleby." "Inexplicable" is certainly one of the connotations of "unaccountable" in Spanish, but unaccountable suggests also that an individual may be irresponsible or not responsible for something. Of course, since Bartleby is an accountant, the word *unaccountable* adds an ironic touch. Borges's choice of *inexplicable* erases all connotations of the word regarding responsibility or accounting. This is consistent with the heightened Kafkaesque air informing Borges's translation. In Borges's rendition, even more so than in the original, Melville's classic tale is that which Borges claimed it is: a precursor to Kafka. The Chestertonian use of the word *inexplicable* sheds light on a number of Borges's short stories, including "The Immortal," a tale directly inspired by Borges's reflections on the history of Homeric translation.

Moments after drinking from the "black" waters of the river of immortality, Cartaphilus remembers that "inexplicably I repeated a few Greek words: *the rich Trojans of Zelea who drink the black water of the Aesepus.*"[32] It is inexplicable that the uncultured Roman warrior would repeat a line from Homer and, even more inexplicable, that he should quote it in what for Borges would be an unfaithful translation. Borges quotes the same phrase, with slight modification, in his "Homeric Versions" to illustrate the strange effects in modern translations of the Homeric epithets ("the rich men who drink the black water of the Aesepus").[33] It is inexplicable, and humorously ironic perhaps, that the uncultured Roman tribune Flaminius Rufus, who lamented he was not responsible for the destruction of Alexandria, would pronounce a text in Greek that corresponds to the text Borges used elsewhere to exemplify the difficulties contemporary readers of Homer may have in understanding the strange Homeric epithet.

The Chestertonian usage of *inexplicable* suggests an apparently fantastic element that will maintain its power of suggestion even after the strangeness can be explained. With hindsight Cartaphilus knows that the words he may have uttered after drinking from the river of immortality come from the *Iliad:* "the Roman, after drinking from the immortal water pronounces a few words in Greek; those words are Homeric and they can be found in the catalogue of the ships."[34]

That the uncultured Roman drinking from the waters that will make him immortal speaks words identical to a Homeric text is inexplicable. Also strange is that Cartaphilus coincidentally remembers the mention of men who drink black water, and that the waters of the immortal river are also black. It is, however, *explicable* that Cartaphilus's language would be permeated with Homeric locutions and that the color of the river in his imperfect memory may have been prompted by his Homeric readings in literal translations. When Cartaphilus rereads his own manuscript, he is convinced he has confused his past with that of Homer and that his language is contaminated by Homerisms.

According to Borges's terminology, the translation is a *literal version,* as the editor of the manuscript indicates, but it is not a *copy,* which would retain all of the relevant features of the original. Had the translation maintained all of the Hellenisms and Latinisms of the original, it would have been a copy, but the translator attests to have eliminated only the Latinisms. The translation, is therefore not a copy. That being said, the Latin idiosyncrasies in the original manuscript were eliminated because they would offer redundant clues about the identity of the protagonist who believes he was a Roman tribune. Importantly in contrast, the Hellenisms retained in the translation are of great interest since they suggest that the character may have been mistaken about his identity, that, in fact, he may have been a Greek rather than a Roman. In short, the translator eliminated the effects that would have stressed the interference of Latinisms in Cartaphilus's written English, but maintained the Hellenic idiosyncrasies throughout the manuscript, among them the repetition of the epithet "black," the color of the water of the immortal river, and the words the character thinks he said as he drank from the river.

Even though Cartaphilus believed he was an ancient Roman who confused his destiny with Homer as he was writing his manuscript, the translation—which underscores the Homeric locutions while omitting the Latinisms—offers the exact opposite impression: that Cartaphilus has probably forgotten he was Homer and confused his own past with that of the tribune Marcus Flaminius Rufus. In retaining the Hellenisms, the translator suggests that Homer has confused his own destiny with an uncultured Roman tribune who celebrated the fall of Alexandria (and the burning of its famous library that might have jeopardized Homer's literary posterity). Borges offers a number of hints that Cartaphilus, after writing the manuscript, may have discovered his true identity, namely that he is Homer. The narrator indicates he returned to Smyrna, where he was born, and was buried in the island of Ios. Those are amongst the areas where the author of the *Odyssey* may have lived.

Whether or not Cartaphilus is Homer or the Roman tribune, his memory has confused the destiny of those two individuals, and both have forgotten the *Odyssey*. Furthermore, Cartaphilus recovered Homer's writings in English translations, among them a copy of Pope's translation of the *Iliad* in which his manuscript was found. Cartaphilus has recovered the Homeric texts by way of translations, and his writing style has been contaminated by them (and perhaps by other texts of the chain initiated by Homer).

In the postscript that follows the manuscript, the editor discusses a book by a Cordovero who claims that "the narration attributed to Cartaphilus" is made up of fragments by other authors.[35] Cordovero detects a number of interpolations and concludes "the document is apocryphal."[36] The editor protests. He does not deny that Cartaphilus's text is plagued with intrusions and pilfering, but he considers it "inadmissible" to call it an apocryphal document.[37] Ronald Christ takes the side of the invented Cordovero over Borges's invented editor in his observation: "Like *Ulysses*, like *The Waste Land*, 'The Immortal' uses allusion not only as a means to an end but as an end in itself."[38] Christ is masterful in his rigorous demonstrations of the multiple web of allusions in Borges's story, but the apocryphal Cordovero may be mistaken, as the editor of the postscript intimates. If the manuscript is an apocryphal game of literary allusions, it is no longer possible to appreciate one of the most significant elements of the story: how translations can contaminate memories and experiences. Cartaphilus could only have composed his text as a hybrid of other texts because his knowledge of Homer and of literature, as Jaime Alazraki would argue, are "one variation of the Homeric text, or perhaps, the reflection of a long chain of reflections produced by the first text."[39]

"Death and the Compass"

Borges's translations often play a role in his creative process. While writing "La muerte y la brújula" ("Death and the Compass"), he was preparing, with Adolfo Bioy Casares, their translations of short stories for their anthology of detective fiction *Los mejores cuentos policiales*, which included "Death and the Compass."[40] The anthology also included their translation of Poe's "The Purloined Letter," Jack London's "The Minions of Midas," and Nathaniel Hawthorne's "Mr. Higginbotham's Catastrophe." Each of these stories may have played a part in the gestation of "Death and the Compass," and Borges certainly intended these translations to be read

with his own story, an assertion supported by the fact that he included them all together in his 1943 anthology of detective fiction,
before the tale appeared in a collection of his own stories in 1944.[41]

Each of the translations deviates from its originals in ways that
illuminate the gestation of Borges's tale. His translation of Poe's
"The Purloined Letter" foregrounds a secondary theme in the original as the backbone of "Death and the Compass." In Borges's tale,
as in his translation of its antecedent, the criminal and the detective
both know that the issues involved in understanding the nature of
the crime are not merely forensic, and they have more in common
than first appearances might suggest.[42] The relationship between
Lönnrot and Scharlach in "Death and the Compass" is prefigured
with more clarity in Borges's translation of "The Purloined Letter"
than in the original, where unspecified intrigues involving a woman,
whose noble status (erased from Borges's translation), matter more
than they do in Poe's tale.

In his version of Poe's "The Purloined Letter" and in "Death
and the Compass," Borges emphasizes the ongoing confrontations
between two minds. His signature tale, like his translation of Poe,
enacts an audacious intellectual confrontation between a detective
and a criminal in an ongoing and open-ended sequence of encounters. In both stories detective and criminal engage in a continuous
series of encounters based on intellectual clues rather than on forensic evidence. In Borges's version of "The Purloined Letter" the
clues involve the mind of the poet, and in "Death and the Compass" they entail the knowledge recently acquired by both detective and criminal of the Hebrew Kabbalah and Hasidism, the religious movement and theology founded by Baal Shem Tov.[43]

In "The Purloined Letter" the revelation that detective Dupin
and Minister D. are close, uneasy acquaintances is gradual. Dupin
feels free to call on the minister at home, but he also knows that
the minister would have killed him if he, Dupin, had recovered the
letter with the minister's knowledge: "D. . . is a desperate man, and
a man of nerve. His hotel, too, is not without attendants devoted
to his interests. Had I made the wild attempt you suggest [to seize
the letter openly], I might never have left the Ministerial presence
alive." Characteristically Borges changes the ending to: "The Min-

ister . . . is unscrupulous and courageous. Furthermore, he does not lack faithful servants. The act that you suggest [to take the letter away when he first saw it] could have cost me my life."[44]

The change from a "desperate man" to an "unscrupulous and courageous" one is the starting point of the metamorphosis of Dupin and Minister D. into Lönnrot and Scharlach. Lönnrot and Scharlach, with the color red imbedded in their Germanic names, have their obvious antecedents in Poe's Dupin and Minister D., who share the letter *D* as the first in their respective last names. Just as Dupin harbors a personal grudge toward Minister D. ("D—, at Vienna once, did me an evil turn, which I told him quite humoredly, that I should remember"), so, too, Scharlach holds a grudge against Lönnrot.

Dupin puts his life at risk by leaving the note with the literary clues indicating that he, and nobody else, had outmaneuvered his worthy opponent. Following in his footsteps, Lönnrot risks his life by going unaccompanied to the scene where he expects a crime will take place. This last point coincides with the denouement of another story Borges translated with Adolfo Bioy Casares, Nathaniel Hawthorne's "Mr. Higginbotham's Catastrophe." In Hawthorne's story a peddler has been investigating a mysterious sequence of clues that take him, as in "Death and the Compass," through displacements that would make a geometric figure on a map, leading him to the scene where a crime is about to be committed.

Until its resolution, Hawthorne's story has a fantastic feel to it because the peddler encounters, on two consecutive days, two different men who furnish him with the exact circumstances of the murder of a Mr. Higginbotham, down to the time at which it allegedly took place. The two accounts differ only over the date of the alleged murder. Each day, the peddler spreads the news he has received, and encounters individuals who claim to have seen Mr. Higginbotham after his murder has supposedly taken place. Hawthorne's tale conveys the feeling of a ghost story until the very end when the mystery is resolved. The two men who informed the peddler know the details of the crime because they participated in its planning with a third man; but on consecutive days each of the two are afraid to execute the plan, postponing the murder attempt to a third day. The peddler saves the life of Mr. Higginbotham by arriving on his property, as per the information he was given by his two informants, at the time and the place the third man was poised to commit the murder.

Borges's most important transformation is in the title he calls "La muerte repetida" ("Repeated Death"). The original "Mr. Higginbotham's Catastrophe" highlights one aspect of the misunderstanding in the story, namely, that Mr. Higginbotham was believed to have been murdered. Borges's title brings into sharp focus an aspect of the story that might not otherwise catch the attention of its readers: the possibility, belied in the last paragraphs of the story, that on consecutive nights Mr. Higginbotham, or his ghost, is killed in precisely the same way.

Had the peddler not spread misinformation about Mr. Higginbotham's murder, Mr. Higginbotham would not have been saved. The title in Borges's translation and the role of misinformation with regard to the apparently fantastic events are two elements of Hawthorne's story featured in "Death and the Compass," where information and misinformation with regard to knowledge of the Kabbalah are factored in by Lönnrot, as he attempts to solve the ongoing series of mysterious crimes, and by Scharlach who knows Lönnrot's investigation involves his scrutiny of books about Jewish mysticism.

Another story that played a role in the gestation of "Death and the Compass" is Jack London's "The Minions of Midas." Borges translated it in 1934 with the title "Las muertes eslabonadas" (The concatenated deaths).[45] A corrected version of the 1934 translation appeared with the title "Las muertes concéntricas" (The concentric deaths), in the anthology of detective fiction Borges published with Adolfo Bioy Casares. Since a general note indicates that Borges and Bioy Casares translated all of the stories in the volume, the corrected version of the 1934 translation by Borges may have been a collaborative effort. This story also played a role in the gestation of "Death and the Compass." The notion of concatenated or linked deaths in the title of the first translation invites the reader to reflect upon patterns in the sequence of murders and suicides that abound in the story. The second title is even more suggestive in implying a geometrical dimension to London's sordid tale of conspiracy and crime. Borges once provided insight about his penchant for using geometri-

cal patterns in stories that have a fantastic element. He used them
to persuade his readers to accept a fantastic situation: "Reason accepts geometry."[46]

London's "The Minions of Midas" opens with a double mystery: Eben Hale, a millionaire, commits suicide and, although he
treasures his family, leaves his fortune to a faithful employee, Wade
Atsheler, who commits suicide soon after. Both suicides are linked
to "a terrible series of tragedies,"[47] which Borges translates as "an
uncontainable series of tragedies."[48] A close friend of Atsheler receives a long letter from his friend written only an hour before his
suicide. In that letter Atsheler resolves the mysteries.

The long letter from Atsheler to his friend begins by reproducing another letter signed "The Minions of Midas" sent to Mr. Eben
Hale. The signatories demand payment of $20 million from Mr.
Hale, at his convenience. The letter explains that "The Minions of
Midas" is a secret organization of anarchists seeking to redistribute
wealth. In their view of history the mind of the "Capitalist Class"
of the industrial era was able to depose the descendants of the feu-
dal world by force of their superior intellect and lack of "foolish
ethical [or] social scruples." They offer the millionaire a period of
approximately six weeks before they kill an innocent man on October 1, 1899, at a location they specify ("on East Thirty-ninth Street"),
to confirm their seriousness.

Mr. Hale interprets the letter as an elaborate hoax, but on October 1 he receives a second letter indicating that they have killed a
man on the appointed day. Atsheler finds confirmation of the crime
in a newspaper indicating that a laborer "was stabbed in the heart
by an unknown assailant." The method of the first crime of London's
story is identical to the method of both the first and second crimes
in "Death and the Compass," in which the kabbalistic scholar Yarmolinsky was found dead with a knife in his chest. In fact, the wording of Borges's translation of "The Minions of Midas" and of his
own story is almost identical: "una puñalada en el corazón" (a knife-
stab in the heart), "una puñalada profunda le había partido el pecho"
(a deep knife-stab had split his chest). The Minions also use gun-
fire in their assaults, just as Borges's new generation of bandits do
in "Death and the Compass." Borges makes much of these two

methods of killing since Daniel Simón Azevedo, the second victim
in "Death and the Compass," was "the last representative of a generation of bandits who knew how to handle a knife, but not the
gun."

Atsheler, at Mr. Hale's request, informs the police inspector of
the Minions' existence, the first murder, and the threat of a second
murder in a particular corner on a particular date. London's inspector responds with laughter and feigns assistance: "I had the pleasure of being laughed at in the Inspector's private office, although
I went away with the assurance that they would look into it and
that the vicinity of Polk and Clermont would be doubly paralleled
on the night mentioned," which Borges simplifies as "I had the pleasure of being laughed at by the Inspector, even though he prom-
ised that the vicinity of the aforementioned corner would be watched
over, especially on the aforementioned night."[49] The inspector's re-
action in "Death and the Compass" to the conjectures of Lönnrot
is laughter and a reluctant concession to assist in the investigation:
"The inspector saw them with fear, almost with repulsion. He then
broke into laughter."

The appointed victim of the Minions' second letter to Mr. Hale
is a policeman, to be murdered exactly two weeks later on the corner of Polk Street and Clermont Avenue. A day after the appointed
date Hale receives yet another letter: "Your second victim has fallen
on scheduled time." The millionaire is told that the Minions will
continue to kill on a weekly basis but "to protect ourselves against
police interference we shall hereafter inform you of the event but a
little prior to or simultaneously with the deed."

As in "Death and the Compass" the police are ineffectual in cap-
turing the criminals or even in understanding the true logic of the
crimes. The police offer armed protection to the millionaire who
receives the following letter by the Minions:

> We are sorry to note how completely you have misunderstood
> us. You have seen fit to surround yourself and your house-
> hold with armed guards, as though, forsooth, we were com-
> mon criminals, apt to break in upon you and wrest away by

force your twenty millions. . . . You will readily comprehend, after a little sober thought, that your life is dear to us. Do not be afraid. We would not hurt you for the world. It is our policy to cherish you tenderly and protect you from all harm. Your death means nothing to us. If it did, rest assured that we would not hesitate a moment in destroying you.

In the original Mr. Hale is willing to hire the best agencies of secret investigators. He seeks the "aid of the Pinkertons and of countless private detective agencies." Borges cannot help himself and signals his personal preference for Poe over Sir Conan Doyle by including Sherlock Holmes (not mentioned in the original) as one of the ineffectual detectives hired to solve the case.[50]

The Minions do not respond to Mr. Hale's futile investigations. Instead, they promise to murder the police inspector Mr. Hale called upon to discuss the crimes. Upon receiving the letter Mr. Atsheler immediately calls the inspector:

Great was my relief when I heard the Inspector's hearty voice. But, even as he spoke, his voice died away in the receiver to a gurgling sob, and I heard faintly the crash of a falling body. Then a strange voice hello'd me, sent me the regards of the M. of M., and broke the switch.

The third and apocryphal murder in "Death and the Compass" might have been inspired by London's story:

The third murder occurred on the night of the third of February. A little before one o'clock, the telephone rang in the office of the inspector Triviranus. With avid secrecy a man with a guttural voice spoke: he said he was called Ginzberg (or Ginzburg) and that he was willing to communicate, for a reasonable remuneration, the facts of the two sacrifices of Azevedo and of Yarmonlinsky. A discord of whistles and of horns drowned the informer's voice. Then, the communication broke.[51]

Borges translates the English "broke the switch" to refer to the end of the telephone conversation as "he hung up" or "cortó" in Spanish. In "Death and the Compass" he also uses the word "cortó" to signal the end of the telephone call.

In keeping with the inexorable tone of his version, Borges translates London's "damnable work" of the Minions as their "inevitable work" (obra inevitable). And if in London's original the millionaire thinks that the deaths of the individuals murdered by the Minions were "due to him," in Borges's version he feels he has "caused" them.

The Minions begin to personalize the crimes even further by promising to kill the daughter of a close friend of Mr. Hale. It is at this juncture that Mr. Hale decides to commit suicide and leave his inheritance to his assistant Atsheler, to protect his family from the harassment of the Minions. Later, before Atsheler himself commits suicide, he returns *his* recently inherited estate to Hale's family and begs his unnamed friend to publish the letter he has written with his confession.

As indicated above, "The Minions of Midas" becomes "The concentric deaths" the second time Borges translated the story, endowing it with a geometric dimension the original lacks. The title invites the reader to speculate in a way that the original does not. Borges, shrewd as always, does not title the story "The concentric murders," which would point only to a sequence of murders that begins with victims without connection to Hale and then continues with his inner circles of acquaintances, friends, and ostensibly family members. Borges's title incorporates series of circles but also suggests the sequence of suicides that unfold as Hale and Atsheler, the owners of vast wealth, commit suicide in a vain attempt to prevent the inevitable, that is to say, the moment in which the extortion must be paid to avoid the danger the Minions pose to their friends and family.

In Borges's translation, as opposed to London's original, the reader is invited to make geometric connections with the events of the story. But in "Death and the Compass" such considerations are shifted from the reader to the characters. Detective Lönnrot includes geometric and even kabbalistic calculations in the thought process that leads to the resolution of the crime, which, as in London's story, is also an intricate suicide.

Another translation that may have played a role in the gestation of "Death and the Compass" is Borges's version of Chesterton's "The Three Horsemen of Apocalypse," also in collaboration with Adolfo Bioy Casares, in which one can trace the personality of Borges's prefect of police. In Chesterton's story an Austro-Hungarian Marshal with no sympathy for poetry seeks to execute a rebel poet before his sentence can be commuted by the prince, who has a weakness for poetry. Marshal Grock sends a horseman to the town where the execution is to take place to insist the order be carried out immediately. The prince arrives in Grock's camp and sends another horseman with his commutation of the sentence. As the prince leaves the camp, Grock orders a third horseman to stop the second one. The third horseman executes the first, thinking he was the second, and the poet's life is saved. Like his Chestertonian antecedent, the prefect of police in "Death and the Compass" is skeptical of intellectual speculations. Chesterton describes Grock as one who

> had never read a line of poetry himself; but he was no fool. He had the sense of reality which belongs to soldiers; and it prevented him from falling into the asinine error of the practical politician. He did not scoff at visions; he only hated them. He knew that a poet or a prophet could be as dangerous as an army.[52]

In the case of "Death and the Compass" Borges was engaged with the detective genre, and several of his translations played a role in his creative process. In the case of "Emma Zunz," translation played a more modest, albeit important, role.

"Emma Zunz"

In the epilogue to *The Aleph*, Borges indicates that the plot of "Emma Zunz" was suggested by his friend Cecilia Ingenieros. The story depicts a woman who has sexual relations with one man, murders another, claims she was raped by the second whom she killed in self-defense, and is believed. Borges's attribution of this plot to Ingenieros is only partially correct. Another important source is his translation, in collaboration with Adolfo Bioy Casares, of Guillaume Apollinaire's "Le Matelot d'Amsterdam" ("The Sailor of Amsterdam"). The translation was included in the first edition of *Los mejores cuentos policiales* but disappeared from all future editions after "Emma Zunz" appeared in print.

In the original, a proper looking English gentleman awaits, in the port of Southampton, a commercial ship from Holland carrying spices and other prized cargo. He accosts a sailor, on a brief shore leave, who has a parakeet on one shoulder, a monkey on another, and is carrying a bundle of fabric from India. With the promise to buy his bird and perhaps some of the cloth from India, the gentleman persuades the sailor to accompany him to his home, far away from the port. At the home the gentleman asks the sailor to enter a room where he can display his fabrics from India, but instead of joining him he locks the door shut, and from a skylight the sailor notices a gun pointing at him. The gentleman orders him to obey and promises a reward for his troubles. He asks him to remove a loaded gun from a drawer on a desk and to pull open a curtain at the end of the room. Behind the curtain the sailor finds a woman bound and gagged. The gentleman orders the sailor to release the woman. In desperation she begs the gentleman for forgiveness. The gentleman orders the sailor to kill his lover in exchange for money and threatens, otherwise, to kill him. The sailor pulls the trigger, and the gentleman immediately kills the sailor. When the bodies of the sailor and the woman are found, the police report indicates that the sailor had killed the woman and subsequently committed suicide.

In Borges's translation the changes are slight and perhaps more effective than the original. Instead of translating "like all the others [the victim's husband] did not understand what had happened,"[53] Borges writes "like the others [the victim's husband] found the case inexplicable."[54] Where the original has the less emphatic "The circumstances of the crime appeared mysterious,"[55] Borges's translates, "The circumstances of the crime were mysterious."[56]

The connections between Apollinaire's "The Sailor of Amsterdam" and "Emma Zunz" are evident in both obvious and subtle ways. There are a number of turns of phrases employed by Borges in his translation that do not appear in the Apollinaire's original but that reappear in "Emma Zunz." Thus, instead of translating the French "tira" (he shot), Borges uses the more colloquial expression "hacer fuego" (fire), which is also the expression he uses when Emma shoots Lowenthal, her employer and victim. As in Apollinaire's story the murder weapon is in a desk drawer, which a murderer picks up as the victim of the crime stares intently at his killer. The most telling connection between the plots of the two stories is summarized in the final lines of "Emma Zunz," in which the narrator indicates that the story is incredible but basically true, that only the circumstances are false, as were a couple of proper names. In Apollinaire's story the police assume that the sailor is both a willing murderer and suicide victim when actually he killed in a situation of duress and was killed in turn. In "Emma Zunz" Emma is assumed to have killed in response to an alleged rape that did not take place. In each story a key character disappears from the purview of the authorities investigating the crime: In "The Sailor of Amsterdam" it is the lover of the murdered woman, and in "Emma Zunz" it is the sailor with whom Emma had sexual relations.

Borges's "Emma Zunz" has levels of psychological insight unavailable in either Apollinaire's original or Borges's translation. Nevertheless, "The Sailor of Amsterdam" offered Borges a means he used to tell the anecdote that Cecilia Ingenieros might have provided him, even as Borges's "Emma Zunz" is more emphatic than Apollinaire's story concerning the tale's ultimately inexplicable nature.[57]

"The Garden of Forking Paths"

Borges draws on some translations to create a plot and on others to generate crucial nuances. The latter is the case with "The Garden of Forking Paths," whose mysteries can be illuminated by sections of Borges's translation of Henri Michaux's *Un barbare en Asie* (a barbarian in Asia).

In an author's note Borges indicates that one of the most mysterious aspects of his tale is not revealed until the end of the story. Indeed, it is not until the final lines of the tale that it becomes clear why Yu Tsun, the multilingual English teacher from China turned spy working for German military intelligence in England during the First World War, is looking for a man named Albert he has never met, yet intends to kill. The last few lines of the story reveal that Yu Tsun knows that when the British newspapers report on the murder of Albert by a Chinese man, military intelligence in Berlin will understand that he is indicating to them the name of a city the Germans must attack.

There are, however, other mysteries not revealed in the story itself. The first of these mysteries involves Yu Tsun's decision to work effectively for the German cause, in the first place, since he considers Germany to be a barbarian nation: "I care nothing for a barbarian nation that has forced me to the abjection of being a spy. . . . I did it because I felt the Chief had little regard for me and those of my race—the innumerable ancestors that converge in me. I wanted to prove to him that a yellow man could save his armies."[58] In his attempt to demonstrate that a Chinese man can be as competent a spy as any German, he assassinates Albert, a victim ingeniously selected purely for the accident of his name. Yu Tsun's murder of Albert is all the more mysterious after he discovers the extraordinary fact that his intended victim is a learned sinologist. Albert happens to be better informed than Yu Tsun in all matters of Chinese literature, history, and culture. In fact, Albert has solved the most intriguing mysteries involving Ts'ui Pên, Yu Tsun's most mysterious ancestor, who gave up political power to build a labyrinth and to write a book. Albert translated the book into English, understands that the labyrinth and the book are one, and knows that Ts'ui Pên succeeded in his project: to write a book registering and prefiguring human existence in all of its possible permutations in space and time.

Even though Albert's understanding of the intricacies of Yu Tsun's ancestors is infinitely greater than Yu Tsun's, he treats his Chinese guest with utmost respect. Yu Tsun is embarrassed for himself, and for his family, for having misunderstood the significance of Ts'ui Pên's designs. He admits having cursed the monk who insisted on the publication of the book his ancestors wanted to burn. Instead of calling attention to his superior knowledge, Albert calls himself an "English barbarian"[59] to allow his astounded Chinese interlocutor to save face. The gesture, as it turns out, is of enormous significance to Chinese culture; this is at least one of the most important cultural observations that Henri Michaux makes in "Un barbare en Chine" ("a barbarian in China"), the longest section of *Un barbare en Asie.*

There is a passage in the section "a barbarian in China" in which Michaux refers to a book called *Teachings of the Painting of a Great Garden Like a Grain of Mustard,*[60] which Borges translates as *El jardín del tamaño de un grano de mostaza* (a garden the size of a grain of mustard).[61] Immediately following that reference, which might have inspired the title of Borges's story, Michaux offers an assessment of Chinese culture that can be read as both a commentary on the subtle ways in which Albert had been transformed by sinology and as an assessment of Yu Tsun's behavior:

> The fear of feeling humiliated is so Chinese that it dominates the whole Chinese civilization. That is why they are so courteous. In order not to humiliate others. They would rather be humiliated than to humiliate. . . . They do not fear to "lose face" as much as they fear making others "lose face." That sensibility sickly, by European eyes, gives a special aspect to their entire civilization. They do not have self-consciousness, but of their appearance, as if they were outside themselves and observed themselves from outside. Even the emperors, when there were emperors, feared humiliation. When speaking of barbarians, of Koreans, they charged their ambassadors: Carry on in such a way that they won't laugh at us. To become the butt of laughter! The Chinese know how to take offense more than any other people, and their literature contains, as one may expect, the most courteous and susceptible men, and the cruelest and most infernal insolences.[62]

In Borges's translation he eliminates the aspects of "Chinese paranoia" that Michaux discusses—and that play no role in Borges's story—but insists on the notion of humiliation at losing face, which is one of the principal motifs of the multifaceted tale "The Garden of Forking Paths."[63]

Humiliation is one of Borges's most salient motifs, as we will have the opportunity to see elsewhere, but in this story, it is developed through face-saving notions inspired by early twentieth-century Western accounts of Chinese culture akin to Henri Michaux's. At the end of his autobiographical text, Yu Tsun expresses his contrition for murdering Albert, an action he found inevitable. The inevitability of a murder, which would in turn jeopardize the lives of many allies in the city of Albert, may well have resulted from a complex face-saving mechanism. Yu Tsun's admiration, respect, and apparent affection for Albert is outweighed by his need to demonstrate to his German superior that he is as good or better than any European spy.

Yu Tsun's defiance of the prejudices Europeans have with respect to the Chinese also make him cruelly indifferent to the innocent lives his spying activities might cost. Yu Tsun seems to exemplify Michaux's claim that Chinese literature contains "the most courteous and susceptible of men, and the cruelest and most infernal insolences."

"The Circular Ruins"

If Borges's translation of Michaux's *Un barbare en Asie* played a role in the fashioning of an aspect of "The Garden of Forking Paths," translation is key to the gestation of "Las ruinas circulares" ("The Circular Ruins"). One of the most stunning and perplexing openings of any Borges story is the beginning of "The Circular Ruins": "No one saw him disembark in the unanimous night, no one saw his canoe. . . ." No one saw *him* disembark because the protagonist—who does not realize it himself, until the very end of the story—is a product of somebody else's dream. The night is "unanimous" perhaps because the word "unánime" in Spanish could be read as a contraction of "una ánima," a single soul or spirit. In any event, the protagonist is the product of someone else's dream.

Borges does not grant his protagonist a name or a past, perhaps because he does not have one, but refers to him with several epithets: "the melancholy man" (el hombre taciturno), "the gray man" (el hombre gris), "the stranger" (el forastero). The man is also called a "magician" because his project is to dream another human being, a young man to be precise, into existence and to bring him into the world of his own awakenings. In the climactic moment of his story, which has covered many years, he arrives at the humiliating realization that he is someone else's dream. The notion of humiliation—so central to Borges's literary world—also becomes the protagonist's concern once he finally finds the means to bring his dream creation (his "son") into the world of his awakenings. He does not want his son to know he is a dream: "He feared his son would meditate upon his abnormal privilege and discover that he was a mere simulacrum. Not to be a man, to be the projection of a dream of another man, what an incomparable humiliation!"[64] It is also humiliation the dreamer feels on realizing he himself belongs to someone else's dream.

This remarkable story, which some literary critics, including Enrique Anderson Imbert, have considered Borges's best, has its origins in Giovanni Papini's "L'ultima visita del gentiluomo malato" (The last visit of the ill gentleman). The first Spanish translation of the story appears in the *Anthology of Fantastic Literature*, edited by Borges, Silvina Ocampo, and Adolfo Bioy Casares. I will analyze it as if it were translated by Borges, as I believe it was.[65] The translation from the anthology was published before Borges wrote "The Circular Ruins." Many years later, he published another version of the same translation, significantly altered, in his *Book of Dreams*, which he edited on his own.[66] Both the early and the later translation offer insights into Borges's creative process.

The original opens with the same air of mystery as Borges's story: "No one ever knew the real name of the man we all called the ill gentleman. . . . No one understood everything he wanted to say. . . . No one asked him after his illness. . . . No one knew where his house was. . . . No one knew if he had a father or brothers. . . . One day he appeared in our city, and another day, a few years later, he disappeared."[67] Once he disappears, the narrator assures his readers, in the very last line of his story, that only "one" (uno) saw him after his disappearance.[68]

In the striking opening line of "The Circular Ruins" Borges compacts the beginning and end of Papini's story, but he also alters the perspective of the story: in Papini's tale the protagonist knows he is someone else's dream, feels humiliated by that knowledge, wonders about his creator, and longs to vanish. Papini's protagonist is aware that "the dream of this one is so lasting, and so intense, that I have become visible also for the men who are awake."[69]

In the Italian story the "ill" gentleman appears one morning on the bedside of the awaking narrator. Papini is brilliantly ambiguous: the gentleman might be an intimate friend of the narrator's; the narrator, himself, might be another character of the dream; or the visitor is at the narrator's bedside simply to enhance the subtle dreamlike quality of the story. Be that as it may, the gentleman arrives at his friend's bedside to make a series of confessions and to seek his assistance. The gentleman reveals to his friend that he is a product of someone else's dream. He discloses his attempts to keep his dreamer dreaming, it having dawned on him that he might vanish forever on his dreamer awaking. He also confesses that, in time, his instinct for survival was superseded by his feelings of humiliation. When he comes to terms with the full significance of the fact that his life is contingent on the dreams of another, he decides to turn his life into a nightmare that might awaken the dreamer, longing to bring the dream and his own humiliated life to an end.

In Papini's story the narrator is terribly frightened by what he is hearing, by the condition of his friend, and by the gruesome confessions of murder and mayhem in which the gentleman has participated to turn his life into a nightmare that might awake his dreamer. In the original the gentleman also confesses that he has consorted with supernatural creatures such as witches and giants. The narrator is unable to assist or console his friend.

Borges's first translation of the story is more elegant and poignant than the original. In his translation the friend listens to the gentleman's tale in disbelief but not horror. Borges erases all the supernatural elements of the original with the exception of the main conceit of the story, that is, the possibility that the gentleman is actually somebody else's dream. Borges also eliminates aspects of the original that would otherwise qualify it as a gruesome tale of horror by cutting details of the crimes the gentleman committed in his attempts to awake his dreamer.

Compare a ghastly passage from the original to Borges's translation:

(Papini)
> No crime was alien to me, nothing abominable was unknown to me, no terror detained me. I murdered innocent old people with refined torture; I poisoned the waters of an entire city; I set fire to the hair of many women; I killed children with my teeth; . . . I threw myself from a mountain into a naked valley surrounded by white bones. . . . But it seems that the one who dreams me is not frightened by that which makes other men tremble.[70]

(Borges)
> I did not avoid any crime imaginable, I did not ignore any evil, no terror made me turn back. I think that he who dreams me does not fear that which makes other men tremble.[71]

Borges makes a similar choice in his translation of the *Prose Edda* in which he omits the gruesome element of the description of an eagle to leave the pathos of a simple scream: (Byock) "The screaming eagle, darkly pale, rips apart corpses"; (Borges) "The eagle screams."[72] Borges often removes gory or distasteful details from his translations, especially when they diminish the impact of another aspect of the literary work.[73] Thus, the tone of wistful mystery imbuing Stevenson's "The Song of the Morrow" is tainted in the original by repugnant details Borges omits, such as lice in the following example: (Stevenson) "And lo the nurse fell upon the beach as it were two handfuls of dead leaves, and the wind whirled them widdershins, and the sand lice hopped between";[74] (Borges) "And the nurse fell upon the beach as if she were a handful of dead leaves and the wind swept them away in the opposite direction and the sand opened up and took her place" (108).[75]

Borges translated Papini's story a second time for his *Book of Dreams* (1976). A great deal of the Spanish text of the second translation is identical to the first, but Borges modified many elements and discarded almost a third of the initial version. The only unfortunate aspect of the second translation is the very beginning, which Borges substantively modified, perhaps to cover his tracks: the new opening is no longer as obviously related to the first line of "The Circular Ruins." The later version transforms his previous "No one ever knew the real name of the man we all called the ill gentleman,"[76] to "Everyone called him the Black Gentleman; no one knew his true name."[77] This unfortunate change aside, the second translation is more elegant and compact than either the original or the first translation. In the second translation both the gentleman and his friend display calmer demeanors, and the suggestion of serious crimes is eliminated. Compare the texts quoted above with the same passage in Borges's second translation: "I did not even avoid crime. But he who dreams me, does he not fear what makes other men tremble?"[78] In the second translation Borges also eliminates all the passages in which the desperate gentleman begs his friend to find a way to force the dreamer from his dream, thus putting him out of his misery. Borges's second version is less dramatic but more poignant. The gentleman seeks only some measure of comfort and consolation from a friend unable to comply:

(Papini)
> Console me a little bit. Suggest a stratagem, an intrigue, a trick that will do away with me. I am asking you with my entire soul. Don't you have some pity for this bored phantom?[79]

(first translation)
> Console me a little bit. Suggest a stratagem, an intrigue, a trick that will make me disappear. Don't you have pity for this bored phantom?[80]

(second translation)
Console me, say something to me, have pity for this bored
phantom. . . .[81]

In the second translation, Borges eliminates the metaphysical speculations of the ill gentleman and focuses on his quiet anxiety, as opposed to the angry and nervous energy of his previous version, which
was already downplaying the desperate gruesomeness of the original story.

Borges's "The Circular Ruins," like the second translation of the
story by Papini, features an air of resignation. In an inspired stroke,
Borges captures the vicissitudes of the gentleman's emotions in a
single moment, when his "taciturn" dreamer feels relief, humiliation, and fear almost instantaneously, when realizing he is a product of someone else's dream and that the dream may be coming to
an end.

Borges transforms Papini's tale from the story of a man aware
he is the product of somebody else's dream to the story of a man
who would like to dream someone else into existence and who eventually discovers he himself is the product of someone else's dream.
"The Circular Ruins," therefore, fuses Papini's tale about the intensity of a dreamer whose dreams can inhabit the world of those
who are awake, with his acknowledged fascination with the golem,
the notion of a human being who longs to usher another into existence. Borges's story is also informed by his version of Chuang-
tzu's dream of the butterfly, in which its protagonist wonders if he
is being dreamt by another, and by his fascination for Schopenhauer's
idea that reality is a recurrent dream of a divine mind.[82]

There are echoes of Papini's conceits in "Ein Traum," a poem
by Borges about a nightmare experienced by Kafka. In the poem
Kafka dreams a female companion into existence who tries to se-
duce Kafka's friend, also a product of Kafka's dreams. The friend
fears that if they consummate their relationship, Kafka will stop
dreaming them. The poem includes the line "Only one knew," alluding to the dreamer when "there was no one left on earth," and
concludes with a sense of disturbing isolation: "Now that the two

are gone, I have remained alone. / I will stop dreaming myself into existence."[83]

Borges would occasionally cut elements from an original he was translating only to use them in one of his own fictions. That was perhaps Borges's way of acknowledging a good literary idea out of place in one text but suitable to another. Thus, for example, Borges omits the following sentence from Papini's story: "Made savage by the will to destroy, I tore apart with my teeth the children I found in my way." The gory passage is poorly suited to the more somber tone of his translation. But he later uses the same idea in a story of his own where the gruesome image is more appropriate. In "La casa de Asterión" ("The House of Asterion") his minotaur devours his victims with his own teeth "without bloodying my hands." Another, more elaborate, instance of Borges's removing elements during translation only to incorporate them later involves his translation of a story by Villiers de l'Isle Adam, itself a rewriting of a story by Poe.

"The Writing of the God"

In his two collections of short stories, *Cruel stories* and *New Cruel Stories,* Villiers de l'Isle Adam explored cruelty in short fiction, as his titles indicate. In some tales he designed to outdo the masters of the genre in the intensity of their cruelty. "The Torture of Hope" heightens the cruelty of Poe's "The Pit and the Pendulum." De l'Isle Adam salutes Poe by quoting an epigraph from Poe's story then attempts to outdo his master. In Villiers's story, as in his American antecedent, a man in a pit is the victim of a torturing Spanish inquisitor. In Poe's version the victim, almost incredibly, escapes the final torture intended to kill him. In the French version the victim thinks he is escaping his torturer, but the escape, anticipated and expected by the inquisitor, happens to be yet another torture, the torture of hope.

Borges considered Villiers's tale more subtle than Poe's in that the French writer had transformed a tale of physical horror into a "moral hell."[84] It is possible to say that Borges's translation is even more successful than Villiers's original in producing the effects the

French writer had intended. Perhaps the most audacious transformation is the change in the title. Borges does not call the tale "La Torture par l'espérance" (the torture of hope) but simply "Hope." In so doing, the reader does not anticipate the resolution from the outset. Borges's translation reads like a rewriting of Poe's story until the very end, when one realizes that the victim's hope for escape is, in fact, the torture. Thus the impact of the translation is more powerful than Villiers's original in transmitting the psychological cruelty of the inquisitor.

Borges leaves traces of his personal style in the translation of Villiers's tale. He eliminates exclamation points and short emphatic phrases, such as "What a frightful silence!" that create a melodramatic tone in the original.[85] He also finds ways to introduce his characteristic vocabulary. Thus, "an excessively long corridor" becomes "it was a corridor indeed, but almost an infinite one."[86]

There is yet another more subtle difference between the original and Borges's version. Borges deletes the indications that the cruelty of the inquisitor may involve his religious differences with his victim—a Rabbi and kabbalist. Borges eliminates entire paragraphs in which Villiers's rabbi implores in vain the Jewish God ("the God of David") for aid or consolation. In the original the inquisitor is a Dominican priest whose torture, in his mind, involves a "fervent charity" toward his Jewish victim. Borges suppresses any mention of charity, or any other theological rationalization for the torture, and erases the mention of the religious order to which the inquisitor belongs. In the original the inquisitor is referred to as "ascetic." Borges eliminates the adjective that would mitigate the cruelty of an individual whose severity might be seen as the result of following the strictures of his order rather than his own nature.

Borges suppresses the theological touches in the story, perhaps because they could suggest a theological difference between the two men which might reduce the cruelty; perhaps because the theological aspects could serve as either a justification or palliative for the cruelty. In any event, the theological elements Borges eliminates have no bearing on the fundamental transformation of Poe's story by Villiers; nor do they impact the outcome of the story as written by Villiers and Borges, which involves an apparent escape as the torture of hope. And yet, Borges's elimination of theological elements allows for a possibility not explored in Villiers's tale. Borges's "La excritura del dios" ("The Writing of the God") is the story of an inquisitor and his victim in which the outcome depends on a theological event.

As with its antecedents, "The Writing of the God" is about an inquisitor's prisoner in a pit. Tzinacan, the protagonist of Borges's story, is not a Rabbi, as in Villiers's, but a Meso-American priest. Borges transposed the character from Villiers's original into a priest because Tzinacan's spiritual practices are kabbalistic. In his cell the priest attempts to decipher the writing of his god, and is aided in the process by the letter-like spots on a tiger kept in a cell next to his.

Borges realizes in his story that which remained a latency in Villiers's: a retelling of "The Pit and the Pendulum" in which theology has a bearing on the outcome. Thus, as the priest deciphers the writing of his god, he gains such extraordinary powers that he can, if he chooses, destroy his torturer. In fact, he can annihilate the universe. And yet, Tzinacan's revelation is so overwhelming that he becomes indifferent to his own body and to the events that will lead to his physical death: "He who has glimpsed the universe, he who has glimpsed the burning designs of the universe, can have no thought for a man, for a man's trivial joys or calamities, though he himself be that man. He was that man, who no longer matters to him."[87]

"The Lottery in Babylon"

Borges took liberties with writers such as Poe and Villiers de l'Isle Adam with ease. This is not the case with Kafka, a writer whose literary resources presented him with far greater challenges. In many of his translations Borges managed to release potentialities the original writer had not fully developed; not so with Kafka. Borges was able to highlight certain aspects of Kafka in his translations, but he leveled others. He adopted and adapted some literary motifs he discovered in his readings of Kafka, but was not able to transcend Kafka the way he had many other writers as he rewrote them into the web of his fictional world. In short, Borges met his match with Kafka.

Kafka always mattered to Borges, and even though he eventually called him the greatest writer of the twentieth century, his initial response was restrained, even as he was actively engaged in writing essays about Kafka, translating many of his works, and publishing stories according to his summations of Kafka's approach to literature.[88] Perhaps owing to his own anxieties provoked by Kafka's brilliance, Borges early on regarded him an interesting minor author. "Perhaps the strength of Kafka," he once wrote, "may lie in his lack of complexity."[89] Borges would resist any interpretation that would confer any transcendence to Kafka's writings and was especially derisive of spiritual interpretations, even as he acknowledged Kafkas's interest in theology: "In and out of Germany theological interpretations of his oeuvre have been rehearsed. They are not arbitrary— we know that Kafka was a devout reader of Pascal and Kierkegaard— but they are not too useful either."[90] In the introduction to Borges's translation of Kafka's parable "Before the Law" (a tale retold verbatim in the famous church scene of *The Trial* and interpreted many times in terms of its Jewish theological overtones), Borges reductively calls it a story in the fantastic genre.[91] For Borges, it was pointless to speculate on the solution to Kafka's mysteries because he believed there is no solution to be found. Once Borges understood the basic situation established in a Kafka narrative, he lost interest.

Borges considered Kafka's greatest merit to lie in his transmutation of Zeno's paradoxes about infinity into "intolerable situations." In his prologue to a collection that includes his translation of "The Great Wall of China" (his favorite tale by Kafka), Borges quotes Zeno to elucidate Kafka's literary technique: "Do you remember the first and the clearest of Zeno's paradoxes? Movement is impossible because in order to reach B we must first pass midpoint C, but before we reach C we must reach midpoint D, but before reaching D . . . the Greek philosophers does not enumerate all of the points, and Franz Kafka does not have to enumerate all of the vicissitudes. It is sufficient that we understand they are infinite."[92] As in Zeno's paradoxes, Borges expected that Kafka's characters would never reach their destinations or achieve their goals. According to Borges, Kafka transformed Zeno's paradoxes into literary works by enacting them in a world of hierarchies that escape the grasp of his characters or readers, a world ruled by secret authorities "who are not known and who are inaccessible."[93]

In his summation of "The Great Wall of China" Borges wrote: "To detain the course of infinitely far away armies, an emperor infinitely remote in space and time orders the infinite generations to raise an infinite wall to surround his infinite empire."[94] Borges's reading of Kafka's tale illuminates those aspects of the story in which infinity becomes an obstacle to the accomplishment of human tasks, but it is also somewhat reductionist. In Kafka's original, as in Borges's translation, the story is constructed on the basis of premises either displaced or reconsidered, and, in typical Kafkaesque fashion, it becomes impossible to distinguish the aspects of the story intended as parables from those that are not, leaving the reader perplexed by a situation that feels both momentous and beyond his or her grasp.

The structure of the story is not solely contingent on the infinite postponements that Borges so splendidly underscores. It depends also on false-starts, contradictions, and non sequiturs. As "The Great Wall of China" opens, the narrator indicates that the edification of the wall had been proclaimed officially complete; he then proceeds to lament that some individuals suspect that the gaps in the wall were never filled; he then indicates that the existence of such gaps cannot be verified; he then assumes that the gaps exist. Toward the opening of the story the narrator discusses the threatening peoples of the North from whom the wall was intended to be a protection, and he claims that those peoples know more about the construction of the wall than the builders. By the end of the story the narrator doubts that the peoples of the North exist at all. The narrator speaks in some detail about an organization he calls "The Direction," ostensibly established in the sacred city of Beijing to administer the building of the wall. During the course of the story the narrator opines differently: the organization may be as old as the universe, and it predates any political structure of the recent past. The narrator also speaks of a truth the builders have kept to themselves, and he finishes his tale refusing to continue with his analysis of a certain unidentified problem, suggesting he has chosen to keep important information to himself.

Notwithstanding Borges's reticence, he owes a great debt to Kafka in those of his tales where a fantastic universe symbolizes dangerous human affairs, sometimes described with resigned stoicism by a narrator who is a victim of the very circumstances he describes. These stories are about worlds ruled by secret and inaccessible authorities and include "Tlön, Uqbar, Orbis Tertius" and "La biblioteca de Babel" ("The Library of Babel"). Borges also spoke of "La lotería en Babilonia" ("The Lottery in Babylon") as one of his attempts to "paraphrase Kafka."[95] The story is about a man escaping a dangerous place run by an organization (as ineffable as "The Direction" in Kafka's "The Great Wall of China"). The organization has arranged a lottery that delivers punishments as well as rewards and whose procedures have become so secret and invisible that it is not longer possible to differentiate their activities from those of destiny or chance. The dangerous and life-threatening aspects of this mysterious organization are expressed by the fears of the narrator, who appears to be fleeing an unbearable and violent land where the controlling institution has apparently gone awry.

Toward the opening of "The Lottery in Babylon" Borges offers a formulation that reads almost like a baroque version of a Zeno paradox, involving the Hebrew alphabet: "The letter [Beth], in the nights when the moon is full, confers upon me power over men whose mark is the letter Ghimel, but it subordinates me to those of the Aleph, who must obey those of Ghimel in moonless nights."[96] In time the institution that supposedly established the lottery (like the emperor in Kafka's tale about the edification of the Chinese wall) transmogrifies into a possible legend or myth. Reality might not be "other than an infinite game of chance."[97] In Borges's story, Zeno's paradoxes are not only a tool of interpretation with which one could, as Borges did with Kafka, elucidate aspects of the tale. In Borges Zeno's paradoxes constitutes the fabric of the story itself and are also explicitly quoted. In fact, Borges refers to Zeno's paradox of the race between Achilles and the turtle to explain the complexity of the lottery in its most advanced stages: "The number of drawings is infinite. No decision is final, each decision has ramifications in other decisions. Ignorant people assume that infinite drawings require infinite time; in fact it is enough for time to be infinitely subdivisible, like the teaching in the famous parable of the contest of the turtle."[98] As with Kafka's "The Great Wall of China" the stories of a company that arranges the lottery are "contaminated with fiction," and the organization becomes so invisible in its practices that it is possible for some to believe it never existed. In fact the story of how it came into being, in a Kafkaesque gesture, may itself be a fiction, a legend, or a fabrication. It is possible to read "The Lottery in Babylon," as Adelheid Hanke-Schaefer has done, as a Kafkaesque parable about Fascist dictatorships of the 1930s and 1940s. The story of the establishment of the institution that has taken over a society reeks of falsehood and deception.[99]

In his translations of Kafka, Borges changes little, but he must have learned more than his somewhat reductionist analysis of Kafka suggests: that it is possible to write a story whose premises and assumptions can be in a process of continuous shift, even as the story is being narrated. He must also have appreciated the literary uses of the non sequitur to produce disquieting effects. "Josephine, or the Mouse Singer," which Borges also translated from Kafka, abounds with such non sequiturs. In describing the relationship of Josephine to her people, Kafka's narrator indicates that her people submitted to her but not unconditionally. The example the narrator uses to illustrate this point is an illogical sequence suggesting just the opposite: unconditional, or even instinctual, submission. We are told that they are incapable of laughing at her ("Es wäre z.B. nicht fähig, über Josephine zu lachen.")[100]

Paul de Man, Ana María Barrenechea, Jaime Alazraki, and others have insisted that the differences between Borges's literary world and that of Kafka's are greater than their similarities. One can admit differences and still recognize that many of the literary means with which Kafka produces a sense of disquiet are identical to those that Borges has used in countless tales to produce the spellbinding illusion of an unreal world. In "The Lottery in Babylon" the narrator describes a lottery wherein prizes are accorded the winning lots, and the narrator continues with a non sequitur: "naturally those 'lotteries' failed. Its moral virtue was void."[101] It does not follow that a lottery offering prizes for winning numbers must fail in favor of a lottery that offers punishments as well as rewards. It is, of course, always possible to take a non sequitur in Borges and find in it an allegorical or a symbolic significance, but the same thing is true of Kafka. The point is simply that Kafkaesque uses of such devices as the non sequitur, the logical gap, and the abandonment of premises and assumptions in the course of the narrative are literary techniques that became part of Borges's repertoire after he translated Kafka. These Kafkaesque gestures support a view I have been defending in this book, that Borges was more of a fabulist than a philosopher in fashioning his literary world, even when drawing on philosophical premises.

Borges slowly relinquished his skepticism of Kafka and apologized for his reductionist readings: "I discovered Kafka in 1917 and I now confess that I was not worthy of his writings. I considered him a minor figure."[102] His first rectification was to recognize that Kafka is a great writer because he expressed the "[theme] of the unbearable loneliness of he who lacks a place, even the most humble one, in the order of the universe."[103] In time Borges began to appreciate the unimaginable beings that inhabit Kafka's world and the invention of a new genre of the fantastic. He admired Kafka's ability to situate, in realistic settings, the inexplicable behavior of his characters. It was through the filter of the inexplicable in an ostensibly realistic setting that Borges then reinterpreted Melville's "Bartleby" as a Kafkaesque tale. In one of Borges's most poignant translations of Kafka, he inverts matters and inscribes aspects of Melville into Kafka. Josephine, in Kafka's "Josephine, or the Mouse Singer," longs to be relieved from work to dedicate herself to singing.[104] Those aspects of the original are eliminated from Borges's translation, including a long sentence in which Kafka's narrator explains how working could adversely affect her voice, and thus her song. Borges reduces the original explanation to a sentence that could almost have been uttered about Melville's Bartleby: "Josephine struggles so that she is not obliged to work."[105]

In time Borges began to believe that Kafka purified "the literature of our era, lost in mere circumstances,"[106] in order to offer "a series of parables whose theme is the moral relation to the divinity and to its incomprehensible universe."[107] A few months before he died, Borges's turnaround was complete: "Kafka's destiny was to transmute circumstances and agonies into fables . . . [His oeuvre] is intemporal and perhaps eternal. Kafka is the great classic writer of our tormented century."[108]

Original Work As Translation

Just as the narrator of "Pierre Menard, Author of the Quixote" begins to read Menard's intentions and idiosyncrasies into the chapters of *Don Quixote* that Menard did not recreate, it is tempting to think of Borges the creative writer as translator at work with respect to works he did not translate. Our first example is his story "Tema del traidor y del héroe" ("The Theme of the Traitor and the Hero"), which bears an obvious resemblance to Chesterton's "The Sign of the Broken Cross."

In the opening of "The Theme of the Traitor and the Hero" Borges's narrator recognizes the debt to Chesterton: "Under the notorious influence of Chesterton (inventor and embellisher of elegant mysteries) . . . I have conceived this plot."[109] Any reader of Chesterton would have to construe the narrator's statement as an indication, on the part of Borges, that he borrowed and embellished "The Sign of the Broken Sword." Borges's tale is, in fact, a baroque version of the story from the Father Brown series in which a man, venerated as a hero, is actually a traitor to his homeland. Father Brown discovers the sordid past of this diabolical man, whose reputation is that of a hero killed in battle. The false hero is in fact killed by his own son-in-law with the assistance of other British patriots. The son-in-law, however, decides that it is in his nation's best interest that the man's treachery remain a secret. He therefore concocts the story that his father-in-law was killed in a heroic battle. Father Brown unravels the mystery by reading between the lines in the existing documents and biographies of the "hero" and his circumstances. The Brazilian general who ostensibly captured and killed him, for example, had a reputation of being a magnanimous man who did not exact revenge upon his enemies: "Almost every other prisoner he had ever captured had been set free. . . . Men who had wronged him came away touched by his simplicity and sweetness. Why the deuce should he diabolically revenge himself only once in his life; and then for the one particular blow that could not have hurt him."[110]

In "The Theme of the Traitor and the Hero" Borges seems to rewrite this passage more concisely: "[Kilpatrick] had signed the death sentence of a traitor whose name has been erased. That sentence is not consistent with the pious habits of Kilpatrick."[111] In Chesterton's story the man who discovers the treason is the hero's son-in-law; in Borges's version it is the hero's best friend. In both cases the hero is reputedly killed by an enemy, whereas he was actually killed by members of the very army he had once led and betrayed. In both cases the main clue that the hero was a traitor involves the fact that a man reputed for clemency decides to exact revenge upon an enemy. In both stories someone who knows the facts writes a biography that attempts to hide them, and in both a shrewd interpreter can read between the lines to unearth the truth.

The basic plots of the two stories are identical. One can read Borges's story as a creative rewriting of Chesterton's story about the reputed hero, who was actually a traitor. First, Borges edits the rambling discussions between Father Brown and his side-kick Flambeau, and second, he complicates the plot by suggesting an eternal return: the periodic repetition, under different historical and literary guises, of a similar sequence of events.

In Borges's adaptation of Chesterton's tale, the man who discovers the treason of the "hero" was also the translator of Shakespeare into Gaelic, James Nolan Ryan, and the plot he concocts to create the legend that his traitor is a hero is inspired, and perhaps prefigured, by the deadly conspiracy in *Julius Caesar*. In Chesterton's story the action takes place in Brazil; in Borges's story "the action takes place in a tenacious and oppressed country: Poland, Ireland, the republic of Venice, some South American or Balkan state. . . ."[112] Somewhat out of context, a line of Borges's story summarizes its relationship with its antecedent: "These parallelisms (and others)

. . . induce Ryan to suppose a secret form of time, a drawing of lines that repeat themselves."[113]

The significance of Chesterton in "The Theme of the Traitor and the Hero" is unambiguous. In other stories, the clues that his creative process is that of a creative translator at work may not be as overt, but one can still detect them with clarity. One can illustrate this point with a careful reading of Borges's "El milagro secreto" ("The Secret Miracle"), one of Borges's tales involving time as a fantastic element. In "The Secret Miracle" God grants a gift to a man about to be executed. The man will die at the appointed time, but a year will transpire, mentally, between the order for his death by firing squad and the execution itself. During the miraculous year, Hladík is able to compose, in his mind, the work of literature he had left unfinished before his death sentence. Borges's "The Secret Miracle" can be read as a rewriting of Ambrose Bierce's "An Occurrence at Owl Creek Bridge." Bierce's story has an identical conceit: the few seconds it takes Farquhar—noose around his neck and pushed from the edge of the bridge—to reach the end of his rope expands in the protagonist's mind. He thinks the rope breaks and imagines both his escape from the bridge and the single day it takes him to travel thirty-five miles before reaching his home beyond enemy lines. As he primes himself to embrace his wife, he reaches the end of the rope and dies from hanging. In both "An Occurrence at Owl Creek Bridge" and "The Secret Miracle," the story takes place in the protagonist's mind; the respective execution squads observe an execution that takes but a few moments.

Borges leaves several clues he may have borrowed from Bierce's tale. Bierce's story, for example, ends with a short single-sentence paragraph beginning, "Peyton Farquhar was dead. . . ."[114] Borges's story also concludes with a short single-sentence paragraph beginning, "Jaromir Hladík died. . . ."[115] Another hint indicating Borges's debt to Bierce involves his protagonist's feelings about execution. Even though the method of execution in the two stories is different, the protagonists share similar fears. In Bierce's story Farquhar ponders, " 'To be hanged and drowned,' he thought, 'that is not so bad; but I do not wish to be shot."[116] In Borges's story, "[Hladík] thought that he would not have feared the gallows, decapitation, or his throat cut, but to die by shooting was intolerable."[117] In both narratives the initial shock of the execution sets off a process that moves from chaos to clarity:

(Bierce)

> He was conscious of nothing but a feeling of fullness—of congestion. These sensations were unaccompanied by thought. The intellectual part of his nature was already effaced; he had power only to feel, and feeling was torment. Then all at once with terrible suddenness . . . the power of thought was restored"[118] [and he goes on, apparently, to escape from his enemies].

(Borges)

> "[Hladík] passed from perplexity to stupor, from stupor to resignation, from resignation to sudden gratitude"[119] [and he goes on to compose his literary work in his mind].

Several lines in Bierce's story even sound Borgesian, such as Farquhar's musings with the stars in the firmament: "He was sure they were arranged in some order which had a secret and malign significance."[120] Other lines recall the bravado of the Borgesian anti-hero: "To die of hanging at the bottom of a river!—the idea seemed to him ludicrous."[121]

The main difference between the two stories is that Farquhar's wish is for survival, whereas Hladík's wish is for the creation of an invisible work: "He did not work for posterity or even for God, of whose literary preferences he knew very little. Meticulously, motionless, secretly, he weaved in time his invisible labyrinth."[122]

In the analysis of "An Occurrence at Owl Creek Bridge" and "The Secret Miracle," we have begun to suggest the potentially rich interplay between translation studies and the traditional methods of comparative literature. It would be possible to continue with other examples, such as the significance of Thomas Mann's "Der Kleiderschrank" (the wardrobe) in Borges's creation of "El Sur" ("The South"), but since such investigations no longer rely on the transformation of one series of words into another, I have come to the natural end point of my analysis of specific works, and we are ready to draw some conclusions about the significance of translation in Borges's approach to literature.

Toward a Poetics of Borges's Oeuvre

Real and fictional translations inform both the global content and form, and many details and nuances, of most of Borges's tales. The use of an imagined translation introduced by a narrator who might not be in a better position than the reader to understand the contents of the text is Borges's preferred opening for a story. Translations, fictional and real, also play a fundamental role in moving his plots forward, as when the translation into Spanish of a German book provides Scharlach with information he needs in order to weave a trap for Lönnrot in "Death and the Compass." Some of Borges's imagined translations have fictional source languages, as with "Ursprache" in the universe of Tlön, or the language of the "apemen" in "Brodie's Report." Real translations play a vital role in the gestation of Borges's works that imagined ones do not: many of Borges's translations, and those of others, are links between the works he translated and his originals. Borges's real translations also serve as commentaries on his stories, and they can even guide fruitful interpretations. It would be possible to construct an illuminating literary poetics of Borges's work by combining his observations about the options available to a translator, his stratagies as a translator, and the types of imagined and real translations that play a role in his fictions.

Conclusion

In public dialogues Borges would readily admit to any connection made by his interlocutors between his own creations and the works of others. His standard response to those who would identify a link between one of his writings and a literary antecedent was to acknowledge the influence and to blame his lack of memory for the borrowing. At other moments he would own up to the charge of plagiarism with ironic pride: "I do not write, I rewrite. My memory produces my sentences. I have read so much and I have heard so much. I admit it: I repeat myself. I confirm it: I plagiarize. We are all the heirs of millions of scribes who have already written down all that is essential a long time before us. We are all copyists, and all the stories we invent have already been told. There are no longer any original ideas."[1] Borges would add that the lack of original ideas is no reason to despair, unless one's aim is to be original, since it is always possible to make versions, combinations, and variations or to change emphasis. Translation, for Borges, is therefore at the core of any literary practice, at least for those who have come so late to literature.

The main purpose of this book has not been to make judgments about the validity of Borges's views on translation, or about his practice as a translator, but to reveal them, to demonstrate their literary impact and their centrality in his views on literature as an art. Borges moved happily between an objectivist aesthetic, according to which the cadences and arbitrary associations of words can produce specific emotions, and a more relativist aesthetic, according to which ideas can be readily transferred and transformed from work to work and reading to reading. Borges's objectivist and relativist approaches to literature engage in an interplay that informs his fundamental views about translation. From his relativist criteria Borges invited writers, readers, and translators to explore possibilities; from his objectivist criteria he did not always appreciate the results.

When pressed on his criteria for favoring some literary works and rejecting others, Borges would appeal to hedonism. Indeed, he was more interested in the pleasures literature could afford than in the efforts of those who interpret it. He was, however, certain of the pleasures he experienced on encountering a work of literature or a literary fragment that mattered to him. He was also certain that an original work does not have, in principle, any advantage over a translation in producing literary effects he would praise or instances of "verbal perfection" he would cherish. He also believed that an original can be as vulnerable or resilient as a translation to the ravages of time and to the vicissitudes of language. Translators cannot control how an original might benefit or suffer from the changes of the language in which it was written: their only responsibility, according to Borges, is to produce a persuasive work of art.

In his most inspired translations Borges exploited possibilities in the original that the original writer did not or, perhaps, could not have envisaged. In lesser hands Borges's methods might produce dire results. His approach to translation depends on a powerful literary mind able to see the latencies and potentialities of a text, and to go beyond it. His methods underwrite the willful transformation of existing works of literature as an approach to literary creation.

Borges remains the most universal of all Latin American writers: more than any other, he transformed the literary tradition into a world of his own. One of his enduring legacies in Latin American literature is the license to rewrite assertively the works of other writers, in the process of fashioning a personal literary world. Gabriel

García Márquez's transformations of Faulkner's Yokanapatha county into his fabled Macondo and his appropriation of the time scheme in Thomas Mann's *Buddenbrooks* as the genealogical backbone of the Buendía family in *One Hundred Years of Solitude* are examples of the Borgesian legacy in Latin American literature. So, too, is Carlos Fuentes's rewriting of Orson Welles's film *Citizen Kane* into the fabric of his novel *The Death of Artemio Cruz*. Mario Vargas Llosa's rewriting of novels by Conrad, Victor Hugo, and others into his fictional world is likewise indebted to Borges. All of these writers have included incarnations of Borges in their works of fiction and have, in fact, rewritten his tales into their own. Some of Vargas Llosa's titles are nods in Borges's direction. One can read *The Storyteller* as a recreation of Borges's "El etnógrafo" ("The Ethnographer"), and *The Feast of the Goat* owes much not only to the history of a Latin American dictator but to the political story "La fiesta del monstruo" ("The Feast of the Monster"), written by Borges with his friend Adolfo Bioy Casares.[2]

Translation looms so large in Borges's writings that even his original Argentine tales are informed by his reflections on the practice. In one of his stories, set in the Argentine pampa, his narrator describes the setting in which a man is waiting to avenge a death committed by a gaucho as "something as untranslatable as music."[3] In another story the narrator describes a sordid adventure involving gauchos as a variation on a biblical text capable of "inexhaustible repetitions, versions, perversions."[4]

Throughout this book I have been arguing that Borges's methods as a translator and his strategies as a creative writer have much in common. I have also been arguing that the study of his translations can spotlight the gestation of many of his works and his approach to literature. I did not claim, however, that Borges's translations have the same status as the creative works he signed as his own, or that the later are indistinguishable from the former. These are not theoretical points, since Borges could have taken even more liberties with his translations than he chose to. His scruples are probably related to his own sense of how far he could push the envelope (given editorial pressures or his sense of what his readership could accept) and to his penchant for downplaying some of his greatest achievements, for he never transformed his published translations beyond recognition. His translations can invariably be read as versions of his originals and are contributions to the history of their reception.

Borges's most radical engagements with an original did not take place in his translations, even in the most daring of them, but in works he signed as his own. Certainly, we have seen in this study instances in which the line between a Borges translation and a Borges original can become somewhat blurred, but in general the differences are clear cut. It would be a mistake, therefore, to think of translation in Borges merely as a loose metaphor for intertextuality. That is why I have concentrated on translation as the remodeling of a series of words into another. To conclude, however, I would like to return to Borges's views about the inevitability, in our belated age, of rewriting those works that have come down to us from the past; which is another way of addressing Borges's views on influence.

In one of the essays from *Historia de la eternidad (History of Eternity),* Borges speculates that our literary experience is inevitably belated: "The first monument of Western literature, the *Iliad,* was composed some three thousand years ago; it is possible to conjecture that, since then, all the essential themes of literature have been noticed and registered."[5] In *El oro de los tigres (The Gold of the Tigers)* he narrows the possible number of stories that can be told to four: the doomed struggle; the return to the homeland; the search; and the sacrifice of a god.[6] In a more wistful moment he reflects, "Perhaps all we are able to rehearse are some moderate, very modest variations on what has already been written: we have to tell the same story but in a slightly different way, changing some of the emphasis, perhaps, and that is all, but this does not have to be for us a source of sadness."[7]

This is a fine image of translation, as conceived by Borges: telling the "same story" but in a slightly different way. For him, as for so many characters in his own fictions, the creator of a literary work is inevitably a recreator or an editor who changes the emphasis or recombines elements of other works. If, as Borges believed, the themes, stories, and metaphors that can be rehearsed in a work of literature have probably already been exhausted, translation is not only a privileged vantage point from which to appreciate a literary practice; it is perhaps the only one. Borges's achievements as translator are a tribute to his humility and craftsmanship; they are like the masterpieces of Pierre Menard—invisible.

Afterword:
Borges and Philosophy

According to an influential view, Borges's most important achievements in literature involve his philosophical insights. To some critics holding this view, translation may seem a side issue, a curiosity. I think Borges was a fabulist, that translation is at the heart of his concerns as a writer, and that his philosophical concerns—even when they inform a story or a poem—are a function of his literary ones.

To clarify my position regarding Borges and philosophy, I must first acknowledge the significance of Ana María Barrenechea's book *Borges the Labyrinth Maker*.[1] Since its publication the reception of Borges has been dominated by two assumptions. First, his works can be read as a self-contained literary universe; second, in his literary world he transforms the real, or that which is assumed to be real, into the unreal: "Borges is an admirable writer pledged to destroy reality and convert Man into a shadow."[2] Barrenechea's book offers a telling account of Borges's metaphysical themes and their impact on his style, and it continues to be an indispensable reference for readers of Borges. Barrenechea, however, downplays the make-believe aspects of Borges's fictions, his creative process, and his penchant for irony. The view that Borges was "pledged to destroy reality" does not take sufficiently into consideration that Borges was fond of exploring ideas for their literary possibilities rather than for their truth, and that, in the footsteps of his admired Kipling, he also wrote fictions informed by propositions in which he did not believe, in some cases by ideas he found ludicrous.

Borges himself, who wrote an amiable preface to the English edition of Barrenechea's book, helped to promote the view that he is a skeptical realist insisting, in many essays and interviews, that literature, metaphysics, and religion have a common source, and that he is unable to draw a clear boundary between fiction and reality: "The outside world is as we perceive or imagine it. It does not exist independently of our minds. Reality and fiction are closely related. Our ideas are creative fictions."[3]

But Borges's skepticism is tinged with irony and contradiction. He carefully cultivated an image of himself in which it is impossible to determine whether his air of perplexity was a mask for philosophical certainties or whether his philosophical affirmations were a mask for his perplexity. Borges was not an enemy of contradiction. On the contrary, as he once said, "Contradiction is often an intimate conviction. I always distrust those who have a univocal point of view, or those whose pronouncements are always consistent. Our reflections are at the mercy of the seasons, they are portraits of particular moments."[4] Borges's irony, coupled with his claim that "unreality is the condition of art," and his skepticism[5] about our ability to draw boundaries between the fictional and the real have been welcomed by many prominent critics of Latin American literature. These critics emphasize either the unreality of the real (which Borges ostensibly transforms), the "realism" of his apparent unreality, or his role in undermining the dichotomy altogether.[6]

Since Borges considered himself first and foremost a creator of literary fictions, his response to the criticism of the metaphysical aspects of his own work has ranged from caustic bewilderment to playful acquiescence. His most common rejoinder to the claim he was more a philosopher than a man of letters was to point out that he used philosophical ideas for his literary purposes, just as he had used religious ones. Borges often cautioned that he did not necessarily take seriously the philosophical ideas that sparked his imagination: "I am fond of the circular form. That does not mean that I believe in circular time, in the hypothesis of Pythagoras, Hume, Nietzsche, or many others. The stoics also held that history repeats itself in exactly the same fashion. I do nothing but take advantage, to the best of my ability, of the literary possibilities of this hypothesis Nietzsche thought he had invented."[7]

Borges also indicated his delight with those philosophers who pretended to take seriously mysteries that were not mysterious to them at all. In an essay about a particular paradox in pre-Socratic philosophy Borges said, "The Greeks only played with perplexity and with mystery."[8] Fernando Savater summarizes Borges's philosophical stance as a "speculative zeal always imbued with an ironic skepticism that liberates him from dogmatic seriousness."[9] According to the Spanish philosopher, Borges has been an inspiration to philosophers of various tendencies, because philosophy enhanced his literary resources. The literary criticism that takes Borges's writings strictly as philosophical reflection can be misleading, however, when it neglects the different literary contexts in which Borges toyed with numerous philosophical ideas he knew to be mutually exclusive, more specifically: his penchant for the non sequitur, for playful contradiction, for intended imprecision to generate a disorienting illusion of precision, for giving literary form and narrative voice to points of view he otherwise deplored or derided, for humor, and for the ambiguous underlying pathos of his ironic refutations of reality.[10]

Borges would sometimes offer an apparently more prosaic explanation for his propensity for philosophical skepticism, seeing it as a consolation for the painful experiences that are all too human: "The denial of temporal succession, the denial of the self, the denial of the astronomical universe are apparent expressions of despair, as well as secret consolations."[11] The pain of an unrequited lover, which abounds in Borges's poetry, may be the rock bottom of his emotional range, even when couched in irony. The feeling of humiliation sublimated into a philosophical exploration is also a recurrent theme in Borges's stories, poems, and essays, including those he devoted to Dante. Borges's view that we have to thank Dante's humiliation by a historical Beatrice of flesh and blood for the *Divine Comedy* may be a projection of his own "ironically absurd pas-

sion," but as Harold Bloom has put the matter, it is an acute projection on the "scandalous disproportion" between the almost vacu-
ous experiences that can provoke a work of literature, and the work
of literature itself. Bloom draws on Borges's insights to argue that
"disproportion is Dante's royal road to the sublime." One could
add that in Borges the disproportion between the poverty of experience and the consolation of literature is a recurrent theme in his
poetry and frames the most intimate of his confessional moments.[12]

It is possible, of course, to ignore the pathos of Borges's pronouncements on the consoling powers of metaphysical speculation
and philosophical skepticism. But it is ever present, as in his famous
couplet where his lyrical voice puts on the mask of the Heraclitus
to lament his fortune: "I, who have been many men, have never
been / The one in whose arms swooned Matilde Urbach."[13] In a
lecture entitled "Spinoza, a Pathetic Figure," Borges argues that
Spinoza's philosophical system may be a consolation in its suggestion that "everything that happens to us is ephemeral, and therefore not important. We ought to love God, but for Spinoza what
does it mean to love God? It certainly does not mean to love an
individual person."[14] The central idea of the lecture echoes a poem
Borges wrote about the philosopher: "The most prodigal love was
bestowed on him / The love that does not hope for love in return."[15] A consolation for unrequited love, invoked by the poem
and the lecture, is not ultimately fulfilling for the fabulist. Borges
ends the lecture with a confessional statement in which he reflects
on the limited solace philosophy can provide for his personal trials:
"Sometimes, far from any philosophical idea, I wonder why the destiny of an individual named Borges who lived in the twentieth century in a city named Buenos Aires, in the southern hemisphere, is
of any interest to myself, why his fate, which is nothing in this universe, interests me so. But it is difficult to console oneself in this
way. I have tried to take Spinoza seriously, but I have never been
able to do so."[16]

Borges gave this lecture on Spinoza in 1981 at the Freudian
School of Buenos Aires. Given his skepticism about Freud, and his
sometimes disparaging remarks about psychoanalysis ("psychoanlysis
involves gossip and indiscretions about sexual life,")[17] his identifi-

cation with Spinoza as a pathetic figure takes on an ironic twist. Is
he making a painful confession, or is he playing a joke on an audience trained to untangle the sublimations of their patients, or is he,
perhaps, poking fun at the literary criticism that purports to read
his fictions as serious philosophical reflection?[18]

Nestor Ibarra said that Borges's confessions are sometimes pathetic to an exaggerated degree because he is being ironic. The disavowal of his philosophical proclivities may well be another in the
repertoire of his literary conceits that are, according to Ibarra, "a
part of him, they are him, and thanks to them he has written some
extraordinary pages."[19] Ibarra points out that it is not necessary to
enter into Borges's game to appreciate his achievements: "I do not
think it is necessary to enter into his game. One must give him the
better part of ourselves, including our refusals. Let us not make it
easy on him; he is better than that. It is against those who object
and who demand that Borges will gain his most significant victo-
ries."[20] In this sense, Rafael Gutiérrez Girardot made an observation of enduring significance, in one of the first books written about
Borges, when he said that the Argentine master began as a skeptic
and ended as an ironist.[21] One could add that Borges expresses his
irony in the amiable tone of an individual fascinated by ideas rather
than in the high-pitched voice of a debunker.[22] Characteristically,
whenever Borges was pressed on his philosophical positions, he
would respond with ironic or humorous rejoinders: "I live com-
fortably baffled, and I am astonished that people take me seriously,
I do not know if I take myself seriously."[23]

IN THIS STUDY I have circumvented both Borges's skepticism and
his irony by approaching his works from the perspective of the role
of translation in his creative process. No skepticism, irony, or even
humor can obscure the central role that translation has played in
every one of his literary pursuits, including the project of incorpo-
rating philosophical material into his fictional world. Nor can anything place in doubt Borges's design, as with other twentieth-
century writers such as Kafka and Beckett, to resist facile interpretation.

Notes

Introduction

1. The letter is in the "Fundación San Telmo" in Buenos Aires.
2. José Miguel Oviedo, *Breve historia del ensayo hispanoamericano* (Madrid: Alianza Editorial, 1991), p. 97.
3. See Salvador Elizondo, "La experiencia de Borges," *Paréntesis* 1, no. 1 (December 1999): 60–62.
4. Mario Vargas Llosa wrote that "in Borges's case I do not consider it rash to acclaim him as the most important thing to happen to imaginative writing in the Spanish language in modern times and as one of the most memorable artists of our age" ("An Invitation to Borges's Fiction," in *A Writer's Reality* [Syracuse, N.Y.: Syracuse University Press, 1991, p. 3]). According to José Emilio Pacheco: "Toda la narrativa hispanoamericana posterior a 1945 salió de Borges y su círculo y especialmente de dos libros: la *Antología de literatura fantástica* y el *Ulises* de Joyce traducido por Salas Subirat" (All Spanish American narrative after 1945 came out of Borges and his circle and especially from two books: *Antología de literature fantástica* and Joyce's *Ulysses,* translated by Salas Subirat) ("Muchos Años Después," in *Los Novelistas como críticos,* ed. Norma Klahn and Wilfrido H. Corral [Mexico City, 1991], 2:459). Carlos Fuentes has indicated that reading Borges was a life-changing experience: "Mi vida cambió. Aquí estaba, al fin la conjunción perfecta de mi imaginación y mi lengua, excluyente de cualquier otra lengua pero incluyente de todas las imaginaciones posibles. Leyendo sus cuentos descubrí para mí mismo, mediante ese descubrimiento personal que ocurre con pararelismo a toda verdadera lectura, que el español ere realmente mi lengua" (My life changed. Here it was, at last the perfect conjunction of my imagination and my language, exclusive of every other language but inclusive of every possible imagination. Reading his stories I discovered for myself, through this personal discovery that happens alongside every true reading, that Spanish really was my language) (in Carlos Fuentes,

"Jorge Luis Borges: La herida de Babel," in *Geografía de la novela* [Madrid: Alfaguara, 1993], p. 42). See also Octavio Paz, "El arquero la flecha y el blanco (Jorge Luis Borges)," in *Convergencias* (Barcelona: Seix Barral), 1991.

5. George Steiner, *After Babel: Aspects of Language and Translation* (Oxford: Oxford University Press, 1992), p. 73.

6. Ibid., p. 76.

7. Borges, prologue to *Fábulas: Translation by Borges and Roberto Alifano* (Buenos Aires: Omnibus, 1983), p. 11.

8. The essay originally published in the *New York Review of Books* in November 1964 has been reprinted in *Jorge Luis Borges,* ed. Harold Bloom (New York: Chelsea House, 1986), and in Jaime Alazraki's *Critical Essays on Jorge Luis Borges* (Boston: G. K. Hall & Co., 1987).

9. Suzanne Jill Levine summarizes Callois's insight, as well as James Irby's, and expands them by exploring Borges's notion of the fictional biography. See her "A Universal Tradition: The Fictional Biography," *Review: Latin American Literature and the Arts* (spring 1973): 24–28.

10. "Literary Pleasure," trans. Suzanne Jill Levine, in Borges, *Selected Non-Fictions,* ed. Eliot Weinberger, trans. Esther Allen, Suzanne Jill Levine, and Eliot Weinberger (New York: Penguin, 1999), p. 31.

11. Borges, "The Homeric Versions," in *Selected Non-Fictions,* p. 69.

12. Jaime Alazraki, "El Golem," in *Expliquémonos a Borges como poeta,* ed. Angel Flores (Mexico City: Siglo XXI, 1984), see especially pp. 235–36.

13. See Ronald Christ, *The Narrow Act: Borges's Art of Allusion* (New York: Lumen, 1995); John T. Irwin, *The Mystery to a Solution: Poe, Borges, and the Analytic Detective Fiction* (Baltimore and London: Johns Hopkins University Press, 1994); Daniel Balderston, *Out of Context: Historical Reference and the Representation Of Reality in Borges* (Durham, N.C.: Duke University Press, 1993).

14. Michel Lafon, *Borges ou la réécriture* (Paris: Seuil, 1990).

15. Another important line of research that has emerged in recent years attempts to show that Borges's achievements ought to be understood in his Argentine context. At its best this line of research has offered illuminating insights into Borges's Argentine milieu, for example Beatriz Sarlo's *Jorge Luis Borges: A Writer on the Edge.* In this study, I am interested in aspects of Borges's literary achievements that transcend his national context.

16. Annick Louis, *Jorge Luis Borges: Œuvre et manœuvres* (Paris: L'Harmattan, 1997), p. 325.

17. I am sympathetic to Lamarque and Olsen's suggestion that, in general, the role of epistemological considerations in the theory of literature has been overestimated. See Peter Lamarque and Stein Haugom Olsen, *Truth, Fiction, and Literature: A Philosophical Perspective* (Oxford: Clarendon Press, 1994).

18. Juan Nuño, *La filosofía de Borges* (Mexico City: Fondo de Cultura Económica, 1987), p. 16. Aimé de Viry thinks that Borges gives literary life to dead philosophical ideas. See de Viry, "Borges ou l'élément romanesque," in *L'Amérique latine et La Nouvelle Revue Française 1920–2000* (Paris: Gallimard, 2001), pp. 468–70.

19. For a discussion of Borges and philosophy see the afterword.

20. Richard Wollheim, *Art and Its Objects* (Cambridge: Cambridge University Press, 1980), p. 142.

21. Borges has made the same point in his essays. See for example the first few lines of his essay "Sobre Chesterton," in *Otras inquisiciones,* in *Obras completas* (Barcelona: Emecé, 1989), 2:72.

22. For biographical information see Emir Rodríguez Monegal, *Jorge Luis Borges: A Literary Biography* (New York: Dutton, 1978); Marcos-Ricardo Barnatán, *Borges: Biografía total* (Madrid: Ediciones Temas de Hoy, 1995); and James Woodall, *Borges: A Life* (New York: Basic Books, 1996). In addition I have received notice that Professor Edwin Williamson from the University of Edinburgh is preparing a major intellectual biography on Borges.

23. The books of essays in question are *Inquisiciones* (1925), *El tamaño de mi esperanza* (1926), and *El idioma de los argentinos* (1928). See note 56 in chapter 2.

24. Borges's penchant for impersonality may have psychological implications that are beyond the scope and the purposes of this book, but they will be briefly addressed in the afterword of this book with respect to his reflections about his own philosophical skepticism. Borges sometimes wrote, perhaps with irony, that his philosophical skepticism (and one could see his bent toward impersonality in literature in similar terms) was a way to protect himself from the pains he suffered from failed interpersonal relationships.

25. The quotation comes from "Elogio al traductor," an introduction to a selection of Borges's translations by Roberto A. Tálice (see *Borges: Obras, reseñas y traducciones inéditas: Diario Crítica 1933–1934,* ed. Irma Zangara [Barcelona: Atlantida, 1999], p. 231).

26.   Nestor Ibarra, *Borges et Borges* (Paris: L'Herne, 1969), p. 72. Petrarch
wrote a letter to ask a friend to emend phrases from his "Bucolicum
carmen." He had recently noticed he had unwittingly pilfered them
from Virgil and Ovid:

> "hec [sc. amata opera michi milies lecta] se michi tam famili-
> ariter ingessere et non modo memorie sed medullis affixa sunt
> unumque cum ingenio facta sunt meo, ut etsi per omnem vitam
> amplius non legantur, ipsa quidem hereant, actis in intima animi
> parte radicibus; sed interdum obliviscar auctorem, quippe qui
> longo usu et possessione continua quasi illa prescripserim
> diuque pro meis habuerim, et turba talium obsessus, nec cuius
> sint certe nec aliena meminerim. Hoc est ergo quod dicebam,
> notiora magis fallere, que siquando forsan ex more recursantia in
> memoriam redeunt, accidit ut nonnunquam occupato et in
> unum aliquid vehementer intento animo non tantum ut propria
> sed, quod miraberis, ut nova se offerant." (Petrarch, *Le Famili-
> ari,* ed. Vittorio Rossi, vol. 4, ed. Umberto Bosco [Florence,
> 1926], xxii, 2, p. 106)
>
> (These [beloved works] have so entered into me, implanted not
> only in memory but in my very marrow, uniting with my talent
> itself, that even if I never in my life read them again they would
> grow there, putting roots into my innermost soul. And at times
> I even forget the author—naturally, since by long use and
> continuous possession, it is as if I had written them once myself
> and possess them as my own property, and thus, besieged by a
> crowd of such passages, do not remember clearly whose they are
> nor even that they are another's. This then is what I was saying,
> that what we know better deceives us more. And now and then,
> as these things return by habit to memory, it can even happen
> that, when the mind concentrates and is closely intent on
> something, they offer themselves not only as one's own but
> even—what will surprise you—as something new.) (I am
> indebted to Karl Maurer, who was a friend of Borges's, for use
> of his elegant translation of this passage from Petrarch.)

     If one were to bracket Petrarch's scruples regarding his unconscious
theft, and his talk of an "innermost soul," his letter reads like a précis
of Borges's appreciation of the literary imagination and of his practice as a translator.

Chapter 1

1. Roberto Alifano, "La traducción," in *Conversaciones con Borges* (Buenos Aires: Torres Aguero, 1994) p. 76.

2. "Mis libros," *La nación*, April 28, 1985, quoted in Julio Chiappini, *Borges y Kafka* (Buenos Aires: Editorial Zeus, 1991), p. 32.

3. The quotation comes from an essay in which Borges explains why he believes the English translation of *Don Segundo Sombra* was able to overcome some stylistic deficiencies of Ricardo Güiraldes's classic Argentine novel. See *"Don Segundo Sombra* en inglés," in Borges, *Obras, reseñas y traducciones inéditas,* p. 205.

4. Nestor Ibarra in his note to Valéry, in Paul Valéry, *El Cementerio marino de Paul Valéry,* trans. Nestor Ibarra (Buenos Aires: Schillinger, 1931), p. 13.

5. "Publicamos para no pasarnos la vida corrigiendo" (we publish so that we don't spend our lives correcting) (in Borges and Roberto Alifano, *Conversaciones con Borges* [Buenos Aires: Torres Aguero, 1994], p. 220).

6. There is no critical edition or intellectual biography of Borges in which readers can gain more information about Borges's work. Sadly, nothing like it exists in Spanish. For a less generous assessment see Annick Louis's "Borges invisible et visible." Louis discovers that the edition (of over 3,000 pages) has been subject to "editorial manipulations."

7. Borges and Alifano, "La traducción," in *Conversaciones con Borges,* p. 80.

8. Ibid., p. 78.

9. *Macedonio Ferndández,* ed. Borges (Buenos Aires: Ministerio de Educación y Justicia, 1961), p. 16. Borges also wrote, "El verso es, entre otras cosas, una entonación, una acentuación muchas veces intraducible" (verse is, among other things, an intonation, an accentuation, in many cases untranslatable) ("La Divina Comedia," in *Siete noches,* in *Obras completas* [Barcelona: Emecé, 1989], 3:209).

10. See "La poesía," in *Siete noches,* in *Obras completas,* 3:259.

11. "Pour jouir convenablement d'une œuvre quelconque, il nous faut la situer dans le contexte de son moment historique. Il y a toutefois, comme le désirait Keats, des bonheurs qui sont singuliers et éternels" (To find appropriate enjoyment of any work, it is important to situate it in the context of its historical moment. There are, all the same, as Keats had desired it, joys that are singular and eternal) (in the author's

preface, *Œuvres complètes,* ed. Jean Pierre Bernès [Paris: Gallimard, 1993], 1:x.

12. "La Divina Comedia," in *Siete noches,* in *Obras completas,* 3:208.

13. Fernando Sorrentino, *Siete conversaciones con Jorge Luis Borges,* 2d ed. (Buenos Aires: El Ateneo, 1996), p. 73.

14. Umberto Eco, "Between La Mancha and Babel," *Variaciones Borges* 4 (1997): 57.

15. Ibid., p. 59.

16. Borges and Osvaldo Ferrari, *Reencuentros inéditos* (Buenos Aires: Editorial Sudamericana, 1998), p. 136.

17. "La obsesión de Joyce por el lenguaje lo convierte en alguien muy difícil, si no imposible, de traducir. Especialmente al español, como descubrí cuando traduje un fragmento del monólogo de Molly en 1925. Las traducciones de Joyce a las lenguas hispánicas de romances han sido hasta la fecha muy pobres. Sus compuestos funcionan mejor en lenguas anglosajonas o germánicas. Y pienso que todas su obras debieran ser leídas como poesía." (Joyce's obsession with language makes him someone who is very difficult, if not impossible, to translate; especially into Spanish, as I discovered when I translated a fragment of Molly's monologue in 1925. Translations of Joyce into Spanish or Romance languages have been very poor to date. His compositions work better in Anglo-Saxon or Germanic languages. And I think that all of his works should be read like poetry) (in Seamus Heany and Richard Kearny, "Jorge Luis Borges: El mundo de la ficción," *Cuadernos hispánoamericanos,* no. 564 [June 1997]: 59 [my translation]).

18. For a discussion on possible responsees to art see Peter Kivy, *Philosophies of Arts: An Essay in Differences* (New York: Cambridge University Press, 1997), p. 95.

19. Borges, "El oficio de traducir," in his *Borges en Sur 1931–1980* (Buenos Aires: Emecé, 1999), p. 321.

20. "Traducción," in Borges, *A/Z,* ed. Antonio Fernández Ferrer (Madrid: Ediciones Siruela, 1988), pp. 264–66.

21. "Préface à l'édition française," in *Œuvre poétique: 1925–1965,* tr. Nestor Ibarra (Paris: Gallimard, 1970), p. 8.

22. Borges and Roberto Alifano, "La traducción," in *Conversaciones con Borges* (Buenos Aires: Tomás Aguero, 1994), p. 79.

23. Marcelo Abadi, "Averroes y su trémula esclava pelirroja," *Variaciones Borges* 7 (1999): 176.

24. "*Don Segundo Sombra* en inglés," *Revista Multicolor de los Sábados* of

the journal *Crítica* (August 11, 1934): 5. The article is reproduced in *Borges: Obras, reseñas y traducciones inéditas,* p. 205. Borges is alluding to Waldo Frank's *Our America* in this sentence.

25.   Waldo Frank was, according to Emir Rodríguez Monegal, instrumental in the establishment of the journal *Sur* when he came to Argentina for the first time in 1931. Borges collaborated regularly with *Sur,* arguably the most important and influential literary journal in the history of Latin American letters. See Emir Rodríguez Monegal, *Jorge Luis Borges: A Literary Biography* (New York: Dutton, 1978), p. 235.

26.   Waldo Frank, introduction to *Don Segundo Sombra: Shadows on the Pampas,* by Ricardo Güiraldes, trans. Harriet de Onís (New York: Farrar & Rinehart, 1935).

27.   "Una vindicación de Mark Twain," in *Borges en Sur 1931–1980,* p. 16.

28.   "*Don Segundo Sombra* en inglés," in *Revista Multicolor de los Sábados* of the journal *Crítica:* 5.

29.   There is also a point of contact between Borges's views on translation and those of Walter Benjamin. In both cases "each language is open to the connotations and visions articulated in other languages" (Rainer Rochlitz, *The Disenchantment of Art: The Philosophy of Walter Benjamin* [New York: Guilford, 1996], p. 25). That said, where Benjamin's vision is messianic, Borges's is ludic, and he therefore is not troubled by willful transformations that may swerve away from the original work as a new work is fashioned.

30.   Borges, *This Craft of Verse,* ed. Calin-Andrei Mihailescu (Cambridge, Mass.: Harvard University Press, 2000), p. 72.

31.   This text appears in his preface to Nestor Ibarra's translation of Paul Valéry's "Cimetière marin," in one of his essays about Joyce's *Ulysses* and in his seminal essay "Homeric Versions," in *Selected Non-Fictions,* ed. Eliot Weinberger, trans. Esther Allen, Suzanne Jill Levine, and Eliot Weinberger (New York: Penguin, 1999).

32.   Borges and Osvaldo Ferrari, *En diálogo,* 2 vols. (Buenos Aires, Editorial Sudamericana, 1998), 2:68.

33.   Ibid. Borges has called plagiarism "one of the forms of tradition" (see André Camp, *Entretien avec Jorge Luis Borges* [Paris: HB Éditions, 1999], p. 24).

34.   *El oro de los tigres,* in *Obras completas,* 2:507.

35.   María Kodama, "Borges y la literatura japonesa," *La Torre* 8 (October–December 1988): 677.

36.   Borges cited Eliot's essay to make the point that "[a writer's] work

modifies our conception of the past, as it will modify the future" ("Kafka and His Precursors," in *Selected Non-Fictions,* p. 365). I thank Alexander Coleman for his observations, in a personal communication, about the significance of T. S. Eliot's "Tradition and the Individual Talent" on Borges's general views about literature.

37. "Tradition and the Individual Talent," in *Points of View* (New York: Faber & Faber, 1941), pp. 25–26.

38. See chapter 3.

39. Borges, "Nota sobre el Ulises en español," *Los Anales de Buenos Aires,* January 1946, p. 49.

40. Ibid., p. 3. Borges would have been delighted that an English translation of Gracian's *Oráculo manual* gained many new readers for Gracián in Spain because of the success of Christopher Maurer's acclaimed version in his plain and elegant English prose. See Baltasar Gracián, *The Art of Wordly Wisdom: A Pocket Oracle,* trans. Christopher Maurer (New York: Doubleday, 1992).

41. Borges, "Nota sobre el Ulises en español," p. 3.

42. Borges, *This Craft of Verse,* p. 74.

43. Borges, "An Autobiographical Essay," in Jaime Alazraki, *Critical Essays on Jorge Luis Borges* (Boston: G. K. Hall & Co., 1987), p. 25.

44. *A/Z,* p. 265. In his survey of the German reception of Borges, Rafael Gutiérrez Girardot has pointed out that some of Borges's translators were too dependent on dictionary definitions, producing a myriad of incoherencies. For example, an "oscuro," a dark horse, was translated as "obscurity," "items of silver" as "stolen silver," and "venality" as "cheap." See Gutierréz Girardot, *Jorge Luis Borges: El gusto de ser modesto* (Colombia, Santafé de Bogotá: Panamericana Editorial, 1998) p. 176.

45. Norman Thomas di Giovanni, "At work with Borges," in *The Cardinal Points of Borges,* ed. Lowell Dunham and Ivar Ivask, p. 69.

46. Carter Wheelock, "Borges's New Prose," in *Prose for Borges,* ed. Charles Newman and Mary Kinzie, with Norman Thomas di Giovanni (Evanston, Ill.: Northwestern University Press, 1974), p. 390.

47. Ibid.

48. Ibid., p. 391.

49. Matthew Howard, "Stranger than Fiction: The Unlikely Case of Jorge Luis Borges and the Translator Who Helped Bring His Work to America," *Lingua Franca,* June/July 1997, p. 42.

50. Albert Bensoussan, "Traducir al francés la poesía de Borges," *Variaciones Borges* 5 (1998): 203–6.

51. "Préface à l'édition française," *Œuvre poétique: 1925–1965*, p. 7.

52. Borges himself must have felt that tension to some degree when he derided the notion of a literary classic as he worshiped the perfection of poets like Virgil and Dante.

53. Sylvia Molloy, *La difusion de la littérature hispano-américaine en France au XXe siècle* (Paris: Presses Universitaires de France, 1972), pp. 205–6.

54. Norman Thomas di Giovanni, in *Borges on Writing*, ed. Norman Thomas di Giovanni, Daniel Halpern, and Frank Macshane (Hopewell, N.J.: Ecco, 1994), p. 158.

55. Borges and Sorrentino, *Siete conversaciones con Jorge Luis Borges*, p. 239.

56. "Las dos maneras de traducir," in Borges, *Textos recobrados, 1919–1929* (Buenos Aires: Emecé, 1997), pp. 257–58. The original essay appeared in *La Prensa* (Buenos Aires), August 1, 1926, p. 258.

57. In the edition that Borges cites, the original reads: "Über die Natur des Wortes. Jedes Wort hat seine eigentümliche Bedeutung, seine Nebenbedeutungen, seine falschen und durchaus willkürlichen Bedeutungen" (Novalis, *Werke*, ed. Hermann Fridamann [Leipzig: Deutsches Verlagshaus, n.d.], p. 207). In the original Novalis also mentions a fourth concept, that of "false meanings" (falsche Bedeutungen), which Borges had mentioned in *El idioma de los argentinos* (1928, pp. 58–59) in a passage where he cites the same fragment by Novalis. This fourth notion is omitted in Borges's essay on translation, and it bears no role in it. In *El idioma de los argentinos*, a book he repudiated, Borges applies those distinctions in favor of contemporary literature and against the classics, a view he would relativize in the future.

58. "The Translators of the *Thousand and One Nights*," in Borges, *Selected Non-Fictions*, p. 104.

59. "Las dos maneras de traducir," p. 258.

60. "En el mismo lugar donde me encuentro, estoy empezando a cantar con guitarra" (in "Las dos maneras de traducir," in *Textos Recobrados: 1919–1929* [Buenos Aires: Emecé, 1997], p. 259).

61. "Aquí en la fraternidad de mi guitarra, empiezo a cantar" (in ibid.).

62. "Las dos maneras de traducir," p. 259.

63. See chapter 2 for the changes Borges underwent in this regard.

64. "Homeric Versions" (translated by Eliot Weinberger), in *Borges: Selected Non-Fictions* (New York: Penguin, 1999), p. 69. Borges's original reads, "un largo sorteo experimental de omisiones y de énfasis"

("Las versiones homéricas," in *Discusión,* in *Obras completas,* 1:239. "Sorteo," which Weinberger translates as a "game of chance," means a "drawing" or "casting of lots" or a "raffle," but it also means the ability to overcome an obstacle; and Borges is playing with both meanings of the word. In Borges's elegant Spanish the word "sorteo" suggests both skillful choice and chance. One could have translated "un largo sorteo" as "a long combinatory game of chance and skill," but this rendering would sound more cumbersome than the original Spanish, which is plain and elegant.

65.   "La loteria en Babilonia," in *Obras completas,* 1:460.

66.   See *Selected Non-Fictions,* p. 95, and *This Craft of Verse,* p. 9.

67.   Borges, in *Borges on Writing,* p. 104.

68.   Borges, *This Craft of Verse,* p. 67.

69.   Ibid., p. 68.

70.   Ibid., p. 65.

71.   "The Homeric Versions," in *Selected Non-Fictions,* p. 71.

72.   Borges, *This Craft of Verse,* p. 73.

73.   Paul Valéry, *El Cementerio marino,* trans. Nestor Ibarra (Buenos Aires: Schillinger), 1931.

74.   Borges, *This Craft of Verse,* p. 60.

75.   Ibid., p. 60.

76.   In *El otro Borges: Entrevistas (1960–1986),* ed. Fernando Mateo (Buenos Aires: Equis Editores, 1997), p. 100.

77.   See *The Concise Oxford Dictionary of Quotations* (Oxford: Oxford University Press, 1981), p. 44; and "Sobre el 'Vathek' de William Beckford," in *Otras inquisiciones,* in *Obras completas,* pp. 107–10.

78.   Whitman escribe (*Song of Myself,* 24):
       Walt Whitman, un cosmos, de Manhattan el hijo,
       Turbulento, carnal, sensual, comiendo, bebiendo, engendrando...

       Felipe 'traduce' (*Canto a mí mismo,* p. 88)
       Yo soy Walt Whitman...
       Un cosmos. ¡Miradme!
       El hijo de Manhattan.
       Turbulento, fuerte y sensual;
       como bebo y engendro. . . .

       La transformación es notoria; de la larga voz sálmica hemos pasado a los engreídos grititos del cante jondo." (In Borges, "Walt Whitman: Canto a mí mismo, traducido por León Felipe

[Editorial Losada, Buenos Aires, 1941]," *Sur* 88 (January 1992): 68–70)

79. Borges would sometimes cite Novalis to make the point that texts that are considered ancient, even if they are not, tend to be read as if they had a greater poetic air.

80. Borges, "The Homeric Versions," in *Selected Non-Fictions*, p. 71.

81. "El agua cenagosa del Esepo."

82. Borges, "Prólogo," in *Las mil y una noches según Galland* (Madrid: Siruela, 1985), p. 11.

83. See chapter 2.

84. In *Selected Non-Fictions*. The 1935 essay was based on several short pieces Borges had been publishing in literary journals at the time.

85. Bloom, introduction to *Jorge Luis Borges* (New York: Chelsea House, 1986), p. 2.

86. "Kafka y sus precursores," in *Otras inquisiciones*, in *Obras completas*, 2:88–90. The essay is translated by Eliot Weinberger as "Kafka and His Precursors," in *Selected Non-Fictions*, pp. 363–65.

87. The Spanish is in "Los traductores de Las 1001 Noches," in *Historia de la eternidad*, in *Obras completas*, 1:411; Esther Allen's English is in "The Translators of the *Thousand and One Nights*," in *Selected Non-Fictions*, p. 107.

88. Borges in *Borges on Writing*, p. 105.

89. "The Translators of the *Thousand and One Nights*," p. 92.

90. Borges's note in *Ficciones*, in *Obras completas*, 1:483.

91. In Borges's story the relative defeats Fierro in a knife fight to the death. In his remarkable critical edition of Borges, Jean Pierre Bernès shrewdly identifies the sections of José Hernández's poem that would justify Borges's assertion. See Jean Pierre Bernès's note in Borges, *Œuvres complètes*, 1:1595.

92. I am grateful to Professor Jonathan Post for his assessment of the passage in a personal communication.

93. "La memoria de Shakespeare," in *La memoria de Shakespeare*, in *Obras completas*, 3:393.

94. The phrase "shifts in the language" is another improvement of Esther Allen's in her translation of the phrase "cambios del idioma," which would translate more literally as "changes in the language" ("The Translators of the *Thousand and One Nights*," p. 93).

95. Borges is quoting the beginning of Shakespeare's *Henry IV, Part 1*, where Henry is planning a crusade against the "pagans" that hold the Holy Land. I thank H. A. Kelly for the reference.

96. Borges in *Borges on Writing*, pp. 159–60.
97. "The Translators of the *Thousand and One Nights*," p. 96.
98. "La memoria de Shakespeare," 3:393.
99. "The Translators of the *Thousand and One Nights*," p. 96.
100. Ibid., p. 98.
101. "The Translators of the *Thousand and One Nights*," pp. 99–100.
102. Ibid., p. 106.
103. Once again Esther Allen improves the Spanish "después de una literatura" with "in the wake of literature" ("The Translators of the *Thousand and One Nights*," p. 108).
104. Ibid.
105. Nestor Ibarra, *Borges et Borges* (Paris: L'Herne, 1969), p. 159.
106. Here I prefer my own translation of the original "¿Qué no haría un hombre, un Kafka, que organizara y acentuara esos juegos, que los rehiciera según la deformación alemana, según la Unheimlichketit de Alemania?" ("Los traductores de Las 1001 Noches," in *Selected Non-Fictions*, p. 413).
107. Sergio Pastormerlo cautions that Borges does not offer hard and fast rules for translating any particular work of literature and recalls his distrust of literary theory including the theory of translation. See his essay "Borges y la traducción," *Voces* 15 (1994): 13–18. Borges's skepticism about literary theory, however, must be understood in the context of his conviction that a literary experience is preferable to an empty abstraction about literature. In short, it is possible to construe Borges's general views on translation, in as much as he outlines both parameters of the practice and criteria to discuss the results.
108. "Pierre Menard, autor del Quijote," in *Obras completas*, 1:446.
109. The original reads "Nur dann zeige ich, daß ich einen Schriftsteller verstanden habe, wenn ich in seinem Geiste handeln kann, wenn ich ihn, ohne seine Individualität zu schmälern, übersetzen, und mannigfach verändern kann" (in Novalis, *Dichter über ihre Dichtungen*, vol. 15, ed. Hans-Joachim Mähl [Passau: Heimeran, 1976], p. 189).
110. "Pierre Menard, autor del Quijote," in *Obras completas*, 1:447.
111. Kristin Pfefferkorn, *Novalis: A Romantic's Theory of Language and Poetry* (New Haven and London: Yale University Press, 1988, p. 53.
112. Since Walter Benjamin was interested in notions such as the essence *(das Wesen)* of a work, his views are fundamentally different from Borges's even if they might both share the view that translation may

give new life to works. See my essay "Walter Benjamin: El Mesianismo y la Traducción," *Teoría/Crítica* 4 (1997): 135–43.

113.   The letter was translated by André Lefevere in *Translating Literature: The German Tradition from Luther to Rosenzeig* (Amsterdam: Van Gorcum, 1977), p. 65. The German original reads: "Übersetzen ist so gut dichten, als eigne Werke zu stande bringen—und schwerer, seltner. Am Ende ist alle Poësie Übersetzung" (in Novalis, *Dichter über ihre Dichtungen*, p. 182).

114.   Willis Barnstone, *The Poetics of Translation: History, Theory, Practice* (New Haven, Conn., and London: Yale University Press, 1993), p. 265.

115.   Following Suzanne Jill Levine (*The Subversive Scribe: Translating Latin American Fiction* [Saint Paul: Graywolf Press, 1991]), Lawrence Venuti is one of the first theorists of translation to give Borges his deserved place in the emerging field of translation studies. See his insightful commentary on Borges's essay on the *Arabian Nights* in his *Translation Studies Reader* (London: Routledge, 2000), pp. 13–14.

116.   Borges, in *Obras completas,* 4:310. Borges has also written that "la creación poética, o lo que llamamos creación [poética] es una mezcla de olvido y recuerdo de lo que hemos leído." ("what we call [poetic] creation is a mixture of forgetting and remembering what we have read") (in *Borges oral,* in *Obras completas,* 4:170).

117.   "Yo había descubierto en ese instante los principios de la memoria imperfecta que se llama imaginación" (in Borges, *Antología de la literatura fantástica,* ed. Borges, Silvina Ocampo, and Adolfo Bioy Casares [Barcelona: Edhasa, 1981], p. 263. Ocampo and Bioy Casares may have collaborated on this translation).

Chapter 2

1.   Another literary work at the time, a possible antecedent for "Pierre Menard, Author of Don Quixote," was a short story Borges purportedly wrote as a child in the style of Cervantes. Carlos García, who has researched Borges's early unpublished work, surmises that the manuscript of the story might be in private hands. See his "Borges inédito: Bibliografía virtual, 1906–1930," *Variaciones Borges* 5 (1998): 265.

2.   Borges has referred to this piece of writing as "the first book or, rather, the first notebook, I ever wrote, a Greek mythology composed in very poor English" (André Camp, *Entretien avec Jorge Luis*

Borges [Paris: HB Éditions, 1999], p. 67). The notebook is in the San Telmo Foundation in Buenos Aires.

3. Borges's text is reproduced in Nicolás Helft and Alan Pauls, *El factor Borges: Nueve ensayos ilustrados* (Buenos Aires: Fondo de Cultura Económica, 2000), p. 99.

4. Borges's first publication, a translation of Oscar Wilde's "The Happy Prince," appeared in the Argentine newspaper *El Pais* on June 25, 1910. Borges's mother, who worked closely with her son on his literary projects until her death, proudly recalled her son's early work: "His first published writing was the translation of a story by Oscar Wilde, 'The Happy Prince,' which he finished here in Buenos Aires, when he was nine years old" (in a testimony by Leonor Acevedo de Borges published in a collective work about Borges; see María Esther Gilio, et al., *Borges* [Buenos Aires: Editorial el Mangrullo, 1976], p. 38).

5. Borges, prologue to *Cuentos de Oscar Wilde,* by Oscar Wilde (Buenos Aires: Editorial Atlántida, 1966), p. 3.

6. Ibid.

7. Ibid.

8. "enamorado," in *Cuentos de Oscar Wilde,* p. 20.

9. "pero mejor bésame en los labios, porque te quiero mucho" in *Cuentos de Oscar Wilde,* p. 24.

10. "bésame en los labios, porque te amo" (in Borges, "El príncipe feliz," *El País,* June 25, 1910).

11. "el más apuesto de los juncos" (in *Cuentos de Oscar Wilde,* p. 18) and "lindísimo junco" (in Borges, "El príncipe feliz," *El País,* June 25, 1910).

12. "la golondrina se sintió solitaria y empezó a cansarse de su novio" (Borges) and "Entonces ella se había sentido sola, y había empezado a aburrirse de su galán" (in *Cuentos de Oscar Wilde,* p. 18).

13. Every Spanish translation of "The Happy Prince" I have consulted, including Ramón Gómez de la Serna's in the Aguilar complete works of Oscar Wilde, changes the gender of the bird from male to female.

14. Jiri Levy has called this phenomenon a "decision process: a series of a certain number of consecutive situations—moves, as in a game—situations imposing on the translator the necessity of choosing among a certain (and very often definable) number of alternatives" (Jiri Levy, "Transation as a Decision Process," in *Translation Studies Reader,* ed. Lawrence Venuti [London: Routledge, 2000], p. 148).

15. The first time I quote from a collaborative translation I will indicate the name of the collaborator. In subsequent references I will often use the name of Borges with the understanding that I am discussing a collaborative effort.

16. See Frances R. Aparicio, *Versiones, interpretaciones, creaciones: Instancias de la traducción literaria en Hispanoamérica en el siglo veinte* (Gaithesburg, Md.: Ediciones Hispanoamérica, 1991), pp. 118–25; and María Elena Bravo, "Borges traductor: El caso de *The Wild Palms* de William Faulkner," *Insula* 40, no. 462 (May 1985): 11–12.

17. María Esther Vázquez, *Borges: Sus días y su tiempo* (Buenos Aires: Javier Vergara), 1984 p. 79.

18. Suzanne Jill Levine, "A Universal Tradition: Fictional Biography," *Review: Latin American Literature and the Arts* (spring 1973): 28.

19. Emir Rodríguez Monegal, *Jorge Luis Borges: A Literary Biography* (New York: Dutton, 1978), p. 107.

20. See Edna Aizenberg, *El tejedor del Aleph: Biblia, Kábala y Judaísmo en Borges* (Madrid: Altalena, 1986), pp. 25–31.

21. "Una versión inglesa de los cantares más antiguos del mundo," in *Textos cautivos,* in *Obras completas* (Barcelona: Emecé, 1996), 4:396.

22. Ibid., p. 396.

23. In her biography of Borges, María Esther Vázquez indicates that "Borges translated one of the fantastic stories from Meyrink's *Fledermäuse*" (*Borges: Esplendor y derrota* [Barcelona: Tusquets, 1999], p. 49) and that he also translated a story of Meyrink's in the journal *Revista Multicolor de los Sábados* of the journal *Crítica*. The only story by Meyrink in the journal is a translation called "Las sanguijuelas del tiempo," published May 5, 1934.

24. Aizenberg, *El tejedor del Aleph,* pp. 95–115. Aizenberg quotes a personal letter in which Gerschom Scholem seems to express polite skepticism about Borges's knowledge of the Kabbalah in its historical context while praising his "intuition about what the Kabbalists might have represented in their own imagination" (p. 113).

25. Compare, for instance, "tödliche Einsamkeit" (deadly loneliness) (in Martin Buber, "Jerusalem," in *Die Legende des Baalschem* [Berlin: Schockin, 1982], p. 94, and "la soledad abrumadora" [oppressive solitude] in Borges's unpublished translation of "Jerusalem").

26. Enriqueta Morillas Ventura argues that Borges's engagements with German Expressionism informed his inclination against realism (see "Borges, el expresionismo y la literatura fantástica," *Insula,* no. 631–632 [July–August 1999]: 27).

27. Linda S. Maier, "Jorge Luis Borges and German Expressionism," *Romance Notes* 28, no. 2 (winter 1986): 143. The references to the four articles are "Lírica expresionista," *Grecia* 47 (August 1, 1920): 10–11; "Antología expresionista," *Cervantes* (October 1920): 100–112; "Lírica expresionista: Wilhelm Klemm," *Grecia* 50 (November 1, 1920): 10— 11; "Horizontes: Die aktions-Lyrik—1914—Berlin," *Ultra* 16 (October 20, 1921). These short essays have been reproduced in Borges, *Textos recobrados 1919–1929* (Buenos Aires: Emecé, 1997).

28. Cansinos-Assens wrote an article in which he expressed his gratitude to Borges for having introduced the poetry of German Expressionism in Spain. The article was reprinted, along with another article by Ramón Gómez de la Serna, in *Jorge Luis Borges,* ed. Jaime Alazraki (Madrid: Taurus, 1976), p. 38.

29. "Su fuente la constituye esa visión ciclópeda y atlética del pluriverso que ritmara Walt Whitman" ("Lírica expresionista: Síntesis," in *Textos recobrados,* p. 52). In a discussion about his early published work with Alexander Coleman, Borges referred to his style of the period as "an absurd style, . . . a baroque style [that might have disguised his] aggressive shyness" (see Borges, *Borges at Eighty: Conversations,* ed. Willis Barnstone [Bloomington: Indiana University Press, 1982], p. 123).

30. The letter to Maurice Abramowicz is not dated, but it was probably written sometime in 1920. See Borges, *Cartas del fervor: Correspondencia con Maurice Abramowicz y Jacobo Sureda (1919–1928),* ed. Cristobal Pera (Barcelona: Emecé, 1999), p. 120, or *Correspondencia,* in *Œuvres complètes,* ed. Jean Pierre Bernès (Paris: Gallimard, 1993), 1:1058.

31. Rodríguez Monegal, *Jorge Luis Borges,* p. 147.

32. José Luis Vega, "Un ejemplo de las traducciones expresionistas de Jorge Luis Borges," *Revista de la facultad de traducción e interpretación, Granada* 5 (1994): 241–48.

33. Ibid., p. 248.

34. "Von Wirklichkeit den Leib so wie von staubiger Rüstung zu entketten" (in Vega, "Un ejemplo de las traducciones," p. 242).

35. "Desnudar la realidad al cuerpo como de un uniforme polvoriento" (ibid., p. 243).

36. Borges, "Acerca del expresionismo," in *Inquisiciones* (Barcelona: Seix Barral, 1994), p. 157.

37. I am quoting from Carlos García's article, which is an excellent introduction to Borges's engagements with Kurt Heynicke's poetry. García points out that Borges transformed Heynicke's poetry, but it is not

his purpose to interpret the changes. See Carlos García, "Borges y el expresionismo: Kurt Heynicke," *Variaciones Borges* 11 (2001): 121–35.

38. "Crepúsculo" (*Textos recobrados*, 53); García, "Borges y el expresionismo," pp. 124–25.

39. "Dos horas infinitas van desplegando minutos" (in *Textos recobrados*, p. 179).

40. Die Batterie erhebt ihre Löwenstimme
Sechsmal hinaus in das Land. Die Granaten heulen.
Stille. In der Ferne brodelt das Feuer der Infanterie,
Tagelang, wochenlang.
(In *Lyrik des Expressionismus*, ed. Silvio Vietta,
[Tübingen: Niemeyer, 1999], p. 127)

41. La batería levanta su voz de león.
Una y seis veces. Silencio.
En los lejos arde la infantería.
Durante días. Durante semanas también.
(In *Textos recobrados*, p. 180)

42. (Original)
Wolke, Schädel ohne Unterkiefer, hobelt das Kraterland.
. . . .
Wie geblähter aufgestochener Darm knallen die Gasgranaten,
stumm wühlen die Rüssel der Masken am Horizontrand ihres
Existenzminimums—
(Alfred Vagt, "Nacht im Trichter,"
Die Aktion 8 [January 1918]: 10–11)
(First version)
Nube, cráneo sin mandíbula inferior, alisa el campo carcomido
de cráteres.
. . . .
Las granadas de gas estallan como un intestino pinchado,
Las proboscis de las caretas limitan su horizonte al mínimum de
existencia.
(In Borges, *Textos recobrados*, p. 64)

43. Un nubarrón, calavera sin la quijada, alias el campo carcomido
de craters.
. . . .
Las granadas dc gas estallan como un intestino pinchado.

> Las trompas de las caretas limitan su horizonte al minimum de
> existencia.
>
> (In *Inquisiciones*, p. 150)

44. "An Autobiographical Essay," in *Critical Essays on Jorge Luis Borges*, ed. Jaime Alazraki (Boston: G. K. Hall & Co., 1987), pp. 29–30.

45. *Cartas del fervor*, p. 74. The letter also appears in Borges, *Correspondencia*, in *Œuvres complètes*, 2:1042.

46. The poem appeared in *Grecia*, a journal published in Seville, on December 31, 1919. It is also in Borges, *Textos recobrados*, pp. 24—26.

47. Borges, *Correspondencia*, in *Œuvres complètes*, 2:1046.

48. Cortínez, Carlos, " 'Himno del mar': El primer poema de Borges," *Revista Chilena de Literatura* 25 (April 1985): 75–77.

49. Prologue to *Elogio de la sombra*, in *Obras completas*, 2:355.

50. "Himno al mar," in Borges, *Textos recobrados*, pp.24–25.

51. "El otro" ("The Other") in *El libro de arena*, in *Obras completas*, 2:15.

52. Emir Rodríguez Monegal, "La palabra del joven poeta," in *Ficcionario: Una antología de textos*, ed. Emir Rodríguez Monegal (Mexico City: Fondo de Cultura Económica, 1985), p. 15.

53. Rafael Olea Franco thinks that Borges's political and aesthetic views of the 1920s can be characterized as "populist" (see his *El otro Borges: El primer Borges* [Mexico City: Fondo de Cultura Económica, 1993], p. 262).

54. Borges, *A/Z*, ed. Antonio Fernández Ferrer (Madrid: Ediciones Siruela, 1988), p. 199.

55. The books in question are *Inquisiciones* (1925), *El tamaño de mi esperanza* (1926), and *El idioma de los argentinos* (1928). The three works have been reissued in recent years. Nestor Ibarra recalls that Borges would go out of his way and pay exorbitant prices for any copies he could find of his first three books of essays in order to destroy them (see Ibarra's note in p. 249 in his translation of Borges's *L'or des tigres* [Paris: Gallimard, 1976]).

56. José Miguel Oviedo, *Historia del ensayo latinoamericano* (Madrid: Alianza Editorial, 1991), p. 97.

57. Borges, *El tamaño de mi esperanza* (Barcelona: Seix Barral, 1993), pp. 128–29.

58. "Nueva versión de Walt Whitman," *Martín Fierro* 4, no. 35 (February 26, 1927): 8.

59. *Borges at Eighty*, p. 136.

60. Although the 1932 version differs from the one he published in 1929, Borges chose to retain the original date at the end of the essay.

61. "El otro Whitman," *La vida literaria* (Buenos Aires), no. 14 (September 1929): 3.

62. Borges, "El otro Whitman," in *Discusión,* in *Obras completas,* 1:209.

63. Whitman, *Hojas de hierba* (Buenos Aires: Editorial Lumen, 1969), p. 22.

64. See Carmen Valero Garcés, "Jorge L. Borges poeta y traductor de Walt Whitman: Análisis de las estrategias en la traducción de poesía," *Torre de papel* 3 (fall 1995): 19–40.

65. "Son traducciones rigurosamente literales que intentan ofrecer al lector hispano un texto lo más fiel posible al original en cuando a lenguaje, orden de palabras, y estructura de versos" (they are rigorously literal translations that attempt to offer the Spanish reader the most faithful text possible to the original in terms of language, word order, and the structure of the verses) (*Versiones, interpretaciones, creaciones,* p. 126).

66. Whitman, *Leaves of Grass,* in *Poetry and Prose* (New York: Library of America, 1996), p. 266.

67. De nuevo me retiene la mano, no quiere que me vaya.
    Vuelvo a verla a mi lado con silenciosos labios, triste, y
        temblando.
                                (Whitman, *Hojas de hierba,* p. 139)

68. Saúl Yurkievich, "Borges, poeta circular," in *Expliquémonos a Borges como poeta,* ed. Angel Flores (Mexico City: Siglo XXI, 1984), pp. 68–88.

69. "La noche cíclica" ("The Cyclical Night"), in *El otro, el mismo,* in *Obras completas,* 2:241. Cyclical themes and infinite regressions abound in Borges's prose and in his poetry. In "El otro" ("The Other"), a story that combines both, an old Borges meets a younger one, and they realize they have little in common. It is clear that the meeting will take place eternally since the younger Borges will age and repeat the encounter. In their conversation, they touch on cyclical matters as the older Borges tells the younger one about the future: "As far as history. . . There was another war with almost the same antagonists. France did not wait long to capitulate; England and France fought the cyclical battle of Waterloo against a German dictator named Hitler. Buenos Aires towards 1946 engendered another Rosas who was very similar to our relative" ("El otro," in *Obras completas,* 2:13). For an

infinite regress in a poem of terror see "Un sueño" ("A Dream"), *Obras completas,* 2:322.

70.   "Para concluir, anuncio lo que vendrá después" (in Whitman, *Hojas de hierba,*" p. 159).

71.   Cuando leas, yo que era visible seré invisible,
      Ahora eres tú, concreto, visible, el que los lee, el que los busca,
      Imaginando lo feliz que serías si yo estuviera a tu lado y fuera tu
         amigo,
      Sé tan feliz como si yo estuviera a tu lado.
      (No estés demasiado seguro de que no esté contigo.)
                                        (In Whitman, *Hojas de hierba,* p. 151)

72.   "A quien está leyéndome," in *El otro, el mismo* in *Obras completas* 2:302.

73.   "G. A. Bürger," in *Historia de la noche,* in *Obras completas* 3:191.

74.   Whitman, *Hojas de hierba,* p. 133; *Leaves of Grass,* p. 264.

75.   "Wieder seh ich Schleier sinken, / Und Vertrautestes wird fremd."

76.   "De nuevo ante mis ojos hay velos que descienden / Se aleja de nosotros lo más eterno e íntimo" ("Cinco poemas de Herman Hesse," trans. Borges and Roberto Alifano, *Proa* 3, no. 6 [October–November 1990]: 37).

77.   "Doch aus früheren Geburten / Zuckt entfernte Ahnung her" (ibid.).

78.   "Algo vago presiento, algo vago y remoto / Que me llega de vidas, de ciclos anteriores" (ibid.).

79.   "Aus zerrissnen Fäden webt sich / Neu und schöner Gottes Kleid" (ibid.).

80.   "La trama se desgarra y el Numen entreteje / Más inasible y bello su renovado ornato" (ibid.).

81.   "Durch des Lebens Wüste irr ich glühend." (original German); "Ciego cruzo el desierto de la vida." (Borges's Spanish) (ibid., p. 35).

82.   "Dass du in dem Getriebe / Des Lebens eine Mitte weisst, / Macht dich und deine Liebe / Für mich zum guten Geist" (ibid., p. 39).

83.   Que en este orbe de caos y de muerte
      Me reveles la senda verdadera
      Y seas mi pastor y mi Virgilio,
      A la luz de tu amor, que será estrella.
                                        (Ibid.)

84. "A percibir las Fuentes primordiales" (ibid.).
85. For an engaging account of Borges's relationship to Dante, see María Rosa Menocal's *Writing in Dante's Cult of Truth: From Borges to Boccaccio* (Durham: Duke University Press, 1991).
86. "Estoy satisfecho, veo, bailo, me río y canto; / Cuando la compañera amorosa que comparte mi lecho duerme a mi lado y se retira al amanecer con pasos furtivos" (in Whitman, *Hojas de hierba*, p. 34).
87. Prologue by Borges to *Cien dísticos del viajero querubínico de Angelus Silesius,* trans. and ed. Borges and María Kodama (Santiago de Chile: Ediciones La Ciudad, 1982), p. 10.
88. See J. Baruzi, *Creation religieuse et pensée contemplative, 2eme part: Angelus Silesius* (Paris: 1951); E. Susini, "Johannes Scheffler (1624—1677)," in *Encyclopedia Universalis,* vol. 14 (Paris, Encyclopedia Universalis France S.A.), pp. 723–24.
89. See p. 40, note 70.
90. Adelheid Hanke-Schaefer, *Jorge Luis Borges zur Einführung* (Hamburg: Junius, 1999), p. 144.
91. The interview published in 1945 is reproduced in Borges, *Borges por el mismo,* ed. Emir Rodriguez Monegal (Caracas: Monte Avila, 1987), p. 151.

92.   *Der Mensch Ists Höchste Ding*

    Nichts dünkt mich hoch zu sein: ich bin das höchste Ding,
    Weil auch Gott ohne mich sich selber ist gering.
    (*Cien dísticos del viajero querubínico de Angelus Silesius,* p. 48)

93.   *Lo más alto es el hombre*

    Nada me parece alto. Soy el más alto.
    Dios no es nada sin mí.

    (Ibid., p. 49)

94.   *Gott Schaut Man mit Gelassenheit*

    Der Engel schauet Gott mit heitern Augen an,
    Ich aber noch viel mehr, so ich Gott lassen kann.

    (Ibid., p. 42)

95.   *Vemos a Dios con el abandono*

    El ángel mira a Dios con ojos serenos. Yo lo
    Veo mucho mehor si puedo agandonarlo.

    (Ibid., p. 43)

96.   *Der Ort Ist Selbst in Dir*

    Nicht du bist in dem Ort, der Ort, der ist in dir;
    Wirfst du ihn aus, so steht die Ewigkeit schon hier.
                                             (Ibid., p. 46)

97.   *El espacio mismo está en ti*

    El espacio está en ti. No estás en el espacio.
    Recházalo. La eternidad ya está aquí.
                                             (Ibid., p. 47)

98.   *Beschluß*

    Freund, es ist auch genug. Im Fall du mehr willst lesen,
    So geh und werde selbst die Schrift un selbst das Wesen.
                          (Hundert Distischen . . . , p. 47)

99.   *Conclusión*

    Ya basta, amigo. Si quieres seguir leyendo,
    conviértete tú mismo en el libro y en su materia.
                                         (Ibid., p. 53)

100. In an interview Borges said that Baudelaire's translation of Poe's work is superior to on account of the French poet's more refined aesthetic sense. See Borges and Osvaldo Ferrari, *Jorge Luis Borges: En diálogo* [Buenos Aires: Editorial Sudamericana, 1998], 2:274.

101. "Quiza el misterio es demasiado simple—dijo Dupin. Y ¿cuál es, por fin, el misterio?—le pregunté" ("La carta robada," in *Los mejores cuentos policiales,* ed. and trans. Borges and Adolfo Bioy Casares [Buenos Aires: Emecé: 1943], p. 26).

102. "Lo sabemos . . . por el carácter del documento y por el hecho de no haberse ya producido ciertos resultados que surgirían si el documento no estuviera en poder del ladrón" (ibid., p. 26).

103. "[N]o he conocido un algebrista . . . que no profesara el clandestino artículo de fe de que $(a + b)^2$ es incondicionalmente igual al $a^2 + 2ab + b^2$. Diga usted a uno de esos caballeros que, en ciertas ocasiones $(a + b)^2$ puede no equivaler estrictamente a $a^2 + 2ab + b^2$, y antes de acabar su explicación eche a correr para que no lo destroce" (ibid., p. 36).

104. Ibid., p. 26.

105. Borges and Roberto Alifano, *Conversaciones con Borges* (Buenos Aires: Torres Aguero, 1994), p. 19.

106. "la dama comprometida" ("La carta robada," in *Los mejores cuentos policiales*, p. 39); Poe, "The Purloined Letter," in *Complete Works*, ed. James A. Harrison (New York: Crowell, 1902; New York: AMS, 1979), 5:176.

107. "El documento—una carta para ser franco—fue recibido por la víctima del posible *chantaje*, mientras estaba sola en la habitación real. Casi inmediatamente después entra una segunda persona, de quien deseaba especialmente ocultar la carta. Apenas tuvo tiempo para dejarla, abierta como estaba, sobre una mesa" ("La carta robada," in *Los mejores cuentos policiales*, p. 27).

108. "la víctima del posible chantaje" ("La carta robada," in Los mejores cuentos policiales, p. 27).

109. "The Purloined Letter," in *Complete Works*, 5:158.

110. "Es evidente . . . que la carta sigue en posesión del Ministro: en esa posesión está su poder. Vendida la carta, el poder termina" ("La carta robada," in *Los mejores cuentos policiales*, p. 28).

111. "The Purloined Letter," in *Complete Works*, 5:157.

112. Ibid., see pp. 155, 172, and 173.

113. In an interview Borges compliments Reyes for writing the best Spanish in the language and for translating Chesterton: "Alfonso Reyes is perhaps the finest prose writer in the language. I do not think the Spanish language ever produced anybody else like Reyes. . . . I knew Reyes personally. He was a very fine man. He translated Chesterton into Spanish" (in Daniel Balderston, "Interview with Borges," *Variaciones Borges* 8 [1999]: 198.)

114. See Robb, James Willis, "Borges y Reyes: Una relación epistolar," in *Jorge Luis Borges*, ed. Alazraki, p. 310.

115. "varios objetos, formando montones separados; objetos tan inexplicables como indiferentes. Un montoncito parecía contener los trozos de un espejo roto. Otro, era un montón de polvo moreno. El tercer objeto era un bastón" ("La honradez de Israel Gow," in *El candor del padre Brown*, ed. and trans. Alfonso Reyes [Buenos Aires: Losada, 1939], pp. 115–16).

116. "varios objetos, objetos tan inexplicables como indiferentes. Uno parecía un montoncito de vidrios rotos. Otro era un montón de polvo pardo. El tercer objeto era un bastón" ("El honor de Israel Gow," in *Los mejores cuentos policiales*, p. 100).

117. James Willis Robb, "Borges y reyes: Una relación epistolar," *Jorge Luis Borges*, ed. Alazraki, p. 311.

118. See chapter 3.

119. Stevenson, *Fables*, p. 56.

120. Antoine Galland, *Les Mille et une nuits* (Paris: Garnier, 1941), 3:210.

121. "Historia de Abdula, el mendigo ciego: Versión de Borges de Antoine Galland," in Borges, *Las mil y una noches según Galland*.

122. In his edition of Borges's complete works, Jean Pierre Bernès has noted the genealogy of Borges's story that first appeared as "An Arabic Legend" in the journal *El Hogar* (June 16, 1939). Borges also published the story in the collection *Cuentos breves y extraordinarios,* ed. Borges and Adolfo Bioy Casares (Buenos Aires: Editorial Raigal, 1955; Buenos Aires: Santiago Rueda, 1967). In that version of 1955 the story is still attributed to Richard Burton.

123. Borges adds another layer of complexity to his assessment when he calls another one of his short stories "Abejacán el Bojarí, muerto en su laberinto" ("Ibn-Hakam Al Bojarí, Murdered in His Labyrinth"), a variation of "The Two Kings and the Two Labyrinths." Here is the full text of this baroque sentence in Borges's postscript to *The Aleph* splendidly rendered by Andrew Hurley: " 'Ibn-Hakam Al Bojarí, Murdered in His Labyrinth' " is not (I have been assured) memorable, in spite of its bloodcurdling title. We might think of it as a variation of 'The Two Kings and the Two Labyrinths,' interpolated into the *1001 Nights* by the copyists yet passed over by the prudent Galland" (*The Aleph,* in *Collected Fictions,* trans. Andrew Hurley [New York: Penguin, 1998], p. 288).

124. Marta Ana Diz, "El mago de Toledo: Borges y Don Juan Manuel," *MLN* 100, no. 2 (1985 March): 291.

125. "La rosa de Parcelso," in *La memoria de Shakespeare,* in *Obras completas*, 3:389–92.

126. In Alastair Reid's brilliant translation of Borges's "Conjectural Poem" (in Borges, *Selected Poems,* ed. Alexander Coleman [New York: Penguin, 2000], p. 159) and "fuggendo a piede e 'nsanguinando il piano" in Dante's original.

127. See Borges, *Selected Poems 1923–1967* (London: Penguin, 1985), p. 319n.

128. At face value, Borges's "Conjectural poem" is a conjecture inspired by a historical event: the death of one of Borges's ancestors, Francisco Laprida, on September 22, 1829. The poem ends with the fateful line "el íntimo cuchillo en la garganta" (the intimate knife on the throat) as Laprida's life is coming to its end. The poem explores the

ironic fate of a man of letters whose "South American destiny" made him a politician and a soldier. The poem is an oblique image of a dilemma Borges had often expressed about himself: his destiny as a man of letters born in Argentina who might have preferred to have lived a life of action. On yet another level, the poem is a subtle commentary on the fifth canto of Dante's *Purgatorio,* where a captain named Buonconte lost his life from a wound to the throat. In his dying moments, Laprida compares his fate with that of Dante's character in a line that includes a literal translation of a line from the *Comedy:*

Como aquel capitán del Purgatorio
que, huyendo a pie y ensangrentando el llano,
fue cegado y tumbado por la muerte
donde un oscuro río pierde el nombre,
así habré de caer.

Borges's lines are inspired by Dante's:

Là 've 'l vocabol suo diventa vano,
arriva' io forato nella gola,
fuggendo a piede e 'nsanguinando il piano.
Quivi perdei la vista e la parola;
nel nome di Maria fini', e quivi
caddi e rimase la mia carne sola.

> (*The Divine Comedy,* vol. 2, *Purgatorio,* trans. and ed.
> John D. Sinclair [with Italian text] [New York: Oxford
> University Press, 1939], p. 72)

Laprida's lines suggest prophetic foreknowledge of the nature of his death, for he expects the cut that will dispatch him, as in the poem by Dante. Borges's poem is not only an oblique commentary on Dante's canto, it presents itself as a compliment, as a kind of bookend to it; for whereas Borges's poem tells the story of the captain until the "intimate knife" touches his throat, Dante's version of Buoconte's demise begins after the throat has been cut.

In each case the destiny of the character is determined as he is facing death; in each a transformation takes place that one could only ascertain conjecturally, which is as much a commentary on the construction of Dante's afterlife as a commentary on the construction of the "Conjectural Poem." Borges's poem makes it clear that Dante did not tell the story of Buonconte's life prior to his dreadful wound-

ing, and Borges's own poem is intended to fill that gap and to complement the story in *Purgatorio*. Read in the light of Dante's story,
Borges's poem tells the story of a military man's life up until a deadly
knife touches his throat; Dante tells the story of the man from the
time he suffers a slit throat until he is taken to purgatory. Borges's
poem is a daring transfiguration of historical and autobiographical
events, as well as a brilliant commentary on Dante. His poem, and
the *Comedy*, explore events that can only be captured conjecturally in
a literary work because they presuppose the perspective of those who
have lost their lives. In Borges's poem, however, there is no certainty
of an afterlife: his poem is told from the perspective of the last few
moments of consciousness before death. Borges is therefore able to
use a literary conceit akin to Dante's without recourse to Dante's
afterlife. One could also add that like the *Comedy*, Borges's poem
also has a political dimension, for it can be read as an oblique protest
against the rise of Peronism in Argentina.

129. See "Cuatro reflexiones," in *Cuentos breves y extraordinarios*, p. 137.
130. See chapter 3.
131. In his "Parábola de Cervantes y de Quijote," Borges offers his variation on Kafka's parable on "The Truth about Sancho Panza." In
Borges's creation Don Quijote is an old soldier who dreamed Miguel
de Cervantes into existence. See *El hacedor*, in *Obras completas*, 2:177.
132. In an informative article, Antonio Fernández Ferrer indicates the significance that Borges gave to the story of Chuang-Tzu and the butterfly, and he discusses the works of many other poets who have also
been interested in the same anecdote. He does not, however, indicate that Borges's versions of the poem are significantly different from
each other, nor does he compare them to the sources that Borges
quoted. See Antonio Fernández Ferrer, "Cercanía de una milenaria
intertextualidad" in *El siglo de Borges: Homenaje a Jorge Luis Borges
en su centenario*, vol. 2, *Literatura-Ciencia-Filosofía* (Frankfurt:
Vervuert, 1999).
133. Borges recalls telling Macedonio Fernández, his Argentine mentor,
the story of the dream of the butterfly. Fernández's response was to
inquire about the date of the text. When Borges pointed out that it
was from the fifth century before Christ, "Macedonio observed that
the Chinese language must have changed so much since that faraway
time that of all the words of the story the word *butterfly* was probably the only one with a certain meaning." See Borges, ed., *Macedonio*

Ferndández (Buenos Aires: Ministerio de Educación y Justicia, 1961), p. 11.

134. "Chuang-Tzu soñó que era una mariposa. Al despertar ignorabe si era Tzu que había soñado que era una mariposa o si era una mariposa y estaba soñando que era Tzu (*Antología de la literatura fantástica*, ed. Borges, Silvina Ocampo, and Adolfo Bioy Casares [first edition 1940; Barcelona: Edhasa, 1981], p. 158). The first version of the translation may have been a collaboration with Bioy Casares and Silvina Ocampo.

135. "El sueño de Chuang Tsu," *Los Anales de Buenos Aires*, March 1946, p. 56.

136. "Chuang-Tzu soñó que era una mariposa y no sabía al despertar si era un hombre que había soñado ser una mariposa o una mariposa que ahora soñaba ser un hombre" (in *Cuentos breves y extraordinarios*, p. 20). Borges indicates that he translated the text from a work by Herbert Allen. His note reads, "De Chuang-Tzu (1889) de Herbert Allen Giles" (*Cuentos breves y extraordinarios*, p. 20).

137. *Chuang-tzu: Nan-hua ching. English. Chuang-Tzu Mystic, Moralist, and Social Reformer,* trans. from the Chinese by Herbert A. Giles (London: Bernard Quaritch, 1889), xxviii, p. 23.

138. "Soñé que era una mariposa que andaba por el aire y que nada sabía de Chuang-Tzu" (*Otras inquisiciones*, in *Obras completas*, 2:146).

139. The translation first appeared in *Revista Multicolor de los Sábados* of the journal *Crítica*, July 21, 1934, and it is reproduced in *Borges: Obras, reseñas y traducciones inéditas: Diario Crítica 1933–1934,* ed. Irma Zangara (Barcelona: Atlantida, 1999), p. 377. The original reads: "Der Traum belehrt uns auf eine merkwürdige Weise von der Leichtigkeit unsere Seele in jedes Objekt einzudringen—sich in jedes sogleich zu verwandeln" (Novalis, *Fragmente* [Heidelberg: Verlag Lambert Schneider, 1957], 1:328).

140. See Jaime Alazraki, "Estructura y función de los sueños en los cuentos de Borges," *Iberoromania* 3 (1975): 9–38. The essay appears in the third edition of Alazraki's *La prosa narrativa de Jorge Luis Borges* (Gredos: Madrid, 1983).

141. See Claudio César Montoto, "Jorge Luis Borges: La literatura como sueño dirigido," *Inti. Revista de Literatura Hispánica*, nos. 49–50 (1999): 39–45.

142. Teodosio Fernández, "Jorge Luis Borges y el destino escandinavo," in *La aurora y el poniente: Borges (1899—1999)*, ed. Manuel Fuentes and Paco Tovar (Tarragona: Gabriel Gibert, 2000), p. 94.

143. All of the English versions of the Prose Edda are based on the manu-script that Jesse Byock of UCLA's Department of Germanic Languages is preparing for Penguin. I also consulted several other translations in English, French, and German, which I cite in the bibliography. I am quoting the original in Anthony Faulkes's edition (*Edda: Prologue and Gylfaginning* [Oxford: Clarendon Press, 1982]).

144. François-Xavier Dillmann, introduction to *L'Edda: Récits de mythologie nordique par Snorri Sturluson* (Paris: Gallimard, 1991).

145. Borges, prologue to *La alucinación de Gylfi*, by Snorri Sturluson, trans. Borges and María Kodama (Madrid: Alianza Editorial, 1984), p. 15.

146. Borges, *Antiguas literaturas germánicas* (Mexico City: Fondo de Cultura Económica, 1951), p. 102.

147. Ibid., p. 104.

148. An example of removing the divine takes place when Borges changes the term "holy places" in the following passage to the more mundane "where Heimdallr lives."

> Himinbijörg, they call it, and there Heimdall, they say, rules over sacred places. There the gods' watchman drinks happily, in his comfortable lodgings, the good mead. (Jesse Byock's translation from the original Old Norse)

> Himinbjörg heita
> en þar Heimdall kveðja
> valda véum.
> Þar vörðr goða
> drekkr í væru ranni
> glaðr hinn góða mjöð. (Original Old Norse, from Faulkes's edition of *Edda: Prologue and Gylfaginning*, p. 26)

> Himinbijörg se llama el lugar en que habita Heimdallr. Ahí el centinela de los dioses bebe alegremente hidromiel. (Borges in original Spanish, *La alucinación de Gylfi*, p. 54)

> The place where Heimdallr lives is called Himinbijörg. There the watchman of the gods drinks mead happilly. (Author's translation of Borges)

149. En sjónhveringar hefi ek gert þér. (Faulkes, *Edda: Prologue and Gylfaginning*, p. 42); "Yo urdí para ti una serie de alucinaciones" (in Borges, *La alucinación de Gylfi*, p. 85).

150. "Gangleri oyó a su alrededor mucho ruido y al mirar vio que estaba a la intemperie en campo abierto y no había ni sala ni castillo. Entonces prosiguió caminando y volvió a su reino y contó esas cosas que había visto y oído, y después de él los hombres siguieron contándolas" (in Borges, *La alucinación de Gylfi*, p. 104); ("Því næst heyrði Gangleri dyni mikla hvern veg frá sér, ok leit út á hlið sér. Ok þá er hann sésk meir um þá stendr hann úti á sléttum velli, sér þá ønga höll ok ønga borg. Gengr hann þá leið sína braut ok kemr heim í ríki sitt ok segir þau tíðindi er hann hefir sét ok heyrt. Ok eptir honum sagði hverr maðr öðrum þessar sögur") (Faulkes, *Edda: Prologue and Gylfaginning*, 54).

151. "Oscuro será el brillo del sol" (in Borges's translation, p. 35); "Svört verða sólskin" (Faulkes, *Edda: Prologue and Gylfaginning*, p. 14).

152. "Dignas de odio fueron para mí las montañas. No estuve en ellas mucho tiempo; nueve fueron las noches. Atroz era el aullido de los lobos después del canto del cisne" (in Borges, *La alucinación de Gylfi*, p. 51);

> Leið erumk fjöll—
> varka ek lengi á,
> nætr einar níu;
> úlfa þytr
> mér þótti illr vera
> hjá söngvi svana.

(Faulkes, *Edda: Prologue and Gylfaginning*, p. 24)

153. "En las playas del mar no pude dormir. Me aturdían las aves marinas. Me despertaban cada mañana cuando venían del océano" (Borges, *La alucinación de Gylfi*, p. 51);

> Sofa ek máttigak
> sævar beðjum á
> fugls jarmi fyrir;
> sá mik vekr
> er af víði kemr
> morgun hverjan; már.

(Faulkes, *Edda: Prologue and Gylfaginning*, p. 24)

154. "En er hann kom inn í borgina þá sá hann þar háva höll, svá at varla mátti hann sjá yfir hana. þak hennar var lagt gyltum skjöldum svá sem spánþak" (Faulkes, *Edda: Prologue and Gylfaginning*, p.7).

155. "Sobre sus hombros los diestros navegantes cargaron las tejas de las

sala de Odín que habían pulido con piedras" (Borges, *La alucinación de Gylfi*, p. 23);

Á baki létu blíkja,
barðir váru grjóti,
Sváfnis salnæfrar
seggir hyggjandi.

(Faulkes, *Edda: Prologue and Gylfaginning*, p. 7)

156. "El hombre en el umbral, in *El Aleph*, in *Obras completas*, 1:612.
157. "El sol no sabía dónde estaba su casa. La luna no sabía su poder. Las estrellas no sabían dónde estaban. Así era antes que la tierra fuera hecha" (Borges, *La alucinación de Gylfi*, p. 31);

Sól þat né vissi
hvar hon saliu átti.
Máni þat ne vissi
hvat hann megins átti.
Stjörnur þat ne vissu
hvar þær staði áttu.

Svá var áðr en þetta væri of jörð.

(Faulkes, *Edda: Prologue and Gylfaginning*, p. 12)

158. "Está hecha de seis cosas: el ruido de la pisada del gato, la barba de la mujer, las raíces de una roca, los tendones del oso, el aliento del pez y la saliva del pájaro. Las divindidades agregan: 'Ves que no te mintimos. Ni las mujeres tienen barba ni los peces tienen aliento; todas las cosas que hemos dicho son tan ciertas como ésas, aunque hay algunas que no es fácil probar'" (Borges, *Antiguas literaturas germánicas*, p. 103).
159. "Estaba hecho de seis cosas: el sonido de una pisada de gato, la barba de una mujer, la raíz de un peñasco, los tendones de un oso, el aliento de un pez y la escupida de un pájaro. Y aunque aún no entiendes bien el asunto, tendrás aquí la prueba de que no miento: sin duda habrás notado que una mujer no tiene barba y que un gato al pasar no hace ruido y que no hay raíz debajo de un peñasco. Y, a fe mía, todo lo que te he dicho no es menos cierto aunue haya algunas cosas que no puedes poner a prueba" (Borges, *La alucinación de Gylfi*, p. 59); (Hann var gjörr af sex hlutum: af dyn kattarins ok af skeggi konunnar ok af rótum bjargsins ok af sinum bjarnarins ok af anda fisksins ok af fogls hráka. Ok þóttu vitir eigi áðr þessi tíðindi, þá máttu nú finna skjótt hér

sönn dæmi at eigi er logit at þér: sét muntþu hafa at konan hefir ekki skegg ok engi dynr verðr af hlaupi kattarins ok eigi eru rætr undir bjarginu, ok þat veit trúa mín at jafnsatt er þat allt er ek hefi sagt þér þótt þeir sé sumir hlutir er þú mátt eigi reyna) (Faulkes, *Edda: Prologue and Gylfaginning*, p. 28).

160. "Larga es una noche, larga la segunda. ¿Cómo hare para esperar tres? Hubo un tiempo en que un mes pasaba más pronto que esta primera noche" (Borges, La *alucinación de Gylfi*, p. 66);

Löng er nótt,
löng er önnur,
hvé mega ek þreyta þrjár?
Opt mér mánaðr
minni þótti
en sjá hálf hynótt.

(Faulkes, *Edda: Prologue and Gylfaginning*, p. 31)

161. "Vive en todos los tiempos" (Borges, *La alucinación de Gylfi*, p. 25); "Lifir hann of allar aldir" (he lives through all ages) (Faulkes, *Edda: Prologue and Gylfaginning*, p. 8).

Chapter 3

1. I use "imagined" translation to mean a translation in a literary work that is not coextensive with a real translation. When, for example, Borges refers to the translations of works by fictional characters of his own invention, they are "imagined translations," as opposed to real translations discussed (and sometimes even quoted) in Borges's fictions, such as Averroës's translations of Aristotle from Latin sources.

2. Nicolás Helft and Alan Pauls have made the point that "translation is the great model of the Borgesian practice." The purpose of this chapter is to demonstrate how translation played a role in his creative process. See Helft and Pauls's informed and wonderfully illustrated *El factor Borges: Nueve ensayos ilustrados* (Buenos Aires: Fondo de Cultura Económica, 2000), p. 110.

3. "Tlön, Uqbar, Orbis Tertius," in *Labyrinths: Selected Stories and Other Writings*, ed. Donald A. Yates and James E. Irby (New York: New Directions, 1964, p. 8). I quote this passage from the splendid translation by James Irby in which he uses the word "English" where "Spanish" is used in the original.

4. It is a thought experiment that can be construed as taking a doctrine akin to that of Nelson Goodman's "ways of worldmaking"—in which versions determine not only names and categories but also what names and categories apply to—to its most absurd consequences.

5. *Obras completas* (Barcelona: Emecé, 1989), 1:442.

6. In 1946 Borges wrote, "El más urgente de los problemas de nuestra época … es la gradual intromisión del Estado en los actos del individuo; en la lucha con ese mal, cuyos nombres son comunismo y nazismo" ("The most urgent problem of our time . . . is the gradual interference of the State in the actions of the individual; [it is an] evil, called Communism and Fascism," in "Nuestro Pobre Individualismo") (in *Otras inquisiciones* [Buenos Aires: Emecé, 1952], p. 45). Borges removed his political essays in future editions of *Otras inquisiciones.*

7. "Tlön, Uqbar, Orbis Tertius," in *Ficciones,* in *Obras completas* 1:443.

8. The full interpolation reads:

> Amplios son los tesoros del olvido, e innumerables los montones de cosas en n estado próximo a la nulidad; más hechos hay sepultados en el silencio que registrados, y los más copiosos volúmenes son epítomes de lo que ha sucedido. La crónica del tiempo empezó con la noche, y la oscuridad todavía la sirve; algunos hechos nunca salen a la luz; muchos hand sido declarados; muchos más fueron devorados por la oscuridad y las cavernas del olvido. Cuánto ha quedado en vacuo, y nunca será reelado, de esos longevos tiempos en que los hombres apenas recordaban su juventud, y más que antiguos parecían antigüedades, cuando perduraban más en sus vidas que ahora en nuestras memorias." ("Quinto capítulo de la 'Hydriotaphia' [1658]," *Sur* III [January 1944: 20])

> (Ample are the treasures of forgetfulness, and innumerable the piles of things in a state close to nullity; many more facts have been buried in silence than registered, and the most copious volumes are but epitomes of what has taken place. The chronicle of time began with the night, and obscurity still serves it; some facts never see the light; many have been declared; many more have been devoured by the obscurity and the caverns of oblivion. How much has been left vacuous, and will never be revealed, of those old times in which men hardly thought about their youth, and more than ancient they seem to be antiquities,

when they lasted longer in their lives than in our memories.)
(My translation of the interpolation)

9. Alentó en Browne el heroísmo paradójico de ignorar la insolencia bélica, persistiendo en empeño pensativo, puesto el mirar en una pura especulación de belleza (*Inquisiciones* [Barcelona: Seix Barral, 1994], p. 34).

10. Borges found this passsage of the highest poetic value: "Es éste . . . más poético que cuantos versos conozco" (this is . . . more poetic than many verses I know) (*Inquisiciones,* p. 37).

11. For a study of the significance of the translation in the context of the work of Bioy Casares and his collaborations with Borges, see Suzanne Jill Levine's *Guía de Bioy Casares* (Madrid: Espiral, 1977), pp. 144–57.

12. Browne, *Religio Medici . . . ,* p. 156.

13. "Ser anónimo en insignes hazañas vale más que una historia infame," in "Quinto capítulo de la 'Hidriotaphia' 1658," *Sur* 14 (January 1944): 19.

14. "A Disturbing Exposition," in *Selected Non-Fictions,* ed. Eliot Weinberger, trans. Esther Allen, Suzanne Jill Levine, and Eliot Weinberger (New York: Penguin, 1999), p. 201. Borges, through his very last writings, continued to express his view that the Russian Revolution was a promising development whose humanistic aspirations were perverted. In one of his last writings he wrote, "la revolución rusa, que fue al principio una generosa esperanza y es ahora el zarismo"("the Russian revolution was first a generous hope; it is now Tsarism") (in "Franz Kafka, *América: Relatos breves,"* in *Biblioteca personal,* in *Obras completas* [Barcelona: Emecé, 1996], 4:454).

15. Ibid., p. 207.

16. "Yo, judío," *Revista Megáfono* 3, no. 12 (April 1934): 60.

17. Suzanne Jill Levine, "Notes to Borges's Notes on Joyce: Infinite Affinities," *Comparative Literature* 49, no. 4 (fall 1997): 341.

18. *Selected Non-Fictions,* p. 209.

19. Harold Bloom, "Jorge Luis Borges," in *How to Read and Why* (New York: Scribner, 2000), p. 60.

20. Christopher Maurer, "The Poet's Poets: Borges and Quevedo," in *Borges the Poet,* ed. Carlos Cortínez (Fayetteville: University of Arkansas Press, 1986), p. 191. Maurer adds: "Among the poets' poets is the seventeenth century Spaniard who, like Borges himself, provides consolation in the face of death" (p. 193).

21. In a pioneering essay Rolando Costa Picazo included a paragraph in

which he indicates that many of Borges's fictions are presented as translations. In this book I am attempting to show the significance of this phenomenon. See Costa Picazo, "Autores que traducen: Borges," *Voces* 15 (1994): 10.

22. Nelson Goodman and Catherine Elgin disagree with the view that Borges's story shows "conclusively that a work cannot be identical with a text—that Cervantes and Menard produced separate works with the same text. . . . Any inscription of a text, no matter who or what produced it, bears all the same interpretations as any other. Menard may in some way have proposed or inspired a new interpretation of the text. . . . So *Don Quijote,* despite its multiple admissible interpretations, is one work, not many" (*Reconceptions in Philosophy and Other Arts and Sciences* [Indianapolis and Cambridge: Hackett, 1988], pp. 62–63).

23. "Pierre Menard, autor del Quijote," in *Obras completas,* 1:446.

24. On several occasions Borges indicated he had translated the first act of Shakespeare's *Macbeth* with his friend Adolfo Bioy Casares, and he recalled, from memory, one fragment of his translation.

25. "La memoria de Shakespeare," in *La memoria de Shakespeare,* in *Obras completas,* 3:398. Soergel's view is not identical to Borges's. In a review of a book that transformed Shakespeare's plays into short narratives, Borges quoted George Bernard Shaw to make the point that Shakespeare's imagination did not consist in his ability to invent stories, but in his ability to transform the stories he had received: "Shakespeare—Shaw wrote—knew how to tell a story very well, provided it had been previously told. The stories in this volume were already ancient when they were taken up on stage; these stories had lived for many centuries in the imagination of men, and in that strange land they will continue to flourish perhaps for always" (in Borges's prologue to *Cuentos basados en el teatro de Shakespeare,* by Charles Lamb [Buenos Aires: Atlántida, 1966], p. 1).

26. Jaime Alazraki, "El Golem," in *Expliquémonos a Borges como poeta,* ed. Angel Flores (Mexico City: Siglo XXI, 1984), p. 223.

27. Marcelo Abadi, "Averroes y su trémula esclava pelirroja," *Variaciones Borges* 7 (1999): 176.

28. "La otra muerte," in *El Aleph,* in *Obras completas,* 1:573.

29. *El libro de arena,* in *Obras completas,* 3:48.

30. "El Inmortal," in *El Aleph,* in *Obras completas,* 1:535.

31. "La secta de los treinta," in *El libro de arena,* in *Obras completas,* 2:38.

32. "El Inmortal," p. 535.

33. "Las versiones homéricas," in *Discusión*, in *Obras completas*, 1:240.
34. "El Inmortal," p. 543.
35. Ibid., p. 544.
36. Ibid., p. 544.
37. Ibid., p. 544.
38. Ronald Christ, *The Narrow Act: Borges's Art of Allusion* (New York: Lumen, 1995), p. 242.
39. Jaime Alazraki, *Versiones, inversiones, reversiones: El espejo como modelo estructural del relato en los cuentos de Borges* (Madrid: Gredos, 1977), p. 69.
40. "Death and the Compass" first appeared in the journal *Sur* in May 1942. It reappeared in the anthology of detective fiction in 1943. See *Œuvres complètes*, ed. Jean Pierre Bernès (Paris: Gallimard, 1999), 2:1589.
41. *Artificios* of 1944 was later integrated into *Ficciones*.
42. See chapter 2.
43. Translation is in the offing again because the oral teachings of Shem Tov, as Arthur Green has pointed out, came to be known, from the start, by way of "translations, abbreviated Hebrew renditions of sermons preached in Yiddish" (Arthur Green, "Teachings of the Hasidic Masters," in *Back to the Sources: Readings in the Classic Jewish Texts*, ed. Barry W. Holtz [New York: Touchstone, 1992], p. 364). Borges's interest in Hasidic literature can be traced to his unpublished 1919 translation of Martin Buber's version of a mystical tale about Shem Tov.
44. "el Ministro . . . es inscrupuloso y valiente. Además, no carece de servidores fieles. El acto que usted me sugiere podía haberme costado la vida" (in "La carta robada," in *Los mejores cuentos policiales*, ed. and trans. Borges and Adolfo Bioy Casares [Buenos Aires: Emecé: 1943], p. 39).
45. This first translation appeared in *Revista Multicolor de los Sábados* of the journal *Crítica*, April 28, 1934, p. 4. It was not reprinted in *Borges: Obras, reseñas y traducciones inéditas: Diario Crítica 1933–1934*.
46. Borges and Osvaldo Ferrari, *En diálogo* (Buenos Aires: Editorial Sudamericana, 1998), 2:163.
47. Jack London, "The Minions of Midas," in *The Complete Short Stories of Jack London*, ed. Earle Labor et al. (Stanford, Calif.: Stanford University Press), 1:434.
48. "la incontenible serie de tragedias" (Jack London, "Las muertes concéntricas," in *Los mejores cuentos policiales*, p. 81).

49. "Tuve el placer de que se riera de mí el comisario, aunque me prometió que la vecindad de aquella esquina sería vigilada especialmente la anoche antedicha" (in "Las muertes concéntricas," in *Los mejores cuentos policiales*, p. 86.)

50. In his version Mr. Hale sought the "aid of Pinkerton, of Holmes. . ." ("La ayuda de Pinkerton, de Holmes y de un sinnúmero de agencias particulares" [in "Las muertes concéntricas," in *Los mejores cuentos policiales*, p. 90]).

51. "El tercer crimen ocurrió la noche del tres de febrero. Poco antes de la una, el teléfono resonó en la oficina del comisario Treviranus. Con ávido sigilo, habló un hombre de voz gutural; dijo que se llamaba Ginzberg (o Ginsburg) y que estaba dispuesto a comunicar, por una remuneración razonable, los hechos de los dos sacrificios de Azevedo y de Yarmolinsky. Una discordia de silbidos y de cornetas ahogó la voz de l delator. Después, la comunicación se cortó." (in "La muerte y la brújula," in *Ficciones,* in *Obras completas,* 1:501-502).

52. G. K. Chesterton, "The Three Horsemen of Apocalypse," in *The Paradoxes of Mr. Pond.* (New York: Dover Publications Inc., 1990), p. 5.

53. "Comme tout le monde, il ne comprenait rien à cette affaire" (in *Apollinaire,* "Le Matelot d'Amsterdam," in *L'Hérésiarque et Cie* [Paris: Éditions Stock, 1967], p. 179).

54. "Como a todos, el caso le parecía inexplicable" ("El marinero de Amsterdam," in *Los mejores cuentos policiales,* p. 93).

55. "Néanmoins, les circonstances du drame paraissaient mystérieuses" (in *Apollinaire,* "Le Matelot d'Amsterdam," p. 178).

56. "Sin embargo, las circunstancias del drama eran misteriosas" (in *"El marinero de Amsterdam,"* in Los mejores cuentos policiales, *p. 93).*

57. For a subtle interpretation of "Emma Zunz" that fleshes out Emma's possible psychological motivations in connection with Borges's labyrinthine complexities, see Herbert Morris, "What Emma Knew: The Outrage Suffered in Jorge Luis Borges's 'Emma Zunz,'" *Indiana Journal of Hispanic Letters,* nos. 10 and 11 (spring–fall 1997): 165–202.

58. "El jardín de senderos que se bifurcan," in *Ficciones,* in *Obras completas,* 1:473.

59. Ibid., p. 477

60. Henri Michaux, *Un barbare en Asie* (Paris: Gallimard, 1967), p. 192.

61. In Henri Michaux, *Un bárbaro en Asia,* trans. Borges (Buenos Aires: Sur, 1941), p. 161.

62.   La peur des humiliations est tellement chinoise qu'elle domine
leur civilisation. Ils sont polis pour cela. Pour ne pas humilier
l'autre. Ils s'humilient pour ne pas être humiliés. . . . Ils n'ont
pas tant peur de perdre la face, que de la faire perdre aux autres.
Cette sensibilité, véritablement maladive aux yeux de l'Euro-
péen, donne un aspect special à toute leur civilisation. Ils ont le
sens et l'appréhension du "on dit." Ils se sentent toujours
regardés. . . . "Quand tu traverses un verger, garde-toi, s'il y a
des pommes, de porter la main à ta culotte et, s'il y a des
melons, de toucher à tes chaussures." Ils n'ont pas conscience
d'eux, mais de leur apparence, comme s'ils étaient eux-même à
l'extérieur et s'observant de là. De tout temps exista dans
l'armée chinoise ce commandement: "*Et maintenant prenez un
air terrible!*"
       Même les empereurs, quand il y en avait, avaient peur d'être
humiliés. Parlant des Barbares, des Coréens, ils disaient à leur
messager: "Faites en sorte qu'ils *ne rient* pas de nous." Être la
risée! Les Chinois savent se froisser comme personne et leur
littérature contient, comme il fallait s'y attendre de la part
d'hommes polis et aisément blessés, le plus cruelles et infernales
insolences. (Michaux, *Un barbare en Asie*, 192–93)

(El miedo a sentirse humillado es tan chino que domina su
civilización china. Por eso son corteses. Para no humillar a los
demás. Se humillan para no ser humillados. . . . no temen tanto
"perder la cara," como hacer que los otros "pierdan la cara."
Esta sensibilidad verdaderamente enfermiza a los ojos del
europeo, da un aspecto especial a toda su civilización. Tienen el
sentido y la aprensión del "qué dirán." No tienen conciencia de
sí mismos, sino de su apariencia como si estuvieran afuera y se
observaran desde afuera. Desde siempre, existe en el ejército
chino esta orden: "*Y ahora tomad un aire terrible.*"
       Hasta los emperadores, cuando había emperadores, tenían
miedo de ser humillados. Hablando de los bárbaros, de los
coreanos, encargaban a sus embajadores: Haced de modo que
no se rían de nosotros. ¡Ser el hazmerreír! Los chinos saben
ofenderse como nadie y su literature contiene, como puede
esperarse de hombres corteses y susceptibles, las insolencias más
crueles e infernales.) (Michaux, *Un bárbaro en Asia*, pp. 161–62)

63. In a recent article Roberto González Echevarría has discussed this story as one proposing contradictory versions that do not cancel out each other. See "Borges en 'El jardín de los senderos que se bifurcan,'" in *Borges: Desesperaciones aparentes y consuelos secretos,* ed. Rafael Olea Franco (Mexico City: El Colegio de México, 1999), pp. 61–74.

64. Borges, "Las ruinas circulares" ("The Circular Ruins"), in *Ficciones,* in *Obras completas,* 1:45.

65. The translation may have been a collaboration with Bioy Casares and Silvina Ocampo. Even in the unlikely event it was not translated or edited by Borges, this particular translation, more than the original, sheds light on the gestation of "The Circular Ruins," and it is also a translation that Borges himself modified in his *Libro de sueños (Book of Dreams).*

66. The first translation I am attributing to Borges appeared in the *Antología de la literatura fantástica,* ed. Borges, Silvina Ocampo, and Adolfo Bioy Casares (Buenos Aires: Editorial Sudamericana, 1940; Barcelona: Edhasa, 1981) in 1940.

67. "Nessuno seppe mai il vero nome di colui che tutti chiamavano il Gentiluomo Malato. . . . nessuno comprendeva tutto ciò che volesse dire. . . . Nessuno gli chiese mai qual fosse il suo male. . . . Nessuno seppe dove fosse la sua casa; nessuno gli conobbe padre o fratelli. Apparve un giorno nella città e dopo alcuni anni un altro giorno scomparve" (Papini, "L'ultima visita del gentiluomo malato," in *Il tragico quotidiano* [Florence: Libreria della Voce, 1919], pp. 83–84).

68. Papini, "L'ultima visita del gentiluomo malato," p. 90.

69. "Il sogno di quest'*uno* è talmente duraturo ed intenso ch'io son divenuto visibile anche agli uomini che vegliano" in Papini, "L'ultima visita del gentiluomo malato" (ibid., p. 86).

70. "Nessun delitto mi fu alieno: nessuna nefandezza mi fu ignota; da nessun terrore mi ritrassi. Uccisi con raffinate torture i vecchi innocenti; avvelenai le acque d'intere città; incendiai nello stesso istante le capigliature di una moltitudine di donne; sabranai coi miei denti, resi selvaggi dalla volontà di annientamento, tutti i fanciulli che trovai sul mio cammino. . . . mi precipitai dall'alto di un monte in una valle nuda e sconvolta, circondata da caverne piene di bianche ossa. . . . Ma sembra che colui che mi sogna non s'impaurisca di quello che fa tremare voialtri uomini" (Papini, "L'ultima visita del gentiluomo malato," pp. 88–89).

71. "No dejé de cometer ningún delito, ninguna cosa mala me fue ignorada, ningún terror me hizo retroceder. Me parece que aquel

que me sueña no se espanta de lo que hace temblar a los demás hombres" (in "La última visita del caballero enfermo," in *Antología de la literatura fantástica*, p. 340).

72. "El águila grita" (in Snorri Sturluson, *La alucinación de Gylfi*, trans. Borges and María Kodama [Madrid: Alianza Editorial, 1984], p. 100); "Örn mun hlakka, slítr nái niðfölr" (Snorri Sturluson, *Edda: Prologue and Gylfaginning*, ed. Anthony Faulkes [Oxford: Clarendon Press, 1982], p. 51).

73. In his translation of William Faulkner's *The Wild Palms*, Borges removes the episode of the abortion, perhaps for similar reasons.

74. In Robert Louis Stevenson, *Fables* (New York: Scribner's & Sons, 1896), pp. 90–91.

75. "Y la nodriza cayó sobre la playa como si fuera un puñado de hojas muertas y el viento las arrastró en sentido contrario y la arena se abrió y tomó su lugar" (in Robert Louis Stevenson, "La canción del mañana," in *Fábulas*, trans. Borges and Roberto Alifano [Buenos Aires: Omnibus, 1983], p. 106).

76. "Nadie supo jamás el verdadero nombre de aquel a quien todos llamaban el Caballero Enfermo" (*Antología de la literatura fantástica*, p. 337).

77. "Todos lo llamaban el Caballero Negro; nadie supo nunca su verdadero nombre" (in "La última visita del caballero enfermo," in *Libro de sueños* [Buenos Aires: Torres Aguero, 1976], p. 56).

78. "Y no dejé de cometer delito. Pero el que me sueña, ¿no se espanta de lo que hace temblar a los demás hombres?" (ibid, p. 57).

79. "Consolatemi un poco; suggeritemi qualche strattagemma, qualche intrigo, qualche frode che mi sopprima! Ve lo chiedo con tutta l'anima. Non avete dunque pietà di questo annoniato spettro?" (in Papini, "L'ultima visita del gentiluomo malato," p. 90).

80. "Consúeleme un poco, sugiérame alguna estratagema, alguna intriga, algún fraude que me suprima. ¿No tiene piedad de este aburrido espectro?" ("La última visita del caballero enfermo," in *Antología de la literatura fantástica*, p. 341).

81. "Consuéleme, dígame algo, tenga piedad de este aburrido espectro" ("La última visita del caballero enfermo," in *Libro de sueños*, p. 57).

82. See the interview with Seamus Heany and Richard Kearny, "Jorge Luis Borges: El mundo de la ficción," *Cuadernos hispánoamericanos*, no. 564 (June 1997): 65.

83. "Ahora que se fueron los dos, he quedado solo. / Dejaré de soñarme" (in "Ein Traum," in *La moneda de hierro*, in *Obras completas*, 2:154).

84. In Borges's prologue to Villiers de l'Isle Adam, *El convidado de las últimas fiestas,* ed. Borges (Madrid: Siruela, 1986), p. 11.

85. "Quel effrayant silence!" (de l'Isle Adam, "La Torture par l'espérance," in *Contes cruels: Nouveaux contes cruels* [Paris: Garnier, 1968], p. 326).

86. "Oui, c'était bien un corridor mais d'une longueur démesurée!" (in "La Torture par l'espérance," p. 326; and "Era realmente un corredor, pero casi infinito" in "La esperanza," in *El convidado de las últimas fiestas,* trans. and ed. Borges [Madrid: Siruela, 1986], p. 20).

87. "The Writing of the God," in *Collected Fictions,* trans. Andrew Hurley (New York: Penguin, 1999), pp. 253–54.

88. Even if Borges himself cast doubt on the 1925 translation of *The Metamorphosis* attributed to him, his numerous translations of Kafka can be traced back to 1938, when he wrote the prologue to the first Spanish version of the short novel along with several shorter pieces he did translate. That year Borges also published a translation of the parable "Before the Law," in the journal *El Hogar.* His translations of Kafka also appeared in his *Anthology of Fantastic Literature,* his *Book of Imaginary Beings,* and his *Cuentos breves y extraordinarios.*

89. Borges and Richard Burgin, *Conversations with Jorge Luis Borges* (New York: Holt, Rinehart, & Winston, 1969), p. 60.

90. Borges's prologue to *La Metamorfósis* (Buenos Aires: Losada, 1938), p. 11.

91. "He aquí, traducido del alemán, uno de sus cuentos fantásticos." The note dated May 27, 1938, is reproduced in *Borges en El Hogar 1935–1958* (Buenos Aires: Emecé, 2000), p. 108.

92. Prologue to Kafka's *La metamorfósis,* p. 11.

93. See Julio Chiappini, *Borges y Kafka* (Buenos Aires: Editorial Zeus, 1991), p. 47.

94. Prologue to Kafka's *La metamorfósis,* p. 10.

95. Chiappini, *Borges y Kafka,* p. 46. He also would include "The Library of Babel" in the same category.

96. "La lotería de Babilonia," in *Ficciones,* in *Obras completas,* 1:456.

97. Ibid., 1:461.

98. "La lotería de Babilonia," in *Ficciones,* in *Obras completas,* 1:459.

99. In her analysis Adelheid Hanke-Schefer also includes "The Library of Babel" in the same context: "Die Lotterie und die Bibliothek können als Parabeln über faschistische Diktaturen der dreißiger und vierziger Jahre verstanden werden, beide Erzählungen enthalten Kafkaesque

Momente" (the Lottery and the Library can be understood as parables about the fascist dictatorships of the thirties and forties. Both stories contain Kafkaesque moments) (*Jorge Luis Borges zur Einführung* [Hamburg: Junius, 1999], p. 63).

100. Kafka, "Josephine, die Sängerin oder Das Volk der Mäuse," in *Sämtliche Erzählungen* (Frankfurt: Fischer, 1995), p. 176.

101. "La lotería de Babilonia," in *Ficciones,* in *Obras completas,* 1:456.

102. "I have written stories that are paraphrases of Kafka, 'The Lottery in Babylon' and 'The Library of Babel,' and I then noticed that this could lead me to a mechanical mode of composition. [In Zeno] infinite delay is a logical impossibility, and in Kafka it acquires a pathetic meaning" (Chiappini, *Borges y Kafka,* p. 46).

103. "Nuestro pobre individualismo," in *Otras Inquisiciones* (1952), p. 45.

104. "Seit Beginn ihren Künstlerlaufbahn, kämpft Josephine darum, daß sie mit Rücksicht auf ihrer Gesang von jeder Arbeit befreit werde" (Kafka, "Josephine," in *Sämtliche Erzählungen,* p. 181).

105. "Josefina," *Antología de la literatura fantástica,* p. 233.

106. Quoted by Julio Chiappini, in *Borges and Kafka,* p. 43.

107. Ibid., p. 41.

108. *Biblioteca personal* (Madrid: Alianza, 1988), p. 13.

109. "The Theme of the Traitor and the Hero, in *Collected Fictions,* trans. Andrew Hurley (New York: Penguin, 1999), p. 183. "Bajo el notorio influjo de Chesterton (discurridor y exornador de elegantes misterios) . . . he imaginado este argumento" (in "Tema del traidor y del heroe," in *Ficciones,* in *Obras completas,* 1:496).

110. Chesterton, "The Sign of the Broken Sword," in *The Complete Father Brown* (London: Penguin, 1981), p. 146.

111. "Kilpatrick . . . había firmado la sentencia de muerte de un traidor, cuyo nombre ha sido borrado. Esta sentencia no condice con los piadosos hábitos de Kilpatrick" (in "Tema del traidor y del heroe," in *Ficciones,* in *Obras completas,* 1:497).

112. "La acción transcurre en un país oprimido y tenaz: Polonia, Irlanda, la República de Venecia, algún estado sudamericano o balcánico. . ." (ibid., 496).

113. "Esos paralelismos (y otros) . . . inducen a Ryan a suponer una secreta forma del tiemo, un dibujo de líneas que se repiten" (ibid., 497).

114. Ambrose Bierce, "An Occurrence at Owl Creek Bridge," in *The Signet Classic Book of American Short Stories,* ed. Burton Raffel (New York: Signet, 1985), p. 192.

115. "Jaromir Hladík murió" (in "El milagro secreto," in *Ficciones,* in *Obras completas,* 1:512).
116. Bierce, "An Occurrence at Owl Creek Bridge," p. 188.
117. "Pensó que no lo hubieran arredrado la horca, la decapitación o el degüello, pero que morir fusilado era intolerable" ("El milagro secreto," in *Ficciones,* in *Obras completas,* 1:509).
118. Bierce, "An Occurrence at Owl Creek Bridge," p. 187.
119. "De la perplejidad pasó al estupor, del estupor a la resignación, de la resignación a la súbita gratitud" ("El milagro secreto," in *Ficciones,* in *Obras completas,* 1:512).
120. Bierce, "An Occurrence at Owl Creek Bridge," p. 191.
121. Ibid., p. 187.
122. "No trabajó para la posteridad ni aun para Dios, de cuyas preferencias literarias poco sabía. Minucioso, inmóvil, secreto urdió en el tiempo su alto laberinto invisible" ("El milagro secreto," in *Ficciones,* in *Obras completas,* 1:512).

Conclusion

1. Jacques Chancel, *Jorge Luis Borges: Radioscopie* (Paris: Éditions du Rocher, 1999), pp. 74, 76.
2. "El etnógrafo" appears in *Elogio de la sombra,* in *Obras completas,* 2:367–68; and "La fiesta del monstruo" appears in *Nuevos cuentos de Bustos Domecq* (with Adolfo Bioy Casares), in *Obras completas en colaboración* (Buenos Aires: Emecé, 1991), pp. 392–402.
3. "El fin," in *Ficciones,* in *Obras completas* (Barcelona: Emecé, 1989), 1:521.
4. "Biografía de Tadeo Isidoro Cruz (1829–1874)," in *El Aleph,* in *Obras completas,* 1:561. "El Evangelio según Marcos" ("The Gospel according to Mark"), and "La intrusa" ("The Interloper"), both in *El Informe de Brodie,* in *Obras completas,* vol. 2, are two more stories set in the Pampas and that involve a reenactment of a biblical text.
5. "La metáfora," in *Historia de la eternidad,* in *Obras completas,* 1:384.
6. "Los cuatro cíclos," in *El oro de los tigres,* in *Obras completas,* 2:506.
7. Borges and Osvaldo Ferrari, *En diálogo* (Buenos Aires: Editorial Sudamericana, 1998), 2:66–67.

Afterword

1. "Borges is an admirable writer pledged to destroy reality and convert Man into a shadow." This influential interpretation, which sees Borges's writings as a "process of dissolution of concepts on which Man's belief in the concreteness of his life is founded–cosmos, personality, time"—has been recast in many guises (Ana María Barrenechea, *Borges the Labyrinth Maker*, ed. and trans. Roger Lima [New York: New York University Press, 1965], p. 144).

2. Barrenechea, p.144.

3. Seamus Heaney and Richard Kearney, "Jorge Luis Borges: El mundo de la ficción," *Cuadernos hispánoamericanos*, no. 564 (June 1997): 55.

4. Jacques Chancel, *Jorge Luis Borges: Radioscopie* (Paris: Éditions du Rocher, 1999), p. 72.

5. "El milagro secreto," in *Ficciones,* in *Obras completas* (Barcelona: Emecé, 1989), 1:510.

6. In *Las letras de Borges* (Buenos Aires: Sudamericana, 1979), Sylvia Molloy swerves away from the reality/unreality dichotomy to underscore a poststructuralist dialectic involving the relationship between the body and writing. Roberto González Echevarría, in turn, aims to undermine the assumption that Borges's writings should be seen in opposition to the regional novel that purports to present the reality of Latin America: "In 'Tlön, Uqbar, Orbis Tertius,' Borges reveals the artifice of the regionalist novel by creating an entirely imaginary country described with the methodological precision of an ethnographer's report. In a sense, what Borges does is to turn the regionalist novel inside out, performing in the process a severe ideological critique of the anthropological mediation" (*Myth and Archive: A Theory of Latin American Narrative* [Cambridge: Cambridge University Press, 1991], p. 162).

7. André Camp, *Entretien avec Jorge Luis Borges* (Paris: HB Éditions, 1999), p. 63.

8. "Dos antiguos problemas," *Revista Multicolor de los Sábados* of the journal *Crítica*, May 12, 1934, p. 5. The article is reproduced in *Borges: Obras, reseñas y traducciones inéditas: Diario Crítica 1933–1934,* ed. Irma Zangara (Barcelona: Atlantida, 1999), p. 27.

9. Fernando Savater, "Borges y la filosofía," in *El siglo de Borges: Homenaje a Jorge Luis Borges en su centenario,* vol. 2, *Literatura-Ciencia-Filosofía,* ed. Alfonso de Toro and Susanne Regazzoni (Frankfurt: Vervuert, 1999), 127.

10.   "[Borges was] a bookish man of our time who thought seriously about the absurdity of the world in which we live, but who refused to take it, or himself, seriously. Precisely for this reason, his comic side erupts often, and often unexpectedly, in even his densest writings. . . . He was a serious writer with a sharp sense of humor" (René de Costa, *Humor in Borges* [Detroit: Wayne State University Press, 2000], p. 132).

11.   "Nueva refutación del tiempo," in *Otras Inquisiciones,* in *Obras completas,* 2:149.

12.   Harold Bloom, *The Western Canon: The Books and Schools of the Ages* (New York: Riverhead, 1994), p. 75.

13.   "Le Regret d'Héraclite," in *El hacedor,* in *Obras completas,* 2:231.

14.   "Spinoza, une figure pathétique," *Europe: Revue littéraire mensuele* 60, no. 637 (May 1982): 75.

15.   "Baruch Spinoza," in *La moneda de hierro,* in *Obras completas,* 2:151.

16.   "Spinoza, une figure pathétique," p. 76.

17.   Borges and Osvaldo Ferrari, *Reencuentro: Diálogos inéditos* (Buenos Aires: Editorial Sudamericana, 1998), p. 188.

18.   In his searching exploration of the possibility that the incest motif illuminates the motivations of the protagonist of "Emma Zunz," Herbert Morris wisely concludes that Borges's is a world "in which it is not this or that but this and that and that, too, an interminable series of possibilities. . . . There is in all this, of course, on the part of the author, a recognition of the elusiveness of simple and definitive answers" (Herbert Morris, "What Emma Knew: The Outrage Suffered in Jorge Luis Borges's 'Emma Zunz,'" *Indiana Journal of Hispanic Letters,* nos. 10 and 11 [spring–fall 1997]: 193).

19.   Nestor Ibarra, *Borges et Borges* (Paris: L'Herne), p. 77.

20.   Ibid., p. 196.

21.   Rafael Gutiérrez Girardot, *Jorge Luis Borges: Ensayo de interpretación* (Madrid: Insula, 1959), p. 82.

22.   Borges had a more polemic and aggressive tone in works from the 1920s, which he repudiated when he found the literary voice that characterizes the works he included in his complete works. See chapter 2 for more on his writings of the 1920s.

23.   Claudio Fabián Pérez et al., "Borges en don Bosco," *Brújula: Periódico de artes* 4, no. 29 (August 1999): 5.

Bibliography

Books by Jorge Luis Borges

Antiguas literaturas germánicas. Mexico City: Fondo de Cultura Económica, 1951.

Autobiografía: 1899-1999. Buenos Aires: El Ateneo, 1999.

Biblioteca personal. Madrid: Alianza, 1988.

A/Z. Edited by Antonio Fernández Ferrer. Madrid: Ediciones Siruela, 1988.

Borges: Obras, reseñas y traducciones inéditas: Diario Crítica 1933-1934. Edited by Irma Zangara. Barcelona: Atlantida, 1999. (This book is an edited version of *Borges en Revista Multicolor: Obras, reseñas y traducciones inéditas de Jorge Luis Borges: Diario Crítica, Revista Multicolor de los Sábados 1933-1934.* Buenos Aires: Atlantida, 1995).

Borges en El Hogar: 1935-1958. Buenos Aires: Emecé, 2000.

Borges en Sur 1931-1980. Buenos Aires: Emecé, 1999.

Borges por el mismo. Edited by Emir Rodríguez Monegal. Caracas: Monte Avila, 1987.

Cartas del fervor: Correspondencia con Maurice Abramowicz y Jacobo Sureda (1919-1928). Edited by Cristobal Pera, prologue by Joaquín Marco, notes by Carlos García. Barcelona: Emecé, 1999.

Collected Fictions. Translated by Andrew Hurley. New York: Penguin, 1999.

Ficcionario: Una antología de textos. Edited by Emir Rodríguez Monegal. Mexico City: Fondo de Cultura Económica, 1985.

El idioma de los argentinos. Barcelona: Seix Barral, 1994.

Inquisiciones. Barcelona: Seix Barral, 1994.

Labyrinths: Selected Stories and Other Writings. Edited by Donald A. Yates and James E. Irby. New York: New Directions, 1964.

Obras completas. Vol. 1, 1923-1949. Barcelona: Emecé, 1989.

Obras completas. Vol. 2, 1952-1972. Barcelona: Emecé, 1989.

Obras completas. Vol. 3, 1975-1985. Barcelona: Emecé, 1989.

Obras completas. Vol. 4, 1975-1988. Barcelona: Emecé, 1996.

Obras completas en colaboración. Buenos Aires: Emecé, 1991.

Œuvre poétique (1925-1965). Translated by Nestor Ibarra, introduction by Jorge Luis Borges. 1965. Reprint, Paris: Gallimard, 1985.

Œuvres complètes. Vol. 1. Edited by Jean Pierre Bernès. Paris: Gallimard, 1993.

Œuvres complètes. Vol. 2. Edited by Jean Pierre Bernès. Paris: Gallimard, 1999.

L'or des tigres. Translation, prologue, and notes by Nestor Ibarra. Paris: Gallimard, 1976.

Otras inquisiciones. Buenos Aires: Emecé, 1952. (This edition includes several essays not included in future editions.)

La rose profonde; La monnaie de Fer; Histoire de la nuit. Translation, prologue, and notes by Nestor Ibarra. Paris: Gallimard, 1983.

Selected Non-Fictions. Edited by Eliot Weinberger. Translated by Esther Allen, Suzanne Jill Levine, and Eliot Weinberger. New York: Penguin, 1999.

Selected Poems. Edited by Alexander Coleman. New York: Penguin, 2000.

Selected Poems 1923–1967. Edited by Norman Thomas di Giovanni. 1972. Reprint, London: Penguin, 1985.

El tamaño de mi esperanza. Barcelona: Seix Barral, 1993.

Textos recobrados: 1919–1929. Buenos Aires: Emecé, 1997.

This Craft of Verse. Edited by Calin-Andrei Mihailescu. Cambridge, Mass.: Harvard University Press, 2000.

Articles, Notes, Prologues, and Reviews by Borges (not included in his books)

"An Autobiographical Essay." In *Critical Essays on Jorge Luis Borges,* edited by Jaime Alazraki. Boston: G. K. Hall & Co., 1987. (The essay originally appeared in English the *New Yorker,* September 1970, and it was cosigned with Thomas Norman di Giovanni).

"La cultura en peligro," *Clarín,* December 13, 1984, p. 21.

"Don Segundo Sombra en inglés," *Revista Multicolor de los Sábados* of the journal *Crítica* (August 11, 1934): 5.

"Dos antiguos problemas," *Revista Multicolor de los Sábados* of the journal *Crítica* (May 12, 1934): 5.

"Nota sobre el Ulises en español," *Los Anales de Buenos Aires,* January 1946, p. 49.

"El otro Whitman," *La vida literaria* (Buenos Aires), no. 14. (September 1929): 3–4.

"Préface à l'édition française." In *Œuvre poétique: 1925–1965,* translated by Nestor Ibarra, pp. 7–8. Paris: Gallimard, 1970.

Prologue to *Cuentos basados en el teatro de Shakespeare*, by Charles Lamb. Buenos Aires: Atlántida, 1966.

Prologue to *Macedonio Ferndández*, pp. 9–22. Buenos Aires: Ministerio de Educación y Justicia, 1961.

Prologue to *Las mil y una noches según Galland*. Translated by Jorge Luis Borges. Madrid: Siruela, 1985.

"Spinoza: Une figure pathétique," *Europe: Revue littéraire mensuele* 60, no. 637 (May 1982): 73–76.

"El sueño de Chuang Tsu," *Los Anales de Buenos Aires* (March 1946): 56.

"Walt Whitman: Canto a mí mismo: Traducido por León Felipe" (Editorial Losada, Buenos Aires, 1941)," *Sur* 88 (January): 68–70.

"Yo, judío," *Revista Megáfono* 3, no. 12 (April 1934): 60.

Interviews with Borges (assuming, in most cases,
the authorship or collaboration of Borges)

Alifano, Roberto. *Conversaciones con Borges*. Buenos Aires: Torres Aguero, 1994.

Balderston, Daniel. "Interview with Borges," *Variaciones Borges* 8 (1999): 187–215.

Banier, François-Marie. "Une semaine avec Borgès," *Le Monde*, January 23, 1983, pp. 17, 19.

Barnstone, Willis, ed. *Borges at Eighty: Conversations*. Bloomington: Indiana University Press, 1982.

Burgin, Richard. *Conversations with Jorge Luis Borges*. New York: Holt, Rinehart, & Winston, 1969.

———. *Jorge Luis Borges: Conversations*. Jackson: University Press of Mississippi, 1998.

Camp André. *Entretien avec Jorge Luis Borges*. Paris: HB Éditions, 1999.

Carrizo, Antonio. *Borges el memorioso: Conversaciones de Jorge Luis Borges con Antonio Carrizo*. Mexico City: Fondo de Cultura Económica, 1997.

Chancel, Jacques. *Jorge Luis Borges: Radioscopie*. Paris, Éditions du Rocher, 1999.

Di Giovanni, Norman Thomas, Daniel Halpern, and Frank Macshane, eds. *Borges on Writing*. Hopewell, N.J.: Ecco, 1994.

Ferrari, Osvaldo. *En diálogo*. 2 vols. Buenos Aires: Editorial Sudamericana, 1998.

———. *Reencuentro: Diálogos inéditos*. Buenos Aires: Editorial Sudamericana, 1998.

Heaney, Seamus, and Richard Kearny. "Jorge Luis Borges: El mundo de la ficción," *Cuadernos hispánoamericanos*, no. 564 (June 1997): 55–68.

Mateo, Fernando, ed. *El otro Borges: Entrevistas (1960–1986)*. Buenos Aires: Equis Editores, 1997.

Pérez, Claudio Fabián, et al. "Borges en don Bosco," *Brújula: Periódico de artes* 4, no. 29 (August 1999): 2–5.

Sorrentino, Fernando. *Siete conversaciones con Jorge Luis Borges.* 2d edition. Buenos Aires: El Ateneo, 1996.

Vázquez, María Esther. *Borges: Sus días y su tiempo.* Buenos Aires: Javier Vergara, 1984.

Translations by Borges

Angelus Silesius. *Cien dísticos del viajero querubínico de Angelus Silesius* (bilingual edition of *Hundert distichen aus dem cherubinischen Wandersmann von Angelus Silesius*). Translated and edited by Jorge Luis Borges and María Kodama. Santiago de Chile: Ediciones La ciudad, 1982.

Apollinaire, Guillaume. "El marinero de Amsterdam." In *Los mejores cuentos policiales,* edited and translated by Jorge Luis Borges and Adolfo Bioy Casáres. Buenos Aires: Emecé, 1943.

Browne, Sir Thomas. "Quinto Capítulo de la 'Hydriotaphia" [fifth chapter of *Urn-Burial] Sur,* no. III (January 1944): 15–26.

Chesterton, Gilbert Keith. "El honor de Israel Gow." In *Los mejores cuentos policiales,* edited and translated by Jorge Luis Borges and Adolfo Bioy Casáres. Buenos Aires: Emecé, 1943.

———. "Los tres jinetes del apocalipsis." In *Los mejores cuentos policiales,* edited and translated by Jorge Luis Borges and Adolfo Bioy Casáres. Buenos Aires: Emecé, 1943.

Galland, Antoine. "Historia de Abdula, el mendigo ciego. Versión de Borges de Antoine Galland." In *Las mil y una noches según Galland.* Madrid: Siruela, 1985.

Hawthorne, Nathaniel. "Las muertes repetidas." In *Los mejores cuentos policiales,* edited and translated by Jorge Luis Borges and Adolfo Bioy Casáres. Buenos Aires: Emecé, 1943.

Hesse, Hermann. "Cinco poemas de Hermann Hesse," translated by Jorge Luis Borges and Roberto Alifano, *Proa* 3, no. 6 (October–November 1990): 35–39.

de l'Isle Adam, Villiers. "La esperanza." In *El convidado de las últimas fiestas.* Edited by Jorge Luis Borges. Madrid: Siruela, 1986.

Joyce, James. "La última hoja del ulises," *Proa,* no. 6 (January 1925): 8–9.

Kafka, Franz. *La Metamorfosis.* Translation and prologue by Jorge Luis

Borges (some critics are skeptical that Borges translated the main body of this translation). Buenos Aires: Losada, 1938.

London, Jack. "Las muertes concéntricas." In *Los mejores cuentos policiales,* edited and translated by Jorge Luis Borges and Adolfo Bioy Casáres. Buenos Aires: Emecé, 1943.

———. "Las muertes eslabonadas." In *Revista Multicolor de los Sábados* of the journal *Crítica,* April 28, 1934, p. 4.

Michaux, Henri. *Un bárbaro en Asia.* Buenos Aires: Sur, 1941.

Papini, Giovani. "La última visita del caballero enfermo." In *Antología de la literatura fantástica.* Edited by Jorge Luis Borges, Silvina Ocampo, and Adolfo Bioy Casares. Buenos Aires: Editorial Sudamericana, 1940; Barcelona: Edhasa, 1981.

———. "La última visita del caballero enfermo." In *El libro de sueños.* Buenos Aires: Torres Agüero, 1976.

Poe, Edgar Allan. "La carta robada." In *La carta robada: Selección y prólogo de Jorge Luis Borges.* Madrid: Siruela, 1985; and in *Los mejores cuentos policiales* (a selection of short stories edited and translated by Jorge Luis Borges and Adolfo Bioy Casares). Buenos Aires: Emecé, 1943.

———. "La verdad sobre el caso de M. Valdemar." In *La carta robada: Selección y prólogo de Jorge Luis Borges.* Madrid: Siruela, 1985; and in *Antología de la literatura fantástica.* Edited by Jorge Luis Borges, Silvina Ocampo, and Adolfo Bioy Casares. Buenaos Aires: Editorial Sudamericana, 1940; Barcelona: Edhasa, 1981.

Stevenson, Robert Louis. *Fábulas.* Translated by Jorge Luis Borges and Roberto Alifano. Buenos Aires: Omnibus, 1983.

Sturluson, Snorri. *La alucinación de Gylfi.* Translated by Jorge Luis Borges and María Kodama. Madrid: Alianza Editorial, 1984.

Whitman, Walt. *Hojas de hierba.* Buenos Aires: Editorial Lumen, 1969.

Wilde, Oscar. "El príncipe feliz," *El País* (Buenos Aires), June 25, 1910.

Original Works Translated by Borges
(not cited under "Translations by Borges")

Apollinaire, Guillaume. "Le Matelot d'Amsterdam." In *L'Hérésiarque et Cie.* Paris: Éditions Stock, 1967.

Browne, Sir Thomas. *Religio Medici, Hydriotaphia, and The Letter to a Friend.* London: Simpson Low, 1869.

Chesterton, Gilbert Keith. *El candor del padre Brown.* Translation by Alfonso Reyes. Buenos Aires: Losada, 1939.

Chesterton, G. K. "The Three Horsemen of Apocalypse," in *The Paradoxes of Mr. Pond*. New York: Dover Publications Inc., 1990

Galland, Antoine. "Histoire de l'aveugle Baba-Abdalla." In *Les mille et une nuits*. 3 vols. Paris: Garnier, 1941.

de l'Isle Adam, Villiers. "La Torture par l'espérance." In *Contes cruels: Nouveaux contes cruels*. Paris, Garnier, 1968.

Manuel, Don Juan. "De lo que contesçió a un deán de Sanctiago con don Yllán, el grand maestro de Toledo." *El Conde Lucanor*. Madrid: Clásicos Castelia, 1971.

Kafka, Franz. *Nachgelassene Schriften und Fragmente*. 2 vols. Edited by Jost Schillemeit. Frankfurt: Fischer, 1992–93.

London, Jack. "The Minions of Midas." In *The Complete Short Stories of Jack London*. 3 vols. Edited by Earle Labor et al., 3:432–44. Stanford, Calif.: Stanford University Press.

Michaux, Henri. *Un barbare en Asie*. Paris: Gallimard, 1967.

Novalis. *Fragmente I*. Heidelberg: Verlag Lambert Schneider, 1957.

———. *Novalis*. Edited by Hans-Joachim Mähl. Vol. 15 of Dichter über ihre Dichtungen. Passau: Heimeran, 1976.

Papini, Giovani. "L'Ultima visita del gentiluomo malato." In *Il tragico quotidiano*. Florence: Libreria della Voce, 1919.

Poe, Edgar Allan. "The Facts in the Case of M. Valdemar." In *The Complete Works of Edgar Allan Poe*. Edited by James A. Harrison. New introduction by Floyd Stovall. Vol. 5. New York: Crowell, 1902. New York: AMS, 1979.

———. "The Purloined Letter." In *The Complete Works of Edgar Allan Poe*. Edited by James A. Harrison. New introduction by Floyd Stovall. Vol. 5. New York: Crowell, 1902. New York: AMS, 1979.

Stevenson, Robert Louis. *Fables*. New York: Scribner's & Sons, 1896.

Sturluson, Snorri. *Edda: Prologue and Gylfaginning*. Edited by Anthony Faulkes. Oxford: Clarendon Press, 1982.

———. *L'Edda: Récits de mythologie nordique*. Translated into French by François-Xavier Dillman. Paris: Gallimard, 1991.

———. *Edda*. Translated from the Icelandic and introduced by Anthony Faulkes. London and Melbourne: Everyman's Library, 1987.

———. *Die jungere Edda*. Translated into German by Gustav Heckel. Jena: Eugen Diedrichs, 1925.

———. *The Prose Edda: Gods of the Norsemen*. Translated by Jesse Byock (manuscript for the forthcoming Penguin edition).

———. *The Prose Edda*. Translated from the Icelandic by Jean I. Young. Berkeley and Los Angeles: University of California Press, 1984.

————. *The Prose Edda.* Translated from the Icelandic with an introduction by Arthur Gilchrist Brodeur. New York: Oxford University Press, 1929.

Whitman, Walt. *Leaves of Grass.* In *Walt Whitman: Poetry and Prose.* New York: Library of America College Editions, 1996.

Wilde, Oscar. "The Happy Prince." In *The Happy Prince and Other Fairy Tales.* New York: Brentano's, 1900.

Edited Anthologies by Borges

Antología de la literatura fantástica. Edited by Jorge Luis Borges, Silvina Ocampo, and Adolfo Bioy Casares. Buenas Aires: Editorial Sudamericana, 1940; Barcelona: Edhasa, 1981.

Cuentos breves y extraordinarios. Edited by Jorge Luis Borges and Adolfo Bioy Casáres. Buenos Aires: Editorial Raigal, 1955; Buenos Aires: Santiago Rueda, 1967.

Libro del cielo y del infierno. Edited by Jorge Luis Borges and Adolfo Bioy Casáres. 1959. Reprint, Buenos Aires: Emecé, 1999.

Libro de sueños. Buenos Aires: Torres Aguero, 1976.

Los mejores cuentos policiales. A selection of short stories edited and translated by Jorge Luis Borges and Adolfo Bioy Casares). Buenos Aires: Emecé, 1943.

Criticism

Abadi, Marcelo. "Averroes y su trémula esclava pelirroja," *Variaciones Borges* 7 (1999): 166–77.

Abadi, Marcelo, N. " 'pinoza' y el otro: Dos poemas de Borges." In *Con Borges (texto y persona),* edited by Carlos Cortínez. Buenos Aires: Torres Aguero, 1988.

Aizenberg, Edna. *El tejedor del Aleph: Biblia, Kábala y judaísmo en Borges.* Madrid: Altalena, 1986.

Alazraki, Jaime. "Estructura y función de los sueños en los cuentos de Borges," *Iberoromania* 3 (1975): 9–38.

————. "El Golem." In *Expliquémonos a Borges como poeta,* edited by Angel Flores. Mexico City: Siglo XXI, 1984.

————. *La prosa narrativa de Jorge Luis Borges.* Gredos: Madrid, 1983.

————. *Versiones, inversiones, reversiones: El espejo como modelo estructural del relato en los cuentos de Borges.* Madrid: Gredos, 1977.

Alazraki, Jaime, ed. *Jorge Luis Borges*. Madrid: Taurus, 1976.

Alegría, Fernando. "Borges's Song of Myself." In *The Cambridge Companion to Walt Whitman*, edited by Ezra Greenspan. Cambridge: Cambridge University Press, 1995.

Aparicio, Frances R. *Versiones, interpretaciones, creaciones: Instancias de la traducción literaria en Hispanoamérica en el siglo veinte*. Gaithesburg, Md.: Ediciones Hispamérica, 1991.

Balderston, Daniel. *Out of Context: Historical Reference and the Representation of Reality in Borges*. Durham, N.C.: Duke University Press, 1993.

Balderston, Daniel, Gastón Gallo, and Nicolás Helft. *Borges: Una enciclopedia*. Buenos Aires: Grupo Editorial Norma, 1999.

Barnatán, Marcos-Ricardo. *Borges: Biografía total*. Madrid: Ediciones Temas de Hoy, 1995.

Barnstone, Willis. *The Poetics of Translation: History, Theory, Practice*. New Haven and London: Yale University Press, 1993.

Barrenechea, Ana María. *Borges the Labyrinth Maker*. Edited and translated by Roger Lima. New York: New York University Press, 1965.

Bensoussan, Albert. "Traducir al francés la poesía de Borges," *Variaciones Borges* 5 (1998): 203–6.

Bloom, Harold, "Jorge Luis Borges." In *How to Read and Why*, pp. 56–60. New York: Scribner, 2000.

———. *The Western Canon: The Books and Schools of the Ages*. New York: Riverhead Books, 1994.

Bloom, Harold, ed. *Jorge Luis Borges*. New York: Chelsea House, 1986.

Bravo, María Elena. "Borges traductor: El caso de *The Wild Palms* de William Faulkner," *Insula* 40, no. 462 (May 1985): 11–12.

Cansinos-Assens, Rafael. "Jorge Luis Borges, 1919–1923." In Jorge Luis Borges, *El escritor y la crítica*, edited by Jaime Alazraki, pp. 34–45. Madrid: Taurus, 1996.

Chiappini, Julio. *Borges y Kafka*. Buenos Aires: Editorial Zeus, 1991.

Christ, Ronald. *The Narrow Act: Borges's Art of Allusion*. New York: Lumen, 1995.

Corvalán, Octavio. "Dos cuentos dos veces contados." In *La letra en el espejo*. Salta, Argentina: Universidad Nacional de Salta, 1982.

Cortínez, Carlos. "'Himno del mar': El primer poema de Borges," *Revista Chilena de Literatura* 25 (April 1985): 73–86.

Costa Picazo, Rolando. "Autores que traducen: Borges," *Voces* 15 (1994): 6–11.

de Costa, René. *Humor in Borges*, Detroit: Wayne State University Press, 2000.

Diz, Marta Ana. "El mago de Toledo: Borges y Don Juan Manuel," *MLN* 100, no. 2 (March 1985): 281–97.

Eco, Umberto. "Between La Mancha and Babel," *Variaciones Borges* 4 (1997): 50–62.

Elizondo, Salvador. "La experiencia de Borges," *Paréntesis* 1, no. 1 (December 1999): 60–62.

Farías, Víctor. *La metafísica del arrabal: El tamaño de mi esperanza, un libro desconocido de Jorge Luis Borges.* Madrid: Anaya, 1992.

Fernández Ferrer, Antonio. "Cercanía de una milenaria intertextualidad." In *El siglo de Borges: Homenaje a Jorge Luis Borges en su centenario.* 2 vols. Vol. 2. *Literatura-Ciencia-Filosofía.* Edited by Alfonso de Toro and Susanne Regazzoni. Frankfurt: Vervuert, 1999.

Fernández, Teodosio. "Jorge Luis Borges, o el sueño dirigido y deliberado de la literatura." In *Jorge Luis Borges: Premio "Miguel de Cervantes" 1979,* edited by Donoán et al., pp. 109–28. Barcelona: Anthropos, 1989.

———. "Jorge Luis Borges y el destino escandinavo." In *La aurora y el poniente: Borges (1899–1999),* edited by Manuel Fuentes and Paco Tovar, pp. 89–95. Tarragona, Spain: Gabriel Gibert, 2000.

Fishburn, Evelyn, and Psiche Hughes. *Un diccionario de Borges.* Buenos Aires: Torres Agüero, 1995.

Fló, Juan. *Jorge Luis Borges traductor de "Die Verwandlung" (Fechas, textos, conjeturas).* Montevideo: Papeles de Trabajo, Universidad de la República, n.d.

Flores, Angel, ed. *Expliquémonos a Borges como poeta.* Mexico City: Siglo XXI, 1984.

Fuentes, Carlos. "Jorge Luis Borges: La herida de Babel." In *Geografía de la novela,* pp. 41–70. Madrid: Alfaguara, 1993.

García, Carlos. "Borges inédito: Bibliografía virtual, 1906–1930," *Variaciones Borges* 5 (1998): 265–76.

———. "Borges y el expresionismo: Kurt Heynicke," *Variaciones Borges,* 11 (2001): 121–35.

Gilio, María Esther, et al. *Borges.* Buenos Aires: Editorial el Mangrullo, 1976.

Di Giovanni, Thomas. "At Work with Borges." In *The Cardinal Points of Borges,* edited by Lowell Dunham and Ivar Ivask, pp. 67–78. Norman: University of Oklahoma Press, 1971.

González Echevarría, Roberto. "Borges en 'El jardín de los senderos que se bifurcan.'" In *Borges: Desesperaciones aparentes y consuelos secretos,* edited by Rafael Olea Franco, pp. 61–74. Mexico City: El Colegio de México, 1999.

————. *Myth and Archive: A Theory of Latin American Narrative*. Cambridge: Cambridge University Press, 1991.

Goodman, Nelson, and Catherine Z. Elgin. *Reconceptions in Philosophy and other Arts and Sciences*. Indianapolis and Cambridge: Hackett, 1988.

Gutierréz Girardot, Rafael. *Jorge Luis Borges: El gusto de ser modesto*. Santafé de Bogotá, Columbia: Panamericana Editorial, 1998.

————. *Jorge Luis Borges: Ensayo de interpretación*. Madrid: Insula, 1959.

Hanke-Schaefer, Adelheid. *Jorge Luis Borges zur Einführung*. Hamburg: Junius, 1999.

Helft, Nicolás, and Alan Pauls. *El factor Borges: Nueve ensayos ilustrados*. Buenos Aires: Fondo de Cultura Económica, 2000.

Howard, Matthew. "Stranger than Fiction: The Unlikely Case of Jorge Luis Borges and the Translator Who Helped Bring His Work to America," *Lingua Franca* (June/July 1997): 41–49.

Ibarra, Nestor. *Borges et Borges*. Paris: L'Herne, 1969.

Irwin, John T. *The Mystery to a Solution: Poe, Borges, and the Analytic Detective Fiction*. Baltimore and London: Johns Hopkins University Press, 1994.

Kodama, María. "Borges y la literatura japonesa," *La Torre* 8 (October–December 1988): 665–79.

Kodama, María. "Oriental Influences in Borges's Poetry: The Nature of the Haiku and Western Literture." In *Borges the Poet*, edited by Carlos Cortínez. Fayetteville: University of Arkansas Press, 1986.

————. "La traducción es una lección de estilo" (interview), *Voces* 15 (1994): 2–4.

Kristal, Efraín. "Borges y la traducción," *Lexis* 23, no. 1 (1999): 3–23.

Lafon, Michel. *Borges ou la réécriture*. Paris: Seuil, 1990.

Levine, Suzanne Jill. *Guía de Bioy Casáres*. Madrid: Espiral, 1977.

————. "Notes to Borges's Notes on Joyce: Infinite Affinities," *Comparative Literature* 49, no. 4 (fall 1997): 337–52.

————. *The Subversive Scribe: Translating Latin American Fiction*. Saint Paul: Graywolf Press, 1991.

————. "A Universal Tradition: The Fictional Biography," *Review: Latin American Literature and the Arts* (Spring 1973): 24–28.

Louis, Annick. "Borges invisible et visible," *Critique* 635 (April 2000): 335–45.

————. *Jorge Luis Borges: Œuvre et manœuvres*. Paris: L'Harmattan, 1997.

Ludmer, Josefina. "¿Cómo salir de Borges?" In *Jorge Luis Borges: Intervenciones sobre pensamiento y literatura*, edited by William Rowe, Claudio Canaparo, and Annick Louis, pp. 289–300. Buenos Aires: Paidos, 2000.

Maier, Linda S. "Jorge Luis Borges and German Expressionism," *Romance Notes* 27, no. 2 (winter 1986): 143–48.

Mandlove, Nancy B. "Chess and Mirrors: Form as Metaphor in Three Sonnets." In *Jorge Luis Borges,* edited by Harold Bloom, pp. 173–83. New York: Chelsea House, 1986.

Maurer, Christopher. "The Poet's Poets: Borges and Quevedo." In *Borges the Poet,* edited by Carlos Cortínez, pp. 185–96. Fayetteville: University of Arkansas Press, 1986.

Menocal, María Rosa. *Writing in Dante's Cult of Truth: From Borges to Boccaccio.* Durham, N.C.: Duke University Press, 1991.

Molloy, Sylvia. *La Difusion de la littérature hispano-américaine en France au XXe siècle.* Paris: Presses Universitaires de France, 1972.

———. *Las letras de Borges.* Buenos Aires: Sudamericana, 1979.

———. "Traducir a Borges." In *Borges desesperaciones aparentes y consuelos secretos,* edited by Rafael Olea Franco, pp. 273–81. Mexico City: El Colegio de Mexico, 1999.

Montoto, Claudio César. "Jorge Luis Borges: La literatura como sueño dirigido," *Inti. Revista de Literatura Hispánica,* nos. 49–50 (1999): 39–45.

Morrillas Ventura, Enriqueta. "Borges, el expresionismo y la literatura fantástica," *Insula,* nos. 631–32 (July–August 1999): 25–27.

Morris, Herbert. "What Emma Knew: The Outrage Suffered in Jorge Luis Borges's Emma Zunz," *Indiana Journal of Hispanic Letters,* nos. 10 and 11 (spring–fall 1997): 165–202

Nuño, Juan. *La filosofía de Borges.* Mexico City: Fondo de Cultura Económica, 1987.

Olea Franco, Rafael. *El otro Borges: El Primer Borges.* Mexico City: Fondo de Cultura Económica, 1993.

Olea Franco, Rafael, ed. *Borges desesperaciones aparentes y consuelos secretos.* Mexico City: El Colegio de Mexico, 1999.

Oviedo, José Miguel. *Breve Historia del ensayo hispanoamericano.* Madrid: Alianza Editorial, 1991.

Pacheco, José Emilio. "'Muchos Años Después.'" In *Los novelistas como críticos.* 2 vols. Edited by Norma Klahn and Wilfrido H. Corral, pp. 459–69. Mexico City: Ediciones del Norte, Fondo de Cultura Económica, 1991.

Pastormerlo, Sergio. "Borges y la traducción," *Voces* 15 (1994): 13–18.

Paz, Octavio. "El arquero la flecha y el blanco (Jorge Luis Borges)." In *Convergencias,* pp. 60–74. Barcelona: Seix Barral, 1991.

Piglia, Ricardo. "Borges: El arte de narrar," *Cuadernos de recienvenido* 12 (1999): 5–19.

Robb, James Willis. "Borges y Reyes: Una relación epistolar." In *Jorge Luis Borges,* edited by Jaime Alazraki, pp. 305–17. Madrid: Taurus, 1976.

Rodriguez Monegal, Emir. *Ficcionario,* Mexico City: Fondo de Cultura Económica, 1981.

———. *Jorge Luis Borges: A Literary Biography.* New York: Dutton, 1978.

Sarlo, Beatriz. *Jorge Luis Borges: A Writer on the Edge.* London: Verso, 1993.

Savater, Fernando. "Borges y la filosofía." In *El siglo de Borges: Homenaje a Jorge Luis Borges en su centenario.* 2 vols. Vol. 2. *Literatura-Ciencia-Filosofía,* edited by Alfonso de Toro and Susanne Regazzoni. Frankfurt: Vervuert, 1999.

Schwartz, Jorge. "Borges y la primera hoja de Ulysses," *Revista Iberoamericana* 93 (1997): 721–28.

Steiner, George. *After Babel: Aspects of Language and Translation.* Oxford: Oxford University Press, 1992.

Stewart, Jon. "Borges on Language and Translation," *Philosophy and Literature* 19 (1995): 320–29.

de Toro, Alfonso, and Susanne Regazzoni, eds. *El siglo de Borges: Homenaje a Jorge Luis Borges en su centenario.* Vol. 2. *Literatura-Ciencia-Filosofía.* Frankfurt: Vervuert, 1999.

Tálice, Roberto A. "Elogio al traductor." In *Borges: Obras, reseñas y traducciones inéditas: Diario Crítica 1933–1934,* edited by Irma Zangara, pp. 231–32. Barcelona: Atlantida, 1999.

Valero Garcés, Carmen. "Jorge L. Borges poeta y traducgtor de Walt Whitman: Análisis de las estrategias en la traducción de poesía," *Torre de papel* 3 (Fall 1995): 19–40.

Vargas Llosa, Mario. "An Invitation to Borges's Fiction." In *A Writer's Reality,* pp. 1–19. Syracuse, N.Y.: Syracuse University Press, 1991.

Vázquez, María Esther. *Borges: Esplendor y derrota.* Barcelona: Tusquets, 1999.

Vega, José Luis. "Un ejemplo de las traducciones expresionistas de Jorge Luis Borges," *Revista de la facultad de traducción e interpretación, Granada* 5 (1994): 241–48.

de Viry, Amé. "Borges ou l'élément romanesque." In *L'Amérique latine et La Nouvelle Revue française 1920–2000,* edited by Fernando Carvallopp, pp. 464–77. Paris: Gallimard, 2001.

Waisman, Sergio Gabriel. "Borges Reads Joyce: The Role of Translation in the Creation of Texts," *Variaciones Borges* 9 (2000): 59–73.

Wheelock, Carter. "Borges's New Prose." In *Prose for Borges*, edited by Charles Newman, Mary Kinzie, and Norman Thomas di Giovanni (consulting editor), pp. 355–92. Evanston, Ill.: Northwestern University Press, 1974.

Woodall, James. *Borges: A Life.* New York: Basic Books, 1996.

Yurkievich, Saúl. "Borges, poeta circular." In *Fundadores de la nueva poesía latinoamericana: Vallejo, Huidobro, Borges, Girondo, Neruda, Paz, Lezama Lima*, pp. 125–46. Barcelona: Ariel, 1984.

———. "Soñar el sueño." In *Brújula: Periódico de artes* 4, no. 29 (August 1999): 11.

Other Works

Bierce, Ambrose. "An Occurrence at Owl Creek Bridge." In *The Signet Classic Book of American Short Stories*, edited by Burton Raffel. New York: Signet, 1985.

Chesterton, G. K. *El candor del padre Brown.* Translated into Spanish by Alfonso Reyes. Buenos Aires: 1939.

Chesterton, G. K. *The Complete Father Brown.* London: Penguin, 1981.

Dillmann, François-Xavier. Introduction to *L'Edda: Récits de mythologie nordique par Snorri Sturluson.* Paris: Gallimard, 1991.

Eliot. Thomas Stearns. "Tradition and the Individual Talent." In *Points of View.* New York: Faber & Faber, 1941.

Frank, Armin Paul. "Theories and Theory of Literary Translation." In *Literary Theory and Criticism Festscrift Presented to René Wellek in Honor of his Eightieth Birthday*, edited by Joseph P. Strelka. 2 vols. Vol. 1: *Theory*, pp. 203–21. Bern: Peter Lang, 1984.

Gracián, Baltasar. *The Art of Wordly Wisdom: A Pocket Oracle.* Translated by Christopher Maurer. New York: Doubleday, 1992.

Green, Arthur. "Teachings of the Hasidic Masters." In *Back to the Sources: Readings in the Classic Jewish Texts*, edited by Barry W. Holtz. New York: Touchstone, 1992.

Güiraldes, Ricardo. *Don Segundo Sombra: Shadows on the Pampas.* Translated by Harriet de Onís, introduction by Waldo Frank. New York: Farrar & Rinehart, 1935.

Hawthorne, Nathaniel. *Twice Told Tales: The Works of Nathaniel Hawthorne.* Edited by William Chravet et al. Vol. 9. Columbus: Ohio State University Press, 1974.

Kivy, Peter. *Philosophies of Arts: An Essay in Differences.* New York: Cambridge University Press, 1997.

Kristal, Efraín. "Walter Benjamin: El Mesianismo y la traducción," *Teoría/ Crítica* 4 (1997): 135–43.

Lamarque, Peter, and Stein Haugom Olsen. *Truth, Fiction, and Literature: A Philosophical Perspective.* Oxford, Clarendon Press, 1994.

Lefevere, André. *Translating Literature: The German Tradition from Luther to Rosenzeig.* Amsterdam: Van Gorcum, 1977

Novalis, *Werke: Dritter Teil.* Edited by Hermann Fridamann. Leipzig: Deutsches Verlagshaus, n.d.

Pfefferkorn, Kristin. *Novalis: A Romantic's Theory of Language and Poetry.* New Haven, Conn., and London: Yale University Press, 1988.

Rochlitz, Rainer. *The Disenchantment of Art: The Philosophy of Walter Benjamin.* New York: Guilford, 1996.

Sontag, Susan. *Against Interpretation.* New York: Farrar, Strauss & Giroux, 1966.

Susini, E. "Johannes Scheffler, (1624–1677)." In *Encyclopedia Universalis,* 14:723–24. Paris: Encyclopedia Universalis France S.A.

Valéry, Paul. *El Cementerio marino de Paul Valéry.* Translated by Nestor Ibarra with a prologue by Jorge Luis Borges. Buenos Aires: Schillinger, 1931.

Vietta, Silvio, ed. *Lyrik des Expressionismus.* Tübingen: Niemeyer, 1999.

Venuti, Lawrence. *The Translation Studies Reader.* London and New York: Routledge, 2001.

———. *The Translator's Invisibility: A History of Translation.* London and New York: Routledge, 1995.

Wilde, Oscar. *Cuentos de Oscar Wilde.* Prologue by Jorge Luis Borges, translated by María O. de Grant. Buenos Aires: Editorial Atlántida, 1966.

———. *Obras completas.* Translated by Ramón Gómez de la Serna. Madrid: Aguilar, 1951.

Wollheim, Richard. *Art and Its Object*s. Cambridge: Cambridge University Press, 1980.

Bibliographies

Becco, Horacio Jorge. *Jorge Luis Borges: Bibliografía total, 1923–1973.* Buenos Aires: Casa Pardo, 1973.

Helft, Nicolás. *Jorge Luis Borges: Bibliografía completa.* Buenos Aires: Fondo de Cultura Económica, 1997.

Index